Praise for
ALL THINGS SHINING

"[*All Things Shining*] offers a meditation on the meaning of life, in a sharp, engaging style . . . [and] fascinating readings of works of literature chosen to illuminate this narrative . . . as well as passionate glimpses of the attitudes toward the world the authors urge us to regain."

—*The New York Times Book Review* (cover review)

"[A]n ambitious book, offering insightful readings of authors including Homer, Dante, Descartes and Kant, as well as the novelists Herman Melville and David Foster Wallace . . . *All Things Shining* repays attention and reflection. It is a fascinating read and deserves an audience far beyond the borders of academia. Even if you don't agree that we are caught in an age of nihilistic indecision, if you attune yourself to the authors' energetic intelligence and deep engagement with key texts in the West, you will have much to be grateful for."

—Michael Roth, *The New York Times*

"[T]his is no bland academic exercise. *All Things Shining* is an inspirational book but a highly intelligent and impassioned one. The authors set out to analyze our contemporary nihilism the better to remedy it . . . compelling."

—*The Wall Street Journal*

"Dreyfus and Kelly would initiate us into a this-worldly piety of wonder and gratitude; of attunement to moments when something transcendentally excellent shines forth in the mundane. The new age that Dreyfus and Kelly hope for is a polytheistic and basically aristocratic corrective to the leveling of modern culture, which they attribute to the mind-sets of monotheism and technology. You will be arrested by their reading of the tradition, and of our current situation."

—Matthew Crawford, author of *Shop Class as Soulcraft*

"The authors successfully leapfrog through literary-philosophical history to suggest how we can reclaim redemptive qualities sacrificed to modernity. . . . A provocative, illuminating and inspirational exhortation to 'Ask not why the gods have abandoned you, but why you have abandoned the gods.'"

—*Kirkus Reviews*

"Fascinating insights about the search for meaning in our time, and the threat of nihilism. *All Things Shining* raises fundamental questions about the religious and ethical developments of humanity since the Axial Age. This book tackles big issues, ones that really matter in our lives today."

—Charles Taylor, author of *A Secular Age*

"Many people in today's world do not recognize 'shining' things when they see them. Instead, feelings of loss, sadness, angst, and despair prevail. Dreyfus and Kelly lament that fact and respond to the situation by introducing (or reintroducing) readers to several literary classics of the Western world. . . . The conclusion is hopeful—that one can live a life worth living in a secular age. It starts with recognizing 'shining' things when we encounter them. This book is proof that some of the Western classics can help us do just that."

—*Booklist*

"Tremendously inspiring. . . . The way Dreyfus and Kelly distill the essence of the thinkers they treat is remarkable."

—Huston Smith, Professor of Philosophy at
four major universities, now retired

"An extraordinary, ambitious, and provocative tour de force that frames one of the central questions of our age: How have we passed 'from the intense and meaningful lives of Homer's world to the indecision and sadness' that too often characterize modern times? In examining the great literary works produced in the history of the West, the authors find new ways of configuring issues of choice, autonomy, fanaticism, solace, and, most important, the ties that bind us to the past. Brief and yet comprehensive, the book delves into the transcendent values of the classic works that have helped to advance modern thought and inform the development of the Western world. I could hardly put it down."

—Vartan Gregorian, President, Carnegie Corporation of New York

"There is a world out there that is as concealed as it is crucial to the good life. Dreyfus and Kelly have lifted the veil with pedagogical skill and striking insights. It's a world of things shining that can lend grace and depth to our lives. The book is itself a shining thing."

—Albert Borgmann, author of *Real American Ethics*

"Stunning! This is one of the most surprising, demanding, and beautiful books I have ever read. My compliments, gentlemen, and I hope thousands of others share my admiration—and awe."

—Charles Van Doren, author of *A History of Knowledge*

ALL THINGS SHINING

Reading the Western Classics to Find Meaning
in a Secular Age

HUBERT DREYFUS

and

SEAN DORRANCE KELLY

Free Press

New York London Toronto Sydney New Delhi

Free Press
A Division of Simon & Schuster, Inc.
1230 Avenue of the Americas
New York, NY 10020

First Free Press trade paperback edition August 2011

FREE PRESS and colophon are trademarks of Simon & Schuster, Inc.

For information about special discounts for bulk purchases,
please contact Simon & Schuster Special Sales at 1-866-506-1949 or
business@simonandschuster.com.

The Simon & Schuster Speakers Bureau can bring authors to your
live event. For more information or to book an event contact the
Simon & Schuster Speakers Bureau at 1-866-248-3049 or
visit our website at www.simonspeakers.com.

Book design by Ellen R. Sasahara

Manufactured in the United States of America

1 3 5 7 9 10 8 6 4 2

The Library of Congress has cataloged the hardcover edition as follows:

Dreyfus, Hubert L.
All things shining: reading the Western classics to find meaning in
a secular age / Hubert Dreyfus and Sean Dorrance Kelly.
p. cm.
1. Religions. 2. Religion. 3. Meaning (Philosophy) I. Kelly, Sean
(Sean D.) II. Title.
BL80.3.D74 2011
200—dc22   2010021750

ISBN 978-1-4165-9615-8
ISBN 978-1-4165-9616-5 (pbk)
ISBN 978-1-4391-0170-4 (ebook)

For Geneviève, whose way of being-in-the-world is my French answer to nihilism

—HUBERT

For Dorrance, Dorothy, Bryan, and Cheryl, Benjamin, Nathaniel

The shining ones who lit the way to here and those who light the way ahead

—SEAN

CONTENTS

If hereafter any highly cultured, poetical nation shall lure back to their birthright, the merry May-day gods of old; and livingly enthrone them again in the now egotistical sky; on the now unhaunted hill; then be sure, exalted to Jove's high seat, the great Sperm Whale shall lord it.

—HERMAN MELVILLE, from *Moby Dick*

A Note to the Reader

THE WORLD DOESN'T MATTER to us the way it used to. The intense and meaningful lives of Homer's Greeks, and the grand hierarchy of meaning that structured Dante's medieval Christian world, both stand in stark contrast to our secular age. The world used to be, in its various forms, a world of sacred, shining things. The shining things now seem far away. This book is intended to bring them close once more.

The issues motivating our story are philosophical and literary, and we come at them from our professional background in these disciplines. But *All Things Shining* is intended for a nonspecialist audience, and we hope it will speak to a wide range of people. Anyone who lives in the contemporary world has the background to read it, and anyone who hopes to enrich his or her life by experiencing it in the light of classic philosophical and literary works can hope to find something here. Anyone who wants to lure back the shining things, to uncover the wonder we were once capable of experiencing and to reveal a world that sometimes calls forth such a mood; anyone who is done with indecision and waiting, with expressionlessness and lostness and sadness and angst, and who is ready for whatever it is that comes next; anyone with hope instead of despair, or anyone with despair that they would like to leave behind, can find something worthwhile in the pages ahead. Or at least that is what we intend.

ALL THINGS SHINING

1

Our Contemporary Nihilism

I T WAS WARM on January 2, 2007. The newspapers reported that week that an optimistic cherry tree at the Brooklyn Botanic Garden had sprouted thousands of blossoms. Throughout the city people gathered spontaneously, drawn together by the hopeful atmosphere of spring.[1] On the subway platform at 137th and Broadway in Manhattan, however, just after lunchtime, the spring mood vanished in the blink of an eye. Cameron Hollopeter, a twenty-year-old film student, collapsed to the ground, his body overtaken by convulsions. According to newspaper reports at the time, a man and two women rushed to help him. As they did, Mr. Hollopeter managed to raise himself, but then stumbled to the platform edge and fell backward to the subway tracks below.[2]

What happened next both inspired and awed the spring-softened world of New York. Wesley Autrey, the fifty-year-old construction worker who initially rushed in to help Mr. Hollopeter, had left his two young daughters, Syshe, four, and Shuqui, six, farther back on the platform. When the headlights of the southbound No. 1 train appeared, however, he did not hesitate. Leaping onto the tracks he pressed his body down on top of Mr. Hollopeter, pushing him into a trough that was about a foot deep. The train's brakes shrieked before them, but the train was unable to stop: five cars screeched over the top of the two men, missing them only by inches, before the train finally came to a halt. As they lay there beneath the train Mr. Autrey heard the screams of terrified onlookers above. "We're okay down here," he yelled, "but I've got two daughters up there. Let them know their father's okay." Cries of wonder and applause erupted from the platform. Later, after cutting the power, workers were able to extricate the two men from beneath the train. Except for the grease that smudged Mr. Autrey's blue knit cap, and some bumps and bruises, both men were unhurt.

The newspapers dubbed Wesley Autrey the "Subway Hero," and he enjoyed a well-deserved spate of popular press. Politicians rushed to be seen with him[3] and scientists and culture commentators debated whether his actions showed that he was "more hard-wired for heroism"[4] than the rest of us, or just that New York City has the same small-town values and caring attitude that you might expect to find in Dubuque.[5] A self-congratulatory public insisted that they too would have acted as Mr. Autrey had, and a solemn police chief advised that New Yorkers take Mr. Autrey's lead and act when people near them are in distress.[6] But throughout it all, Mr. Autrey himself insisted that he was no hero, had done nothing out of the ordinary. "I don't feel like I did something spectacular," Mr. Autrey said. "I just saw someone who needed help."[7]

Not only a hero, one might think, but humble too! And there is no doubt that Mr. Autrey's actions are indeed inspiring and heroic. But it may be that what comes across as humility is really just Mr. Autrey's honest report of his own experience. As it happens, although heroic actions like this are of course rare, it is not at all uncommon for the people who perform them to report that they were just doing what anybody in their situation would have. As Dr. Charles Goodstein, a clinical professor of psychiatry at New York University School of Medicine, said at the time:

If you look at the history of most people who are designated heroes in the military and in other places, most of the time they say the reaction they had was without any mental preparation. It was spontaneous, it was without much consideration for the practicalities, the realities of the moment. I think they're honest when they say they don't think of themselves as heroes, they just reacted to something they saw as an emergency.[8]

The point here is not that anyone in a similar situation actually would do the same thing. There is ample evidence that most people would not. But perhaps what Mr. Autrey and others are honestly reporting is that when they are in the midst of acting heroically, they do not experience themselves as the source of their actions. Instead, the situation itself seems to call the action out of them, allowing for neither uncertainty nor hesitation. As Mr. Autrey said, "I just saw someone who needed help."

THIS SENSE OF CERTAINTY is rare in the contemporary world. Indeed, modern life can seem to be defined by its opposite. An unrelenting flow of choices confronts us at nearly every moment of our lives, and most of us could admit to finding ourselves at least occasionally wavering. Far from being certain and unhesitating, our lives can at the extreme seem shot through with hesitation and indecision, culminating in choices finally made on the basis of nothing at all.

The truly extreme version of this, of course, is a parody. The paralyzing level of neurosis to which a Woody Allen character descends, for example, is fortunately not the lot of most. Or consider T. S. Eliot's famous version of this parodic extreme. J. Alfred Prufrock is so unable to take action that to him a single moment before tea consists of an almost immeasurable series of uncertainties:

Time for you and time for me,
And time yet for a hundred indecisions,
And for a hundred visions and revisions,
Before the taking of a toast and tea.

And yet if these are parodies, they resonate precisely because there is some recognizable element of truth in them. We are not constantly paralyzed by the choices that confront us, thank heavens, but we recognize their constant flow. And sometimes we wonder on what basis we should choose among them.

The choices that confront us are recognizable to all. Some of them seem trivial: Should I hit the snooze bar again? Is this shirt too wrinkled? Fries or a salad? And so on. But some of the choices we confront, perhaps even regularly, seem deeper and more troubling. It can feel as though they cut to the core of who we really are: Is it time to move on from this relationship? This job? Shall I pursue this opportunity or that one? Or none at all? Shall I align myself with this candidate, this co-worker, this social group? Shall I choose this part of the family over the rest? Many of our lives seem rife with these kinds of choices. We wonder on what basis to make them; we regret or rue or celebrate the ones we have made.

Many will point out that the freedom to choose is one of the great signs of progress in modern life. And there is certainly some truth to this. Those who live in abject poverty worry very little about which kind of food to eat precisely because there are no choices before them. The freedom to choose one career over another is not available when a poor economy has stripped all the jobs from the area. And yet the characteristic feature of the modern world is not just that many of us have a wider range of choices than ever before—choices about who to become, how to act, with whom to align ourselves. Rather, it is that when we find ourself confronted with these kinds of existential choices, we feel a lack of any genuine motivation to choose one over the others. Indeed, about our own lives, our own actions, it is rare to find the kind of certainty that Wesley Autrey felt when confronted with a person in distress.

THERE ARE AT LEAST two kinds of people who manage to avoid the contemporary burden of choice, but in the wrong way. First, there is the man of self-confidence (usually it is a man). He plunges forth assuredly into every action he takes. He presents the world as obvious—"How could anyone wonder about the right move here?" he seems to ask—and in certain cases his assurance draws others along with him.

The man of self-confidence is often a compelling figure. Driven and focused, he is committed to bringing the world into line with his vision of how it should be. He may genuinely believe that his vision for the world is a good one, that the world will be a better place if he can shape it to his will, and sometimes he is capable of making changes for the better. But there is a danger to this attitude as well. Too often it turns out that the blustery self-confidence of such a person hides its own darker origins: it is really just arrogance combined with ambition, or worse yet a kind of self-delusion. As a result, when his plans fail, as they are bound to do at least some of the time, the self-confident man is often unable to recognize the failure. Stubbornly and inflexibly committed to his vision of how things ought to be, he has no ability to respond to the world as it actually is. The self-confident man believes that confidence is its own virtue; at the extreme, this kind of self-confidence can lead to fanaticism, as we'll see in the monomaniac Captain Ahab that Melville portrays in *Moby Dick*.

Perhaps a good example of such a willful character can be found in Orson Welles's portrayal of the newspaper magnate Charles Foster Kane in his great movie *Citizen Kane*. Welles's Kane is charming and powerful, and he demands total loyalty and obedience from those around him. He is astonishingly successful, enormously wealthy, and through the influence of his newspapers he claims even to be capable of directing the course of history. As he says, in a famous line from the movie, "You provide the prose poems, I'll provide the war." Kane is a man who never looks back, who would never dream of a moment of weakness, and who despises those who are incapable of moving with enough alacrity and force to rebut his attacks. Eventually, however, his arrogance and his lust for power become his undoing. When an affair ruins both his marriage and his political aspirations, Kane's life spirals out of control. His dying word, "Rosebud," turns out to be a wistful reference to the only time in his life when he lived in poverty, when his self-confidence wasn't itself sufficient to ensure the satisfaction of his every desire.

Kane's self-confidence allows him to avoid the burden of choice. He is clear about his desires and forges ahead in fulfilling them. But the self-confidence upon which he bases his existence turns out to be empty, grounded in nothing but his own lust for power, and in the end it is insufficient soil for a worthwhile life. In contrast with this, a genuine confidence of the sort that seems to have directed Mr. Autrey's actions is driven not by some internal set of thoughts or desires, nor by a calculated set of plans or principles. Indeed, as in the case of Mr. Autrey, it is experienced as confidence drawn forth by something outside of oneself. It is grounded in the way things actually are, not in the confident person's perhaps self-serving characterization of them. The genuinely confident agent does not manufacture confidence, but receives it from the circumstances.

THERE IS A SECOND WAY to avoid the contemporary burden of choice, but it is at least as unattractive as the path of manufactured confidence. We are thinking here of the person who makes no choices about how to act because he is enslaved by obsessions, infatuations, or addictions. Such a person is, it is true, drawn by something beyond himself to act in the way he does. But there is a world of difference between him and the heroic Mr. Autrey.

The case of addiction is well known in the modern world, and there is no need to mention its various forms. As always, there are drugs, entertainments, and manifold other temptations in the face of which we can lose all sense of ourselves. But the peculiar phenomenon of addiction is highlighted well by a modern form unknown before the technological age: blogs and social networking sites. Many people have experienced the draw of these sites. At first there is an excitement associated with them. When one discovers the world of blogs, for example, one finally feels as though one can be up-to-the-minute with respect to every breaking event on the current scene. Suppose that politics is your bailiwick. All of a sudden it seems possible to keep up with precisely what is happening on Capitol Hill. Not just this week but this very moment; not just today but somewhere between the onset of one breath and the conclusion of the next. Similarly with social networking sites. Finally one feels completely in touch with all of those friends you didn't realize you had been missing for so long.

If one falls into the grip of these kinds of obsessions, its phenomenology has a sinking dimension. For one finds oneself constantly craving the newest, latest post, wondering what the most recent crisis or observation or tidbit could be. One cycles through the list of websites or friends waiting for the latest update, only to find that when it is completed one is cycling through the sequence once again, precisely as expectant and desiring as before. The craving for something new is constant and unceasing, and the latest post only serves to make you desire more. With this kind of addiction there is a clear sense of what one must do next. But the completion of the task fails entirely to satisfy the craving that set you on your way. By contrast with this, the heroic actor experiences a heightened sense of joy and fulfillment when a noble and worthy action draws him to its side.

The burden of choice is a peculiarly modern phenomenon. It proliferates in a world that no longer has any God or gods, nor even any sense of what is sacred and inviolable, to focus our understanding of what we are. What we have seen just now, though, is that not every way of resolving choice is equal. Although willful self-confidence and addictive loss of control are both ways of shirking the burden—the first because it refuses to recognize alternatives and the second because it is incapable of doing so—neither of these conditions characterizes the experience of the unthinking heroic actor.

WHAT CAN IT BE like to act with certainty in the way that Mr. Autrey did—to act but not experience oneself as the source of one's actions; to be drawn by a force outside oneself but not enslaved to it? In fact, although we do not pay attention to it, a mild version of this is familiar to us in everyday life. The morning commuter all of a sudden realizes that he has gotten on the bus, but doesn't remember doing so. The long-distance truck driver all of a sudden realizes that he has been driving for some miles without "paying attention." Stumbling home from a long day's work, the tired worker finds herself in a favorite chair, but then realizes that she never decided to sit there. Habitual actions of these sorts can occur "offline," as one might say, without the agent even noticing that she is performing them. And yet it is part of the habitual action that the person performing it can break in at any moment and resist. In some sense the habitual actor, like the heroic one, is neither willful agent nor unwilling slave.

But habitual action is not heroic. The difference is that whereas the habitual actor lacks a sense not only of himself but of his surroundings, the heroic actor by contrast has a heightened awareness of what the situation calls for.

This sense for what the situation demands is nothing like an objective awareness of what is happening. The other bystanders on the subway platform presumably saw *that* Mr. Hollopeter was in distress; in this sense they were good, objective witnesses to the event. Many of them presumably saw, in addition, *that* the situation called for some kind of action. Presumably many of them even felt an urge to act themselves. But they were not sufficiently motivated to act on his behalf. Their experience allowed for hesitation; Mr. Autrey's did not.

It is hard to blame someone who responds in a nonheroic way to such a situation; most of us are familiar with their experience. Perhaps they thought desperately to themselves, "Oh my God! That poor man has fallen on the tracks—somebody do something!" They were not lacking empathy for the victim, we can assume, and indeed perhaps they felt strongly that something must be done to help him. But if we are to take Mr. Autrey at his word, then none of these desperate thoughts ran through his head, and he therefore never *decided* to do anything at all in response to them. Rather, it was Mr. Hollopeter's distress itself that drew him to act without hesitation. In this way his experience was different from that of people acting habitually with no experience of their surroundings at all. He differed from the bystanders at the scene as well, since the experience they had of the situation allowed them to wonder what must be done. By contrast with both of these, Mr. Autrey not only experienced his surroundings, he experienced them directly in terms of what they demanded from him.

This can sound like a bizarre phenomenon, and we admit that it is rather rare. In the extreme form, indeed, it is about as rare as heroic action itself. But if we pay attention we can find versions of it in our daily lives. Perhaps the most common version is found in the domain of sports. Indeed, some of our everyday locutions even emphasize this phenomenon. When someone is playing very well, for example, we can say that they are playing "out of their head"; they have left the domain of thought altogether, in other words, and are carried along by the flow and demands of the game. A master athlete at the top of his game has a heightened awareness of his surroundings not unlike what Mr. Autrey experienced.

One of the great descriptions of this kind of athletic mastery is found in John McPhee's *A Sense of Where You Are*.[9] McPhee's book profiles the college basketball career of Bill Bradley, whom he describes as perhaps the best college basketball player ever. Bradley went on, of course, to be a Rhodes scholar, a Hall of Fame basketball player for the New York Knicks, and eventually a U.S. senator and presidential candidate. But McPhee's book is about Bradley's presence on the college court, and here he describes the phenomenon we are after.

One of the most impressive features of Bradley's game, according to McPhee, was his ability to be aware of everything that was going on in the game at once. He had this awareness without needing to look, as in the case of a certain shot he had perfected:

> The over-the-shoulder shot had no actual name. He tossed it, without looking, over his head and into the basket. There was no need to look, he explained, because "you develop a sense of where you are."[10]

This kind of vision for the court allowed Bradley to be aware of everything going on around him until the moment he let himself be drawn in directly by an opportunity in the game. As McPhee describes:

> His most remarkable natural gift, however, is his vision. During a game, Bradley's eyes are always a glaze of panoptic attention, for a basketball player needs to look at everything, focusing on nothing, until the last moment of commitment.[11]

The vision that is a "glaze of panoptic attention," in McPhee's delightful phrase, is precisely not the kind of awareness that the eyewitness has. It is attentive to opportunities for action, not to details of the scene. It is what allows a master player like Bradley to perform, in the biggest game of his career, against the top-ranked team in the nation, before thousands in Madison Square Garden, like this:

> Michigan played him straight, and he played Michigan into the floor. . . . He stole the ball, he went back door, he threw unbelievable passes. He reversed away from the best defenders in the Big Ten. He held his own man to one point. He played

in the backcourt, in the post, and in the corners. . . . Once, he found himself in a corner of the court with two Michigan players, both taller than he, pressing in on him shoulder to shoulder. He parted them with two rapid fakes—a move of the ball and a move of his head—and leaped up between them to sink a twenty-two-foot jumper. The same two players soon cornered him again. The fakes were different the second time, but the result was the same. He took a long stride between them and went up into the air, drifting forward, as they collided behind him, and he hit a clean shot despite the drift. . . . [When he fouled out toward the end of the game, he had to watch the rest] from the bench. As he sat down, the twenty thousand spectators stood up and applauded him for some three minutes. It was, as sportswriters and the Garden management subsequently agreed, the most clamorous ovation ever given a basketball player, amateur or professional, in Madison Square Garden. . . . [D]uring the long applause the announcer on the Garden loudspeaker impulsively turned up the volume and said, "Bill Bradley, one of the greatest players ever to play in Madison Square Garden, scored forty-one points."[12]

Greatness of this sort is nearly mystical to apprehend. It is characterized by the kind of sustained responsiveness to the demands of the situation that the Subway Hero embodied when he leapt onto the tracks. It is unflinching, unhesitating, and unwavering, and it has these certain qualities precisely because the activity flows not *from* the agent but *through* him. As a spectator of heroic activity one has the sense of watching something nearly inevitable, as though it is ordained by some force beyond the mere whim of human self-assertion. Indeed, one indication of the similarity between Bradley and Autrey is the spontaneous eruption of applause that both performances elicited from witnesses to the events. It is clear to all those present that something superhuman has been achieved.

One name we have for the superhuman is the heroic, and there is a sense in which both Bradley and Autrey are properly considered heroes. There is an important difference between them, however. Bradley's activity, superhuman as it may have been, took place only in the context of the limited domain of basketball. Autrey's actions took place in the broader domain of life. But for the moment it is the similarity between the cases that we would like to emphasize. Both are at the pinnacle of human possibility precisely because they leave no room for the kind of human indecision that plagues us all.

THE BURDEN OF CHOICE, as we have called it, can seem like a necessary feature of human existence. Even if heroic actors such as Bradley and Autrey can escape it for moments, in certain circumstances, the broader existential form of this burden seems to weigh heavily upon all of us. In the most basic case it amounts to profound questions: How, given the kinds of beings that we are, is it possible to live a *meaningful* life? Or more particularly, where are we to find the significant differences among the possible actions in our lives? For it is these differences that provide a basis for making decisions about who we are to be or become. At a certain stage in life these questions can seem unavoidable. The college students we teach everyday, for example, cannot keep from asking them. When they wonder whether they want to become doctors or lawyers, investment bankers or philosophers, when they try to decide whether to major in this or that, when they ask themselves whether they want to advocate liberal or conservative political positions, or associate themselves with a place of worship, or remain faithful to their boyfriend or girlfriend back home—all of these questions ultimately seem to lead them back to the basic one: On what basis should I make this choice?

But it is not only the maturing adult who is confronted with these kinds of existential choices. Even if we are firm in our identities— father or mother, businessperson or software designer—even if we have already made our political or religious commitments, we are always susceptible to good reasons for rescinding these commitments. And even if we were not so susceptible, the question of identity is never concluded. Feeling a certain commitment to my identity as the father of my son doesn't by itself tell me how to take up that role. The basic question always seems to be just around the corner: On what basis am I to make this choice? The heroic certainty of a Bradley or an Autrey seems a distant hope in this existential domain.

Although the burden of choice can seem inevitable, in fact it is unique to contemporary life. It is not just that in earlier epochs one knew on what basis one's most fundamental existential choices were made: it is that the existential questions didn't even make sense.

Consider the Middle Ages, for example. During this period in the Christian West a person's identity was determined by God. To say this is to take no stand on whether there actually was a God in the Middle Ages. The classic metaphysical arguments for the existence of God, or for the necessity of his various attributes, are irrelevant here. What matters instead is that in the Middle Ages people could not help but *experience themselves as* determined or created by God. Indeed, it was so much a part of the way they understood the world they lived in, so taken for granted by everything that made sense to them, that it was virtually inconceivable that one's identity might be determined in any other way. This was true, of course, about kings and queens. To say that they ruled by divine right, as was commonly understood in the Middle Ages, is to say that they were chosen specifically by God to be the rulers of society. But it was not only the kings and queens who were chosen by divine right: everyone else fell into a place in society according to the divine plan of God himself. Indeed, not just people but every item in creation had its place in the divine order, in the Great Chain of Being: kings above noblemen, noblemen above townspeople, all these above serfs, and so on, but also all people above all other animals, all animals above all inanimate objects, and all these, including people, below the angels and ultimately below

God. This order of things was not a *belief* that anyone argued for or a worldview that anyone proposed; it was simply taken for granted by everyone worth talking or listening to. Members of this society made sense of everything in terms of this fundamental idea—one could explain a victory in battle, for instance, or an untimely storm in terms of the will of God—but the idea that everything had its proper place in God's divine plan was not itself a *belief* one could accept or reject. It was an entire way of life.

The way of life of a culture is not an explicit set of beliefs held by the people living in it. It is much deeper than that. A person brought up in a culture learns its way of life the way he learns to speak in the language and with the accent of his family and peers. But a way of life is much broader than this. It involves a sense for how it is appropriate and inappropriate to act in each of the social situations one normally encounters; a familiarity with how to make sense of things and of how to act in the everyday world; and most general of all, a style, such as aggressive or nurturing, that governs the actions of the people in the culture although they are normally not aware of it. We can think of it as a cultural commitment that, to govern people's behavior, must remain in the background, unnoticed but pervasive and real. In the Medieval World, when this commitment involves a sense of God's divine plan, there is simply no question on what basis a person should choose who he is or is to become. For after all, that one *chooses* one's identity at all is inconceivable.

That is not to say that in the Middle Ages one never made any choices. One could always willfully turn away from God's plan and pursue a course that deviated from his desires. Or one could aim for the course of right action and fall short. In the terminology of medieval Christendom there were not only Saints but Sinners too, not only those who lived Virtuous lives but those who succumbed to the perilous attractions of Vice. Dante's *Inferno,* which we shall discuss in greater detail in chapter 5,[13] contains a large and informative discussion of the various ways a person of the Middle Ages could go astray. (Dante wrote around 1300, at the height of the Late Middle Ages.) Despite their extraordinary variety, what is characteristic of all of Dante's sinners is that their actions involve deviations from or perversions of a path already understood to be laid out by God.

Consider a characteristic example. In the second circle of Hell Dante discovers Paolo and Francesca, two lovers who in life were overcome by their overwhelming desire for one another. After being caught together by Francesca's husband, who was also Paolo's brother, and killed by him for their adulterous affair, the two were condemned to spend eternity blown about by the tempestuous wind of their uncontrollable passion for one another. We shall consider this example again in our discussion of Dante later, but for the moment all we need to notice is the medieval conception of sin that it illustrates. Dante's presentation of the case makes it clear that there was one right path of action for Paolo and Francesca—to avoid the adulterous affair—and that their sin lay in succumbing to the attractions of Vice. It has always been difficult, in certain situations, to act in accord with the standards for living well—the Greek philosophers called this difficulty *akrasia,* or weakness of the will; it is the inability to do what we know to be the right thing. At least some of Dante's sinners are victims of this kind of incontinence.

But in the contemporary world we face a deeper and more difficult problem. It is not just that we know the course of right action and fail to pursue it; we often seem not to have any sense for what the standards of living a good life are in the first place. Or said another way, we seem to have no ground for choosing one course of action over any other.

Consider, by contrast with Paolo and Francesca, the more modern, nineteenth-century case of Emma Bovary. In Flaubert's *Madame Bovary* we are told the story of Emma, who is married to the boring and talentless country doctor Charles. To escape her superficial, banal, and empty life in the provinces, Emma has adulterous affairs and lives beyond her means. Things end up badly, of course, but even so it is not obvious that Emma's adulterous affairs themselves are what was wrong. We have some sympathy with her desire to get more out of life, little sympathy for Charles and his empty mode of existence, and in some sense are meant to understand and endorse Emma's desire for escape. The lust for life that she exhibits seems admirable, and provides a creditable counterweight to the commitment her marriage engages her in.

Although in some general sense Emma's adulterous affairs share much with that of Paolo and Francesca, Flaubert's treatment of the situation could not differ more radically from Dante's. For Emma is presented by Flaubert as having been faced with the kind of existential question that Paolo and Francesca, as characterized by Dante, were not. The medieval couple *knew* that it was wrong to engage in an adulterous affair—there was no question about it; unfortunately, they couldn't resist the sinful passion of lust. Emma's situation is much more complicated. Do we really believe that she should stay with Charles? On the contrary, not only can we understand her desire to leave him, it seems at least possible that it could be for the best. Indeed, Charles himself recognizes her actions as admirable: he continues to idolize her after she dies, never criticizing her, and indeed he attempts to adopt her way of life. So the question of whether Emma's actions were admirable or not is a vexed one, and the confusion she felt about her course of action is supposed to be immediately recognizable to us. After all, she felt the burden of choice that nowadays seems so obvious to us all.

How DID WE GET from the fixed certainty of Dante's world to the existential uncertainty of our own? The story is long and complicated, and this book is devoted to articulating the bones of that story. But it may help to get at least a brief sense for one of the major transition points, which occurred at the beginning of the seventeenth century, in what is known as the early modern period of the West.

By 1600 the Medieval World was breaking down. In particular, it was no longer possible to take it for granted that God's will structures the universe. Very few people at the time, if any, explicitly recognized this development. Practices that a whole culture takes for granted are extremely difficult to identify. But we can find the clues to this historical development throughout the literature and philosophy of the time. Let us take two examples.

First, Shakespeare himself seems to have been nearly obsessed with the breakdown of the divine order. Whether he knew it or not, this development motivates many of his plays. As a great and sensitive artist, Shakespeare seems intuitively to have sensed that the breakdown of the divine order was one of the world-historical issues of his day. Many of his most successful characters confront this modern development in one way or another. Consider Macbeth, for example. Here we find an individual who by his "o'ervaulting ambition" alone hopes to leap beyond his natural place in the divine order into a new and higher place as king. The very idea that one should, by one's own will and desire, transform the divine order of the universe would have been anathema to Dante in the world of the Middle Ages. Indeed, we shall see that the character whom Dante most associates with this kind of self-directed ambition is Satan himself, who attempts to substitute his own will for God's, and is banished to the bottom of Hell for the attempt. Far from condemning Macbeth's ambition, however, Shakespeare seems fascinated by the way it pulls our intuition in different directions. On the one hand, Macbeth is in some ways a sympathetic character: his ambition to improve his position in the world seems understandable even if his particular strategy for doing so does not. Indeed, it is not just that Macbeth is in fact a sympathetic character; the very success of the play absolutely depends on our finding him so. This is because the tragedy of the play cannot get a grip on us unless we are rooting for its main character to succeed; there is no tragedy in a purely evil character getting his due. Despite being in some way sympathetic, however, Macbeth is doomed to failure. For better or for worse, the divine order is tenaciously resisting the rise of self-directed ambition. It is as if Shakespeare can see this ambition as a potentially admirable trait even though the world he lives in will not yet support this way of life. The divine order is tenaciously resisting the rise of self-directed ambition, for better or for worse. In other plays, such as *Troilus and Cressida,* the breakdown of the divine order is presented as comical at best, and very likely as unambiguously bad. In general, it seems Shakespeare can see that the way of life based on a divine plan is crumbling but he can't figure out exactly what to think about it.

Or consider the case of Hamlet. His famous soliloquy from Act III Scene 1, "To be or not to be, that is the question," takes on the fundamental issue of whether he should choose to live or choose to die. The very idea that he understands this as a choice open to him indicates that his culture no longer takes it for granted that God determines these fundamental facts of our existence. This is not to say, of course, that nobody ever contemplated suicide before Hamlet. But the cultural interpretation of what one is up to when one is contemplating such a thought is radically different for Hamlet than it would have been for a character of the Middle Ages. In the medieval tradition suicide is understood as an act of rebellion against God, an attempt to take over from God a decision that is rightfully his. (Indeed, Dante puts the suicides in the seventh of the nine circles of Hell, sitting right beside the blasphemers against God.) Once again, we find an act of rebellion of the same sort that Satan engaged in when he tried to organize a rebellion of the angels against the Lord. For Hamlet, by contrast, the thought that suicide would be an affront to God never seems to occur. The question is simply "whether 'tis *nobler in the mind* to suffer the slings and arrows of outrageous fortune / Or to take arms against a sea of troubles. / And by opposing, end them?" The question, in other words, is not whether it is an affront against God, and therefore obviously the wrong thing to do. The question is whether *it's a better decision*—"nobler in the mind"—to suffer or to commit suicide. God, or the understanding of God as the divine planner of the universe, offers no help to Hamlet in considering this question. The breakdown of the divine order of the Middle Ages, in other words, has opened up the possibility for genuine existential questioning.

The freedom to choose who we are to be, however, comes with a heavy burden. For without God's divine plan to ground us, on the basis of what are we to make our existential choices? The desire for a fundamental ground, for some unshakeable conviction on the basis of which to build our understanding of ourselves and the universe, can be seen most clearly in the philosophical tradition.

René Descartes, surely the most important philosopher in the history of modern philosophy, was writing in France approximately one generation after Shakespeare wrote in England. (Descartes' most important works were written around 1630.) One of his main philosophical projects was to show that it is possible to know *for certain,* and *without any doubt at all,* the most basic things that we know. That there is an external world, for instance, or that people other than ourselves exist. It turns out to be very difficult to prove these things with absolute certainty. The characters in the movie *The Matrix,* for example, seem to be living lives just exactly like ours; it turns out, however, that although they are having the very same kinds of experiences that we all have, in their case there is no world at all of the sort they seem to be experiencing. The idea that the world is as it seems to be is a very basic idea. Descartes showed, however, 350 years before Hollywood, that it is very difficult to know this basic fact *without doubt.* But the idea that this is the kind of thing we could doubt at all, and the even more extreme idea that we should have to try to find out whether we could *know* this kind of fundamental thing *for certain,* is an idea that wouldn't occur to someone who lived in a world in which these kinds of questions don't really make sense. The Cartesian project itself would be understood as an act of hubris in the Middle Ages. The idea that we have to prove to ourselves that God *isn't* tricking us takes as a background assumption that, well, for all we know God *is* tricking us. But this kind of assumption doesn't even make sense in a world in which God is from the start understood to be the divine and benevolent architect of the universe. The fact that Descartes not only could ask the skeptical question, but could be taken seriously—indeed, could be held up as a paradigm of philosophical thinking—shows that by the time he was writing in the early 1600s the medieval assumptions were no longer taken for granted. And if something so basic as whether there is an external world at all can be shown to be in need of philosophical grounding, then how much less grounded must be our existential choices about how to act?

FRIEDRICH NIETZSCHE, the great German philosopher of the late nineteenth century, famously claimed that God is dead. What he meant by this is that we in the modern West no longer live in a culture where the basic questions of existence are already answered for us. The God of the Middle Ages played the role of answering existential questions before they could be asked; but such a role is no longer conceivable. This is true for modern religious believers and skeptics alike, as the contemporary philosopher Charles Taylor points out.[14] Even if there is, as some have claimed, a Third Religious Awakening in the modern United States, the kind of religious belief available in our culture today is not sufficient to quell existential questioning. It is no longer taken for granted that nonbelievers are outside the realm of the human. That was the case in medieval Christendom: to be a nonbeliever was ipso facto to be evil, to have set yourself against the delights of all that is humanly worth attaining. Perhaps there are some fanatical religious subcultures that manage to sustain this exclusionary belief today. But insofar as a religious believer's belief in God is consistent with the idea that there are admirable people who nevertheless do not believe, as for the most part is the case in the modern West, then religious belief cannot by itself close off existential questioning. For the idea that a nonbeliever is not ipso facto execrable means that nonbelief is a choice that even a believer must take seriously. To say that we live in a secular age in the modern West is to say that even religious believers face existential questions about how to live a life.

Facing existential questions is not such a bad thing if one has the resources to answer them. Perhaps some religious believers in the modern West do have such resources; Taylor's recent work begins from this premise. Indeed, Taylor sees the radical proliferation of religions and spirituality—a veritable explosion of religious lives—as the central feature of the modern age. The idea that there is no reason to prefer any answer to any other, however, is called nihilism, and Nietzsche thought this the better description of our current condition after the death of God.

Nietzsche thought that nihilism was a great joy, since it frees us to live any life we choose, but many find it horrifying instead. As Dostoyevsky puts it, "If there is no God, then everything is permitted." Our view is that nihilism is every bit as closed-minded as fanaticism, and that neither is a sufficient ground on which to base a livable life. But we are more skeptical than Taylor that Judeo-Christian monotheism can be culturally satisfying in the modern age. Even if it could be, there are other religious traditions in the history of the West that allow one to live a life guided by something experienced as beyond oneself. Chapter 3 considers one such tradition, the tradition of Greek polytheism as it is portrayed by Homer. Before we turn to that, however, we will look at the most sensitive current account of the sadness and lostness of the present age.

2

David Foster Wallace's Nihilism

Wonder is the feeling of a philosopher,
and philosophy begins in wonder.

—PLATO

DAVID FOSTER WALLACE was the greatest writer of his generation; perhaps the greatest mind altogether.[1] He wrote enormous, ambitious novels, stories, and essays that were dedicated to showing his readers how to live a meaningful life. "Fiction's about what it is to be a fucking human being," he once said. Good writing should help readers to "become less alone inside."[2]

David Foster Wallace hanged himself on September 12, 2008. He was forty-six years old.

What can we make of Wallace's suicide? Not much, probably. It is well known that he had suffered from depression for decades, that he had been treating his condition with the antidepressant medication Nardil for nearly twenty years, and that he had undergone many courses of electroconvulsive therapy, including fully a dozen during the months leading up to his death.[3] It is also well known that Wallace's final descent coincided with his attempt once and for all to wean himself from Nardil, the medication that James Wallace said "had allowed his son to be productive."[4] There is no doubt that there are neurophysiological and neurochemical aspects to severe depression, and it seems natural to conclude that Wallace finally succumbed in the face of the biological odds.

And yet.

There is also some truth to the claim that Wallace's writing captured, and Wallace himself embodied, some of the prevailing moods of the modern age. His doorstop of a masterpiece, *Infinite Jest,* is a stylistic embodiment of modern self-consciousness. It is filled with paragraph-long sentences that are constantly undermining themselves, bringing their own premises into question, and then coming back ouroboros-like to eat their own tails. Many of these sentences are complemented by lengthy endnotes that continue the process, as if to say that this is the way we are aware of ourselves in the modern age: we say something, wonder about what we've said, unsay it, ask about it again, circle back to it from a different perspective, qualify it, unqualify it, and so on, footnoting our endnotes and endnoting our footnotes to infinity. We conclude, if at all, without resolution.

Even Wallace's relationships seem to have had this character. At the age of forty-two Wallace did finally marry a visual artist named Karen Green, and their marriage was by all accounts a happy one until his final year. But Wallace had many unsuccessful relationships before that, including a serious, and seriously volatile, relationship with the poet and memoirist Mary Karr.[5] Despite its volatility, or perhaps because of it, Karr was important enough to him that he tattooed a heart upon his arm with her name in it. When eventually, years later, he and Karen Green fell in love, this remnant presumably became something of an embarrassment. He tattooed a strikeout through Mary's name and an asterisk beneath the heart. Further down his arm he added another asterisk and Karen's name, "turning his arm," as D. T. Max writes, "into a living footnote."

Perhaps it's too obvious to recall Melville's tattooed native Queequeg here. But if Melville is right that we wear the sacred practices of our culture tattooed upon our body, as our argument shall claim, then

Wallace's life must be seen as a cautionary tale. What we hold sacred, he seems to be saying, is the ability to footnote our commitments—to qualify them, change them, and take them back. Our most sacred commitment, in other words, is the freedom to choose our commitments. And the freedom to unchoose them again, when that is what we choose to do.

Infinite Jest clocks in at a full 1,079 pages, including almost 100 pages of weighty endnotes, and it now stands as the principal contender for what serious literature can aspire to in the late twentieth and early twenty-first centuries. The novel takes on addiction, depression, consumerism, terrorism, and tennis academies, among many other characteristic late-twentieth-century problems. It is—both stylistically and substantively—a detailed and deeply perceptive attempt to say what it is to be a fucking human being in America at the turn of the millennium.

And what exactly is that like? "There's something particularly sad about it," Wallace said, in a 1996 interview with the online journal *Salon,*

> something that doesn't have very much to do with physical circumstances, or the economy, or any of the stuff that gets talked about in the news. It's more like a stomach-level sadness. I see it in myself and my friends in different ways. It manifests itself as a kind of lostness.

This lostness may simply have been the physiological depression that Wallace had battled his whole adult life. But there is another possibility too. Perhaps Wallace was not so much describing his own personal depression as he was describing aspects of the culture that that depression made him sensitive to. Aspects that others might well overlook, or cover up, or otherwise avoid—aspects of modern existence that we all live through but fail to see. Perhaps, in other words, his depression made him peculiarly sensitive to something that pervades the culture, something not personal and individual but public and shared. And perhaps his job as a writer was to reveal that aspect of ourselves to us. That, at any rate, is how Wallace seems to have seen it:

> The sadness that the book is about, and that I was going through, was a real American type of sadness. I was white, upper-middle-class, obscenely well-educated, had had way more career success than I could have legitimately hoped for and was sort of adrift. A lot of my friends were the same way. Some of them were deeply into drugs, others were unbelievable workaholics. Some were going to singles bars every night. You could see it played out in 20 different ways, but it's the same thing.[6]

And later in the interview he talks about this sadness and lostness as a mood—an American mood—that results from the inability of our culture, or certain segments of our culture, to confront the deepest questions about who we are:

> I get the feeling that a lot of us, privileged Americans, as we enter our early 30s, have to find a way to put away childish things and confront stuff about spirituality and values.

There is no doubt, then, that underlying biological facts played an important role in Wallace's severe depression and ultimate suicide. But to the extent that his work captures something of the modern age—as its success must indicate—then perhaps the mood to which he was attuned is something more than a result of his personal physiological makeup. Perhaps it is an indication of our metaphysical makeup, of the way our age fails to allow us to tell a coherent story about the meanings of our lives. As Wallace told *Whiskey Island,* a literary magazine, in 1993, "This is a generation that has an inheritance of absolutely nothing as far as meaningful moral values."[7]

If Wallace is right about this, and if it is this cultural fact to which he was deeply sensitive, then his suicide is much more than the loss of a single, talented individual. It is a warning that requires our most serious attention. It is, indeed, the proverbial canary in the coal mine of modern existence.

IN THE TIDAL WAVE of commentary devoted to Wallace's work, it is a fair bet that no serious person has considered its relation to that other canonical engagement with American culture: chick lit. Elizabeth Gilbert, arguably, is the reigning queen of this genre. Her 2006 memoir *Eat, Pray, Love* has over five million copies in print, and it spent more than a year as the number one bestseller on the *New York Times* Paperback Nonfiction list. The rising tide of Gilbert's fame has lifted even the pseudonymous characters in her story out of obscurity. Richard from Texas, for example, the drawling former junkie she meets at an ashram in India, has already appeared on *Oprah*. Twice.

Gilbert takes up the mantel of chick lit queen with some ambivalence. Uncertain what the genre consists of precisely, but certain that it is not meant to be a compliment, she chafes a bit at the description. Still, she accepts that there is something apropos about it as well.

Despite the almost unimaginable gulf between chick lit and the avant-garde, however, Gilbert's approach to writing is driven by the same kind of human ambition that motivated Wallace. "Writing has always been my particular way of translating life," she explains. "Of taking experiences out of the ephemeral and digesting them, making them real."[8] And as avant-garde as Wallace's work is, as postmodern and experimental and contemporary as the style and substance of his writing can be, he has a similar goal in mind. Like Gilbert, Wallace wants to unpack the world as it really is. "I've always thought of myself as a realist," he said in the *Salon* interview.

The world that I live in consists of 250 advertisements a day and any number of unbelievably entertaining options . . . I use a fair amount of pop stuff in my fiction, but what I mean by it is nothing different than what other people mean in writing about trees and parks and having to walk to the river to get water a 100 years ago. It's just the texture of the world I live in.

Elizabeth Gilbert's world is different from Wallace's, no doubt, but not because it is lacking the anxiety, depression, and downwright sadness that Wallace saw. The opening pages of her memoir find her sobbing inconsolably on the bathroom floor of her big house in the suburbs of New York.

Moreover, Gilbert's unhappiness is motivated by precisely the kind of lostness that Wallace sees everywhere. Hers is one particular manifestation of this modern American lostness, of course, one particular way of being adrift. But it is a species of the Wallacian phenomenon nevertheless. As Wallace himself said: "You could see it played out in twenty different ways, but it's the same thing." Liz Gilbert on that bathroom floor could have been a character in a Wallace scene.

Now, there is something to the idea that Gilbert's motivating issue speaks more naturally to women than men. She is confronted, after all, with a problem that many modern American women face: the cultural expectation that she should want to have a baby, combined with the personal realization that this is not for her. It may be true that in the modern world the tension between family and professional commitments, and between both of these and personal happiness, is felt more keenly by men than it was in the past. But there is no denying that Gilbert has the female experience in mind, and in this sense it is probably right to say that she is writing for a female audience. Still, prescinding from the details of her case we can see Wallace's general theme—the tension between commitment and choice—shining through. As she says, summing up her predicament:

I couldn't stop thinking about what my sister had said to me once, as she was breastfeeding her firstborn: "Having a baby is

like getting a tattoo on your face. You really need to be certain
it's what you want before you commit."[9]

Besides an ambivalent relationship to tattoos, Wallace and Gilbert
share something else. Although each is motivated by a deep sense of
confusion and lostness, a sense that the darkness of being adrift is
a central feature of the age, nevertheless each feels strongly that the
writer's responsibility is to show the way forward, to offer a vision of
the hopeful possibilities available in the modern world. It is striking,
for instance, that although Gilbert's story begins with the breakup of
her marriage, she refuses to talk about the details of that dark period
in her life. Her memoir takes off from the assumption that we all
know what that kind of darkness is like—it is only, and needs only
to be, drawn in the broadest and dimmest of strokes. The burden of
her story, instead, is to show us how one can go forth from that dark
place, to tell us what it takes to emerge into the light.

So too, Wallace. Early on in his career, he insisted that his goal as a
writer was to show us a way out of our predicament, not to glamorize
its awfulness. As he told Larry McCaffery in a 1991 interview:

Look man, we'd probably most of us agree that these are dark
times, and stupid ones, but do we need fiction that does nothing but dramatize how dark and stupid everything is? In dark
times, the definition of good art would seem to be art that lo-
cates and applies CPR to those elements of what's human and
magical that still live and glow despite the times' darkness. Really good fiction could have as dark a worldview as it wished,
but it'd find a way both to depict this world and to illuminate
the possibilities for being alive and human in it.[10]

That is the real reason that Wallace and Gilbert are appropriate for
this book: not because they sense the lostness of the age—this dark
vision was alive already in Eliot's *Wasteland* and Beckett's *Endgame,*

and countless other testimonies from the early part of the twentieth century. No, what makes these contemporary authors worth reading instead is that they are trying to find a way into the light. In seeing how they fail, we will prepare ourselves to search for the sacred possibilities still alive in the modern world.

WALLACE'S FINAL, UNFINISHED MASTERPIECE has at its center the deep spiritual struggle of a dedicated, nearly monastic group of IRS tax return examiners. Referred to as *The Pale King,* the project was increasingly unwieldy and had swelled to enormous proportions. Wallace complained of being unable to get its racing narrative under control. It's like "trying to carry a sheet of plywood in a windstorm," he moaned.[11] In a January 2006 email to his friend the author Jonathan Franzen, Wallace spoke of "many, many pages written, then either tossed or put in a sealed box."

> The whole thing is a tornado that won't hold still long enough for me to see what's useful and what isn't. I've brooded and brooded about all this till my brooder is sore.[12]

One problem with the narrative was structural. Wallace had deliberately hamstrung himself by choosing the most boring characters imaginable: people who sit for eight hours a day reviewing other people's tax returns. As Michael Pietsch, Wallace's friend and editor, points out, the author had "posed himself the task that is almost the opposite of how fiction works."[13] Normally driven by the directive to leave out the boring parts of life, Wallace's project, by contrast, was meant to focus on them.

But the structural problem was not arbitrary, either; indeed, in Wallace's view it seems to have been absolutely essential. The struggle of the IRS examiners was Wallace's own struggle with writing, and it was the struggle he saw at the center of modern existence as well.

In part, this was the struggle to focus on one's task despite the ever-present and constantly beckoning distractions from it that increasingly constitute the social world in which we live. As Wallace said in a 1997 interview with Charlie Rose, describing an upcoming sabbatical year:

> CR: And so what would you do with that year?
>
> DFW: If past experience holds true I will probably write an hour a day and spend eight hours a day on biting my knuckle and worrying about not writing.
>
> CR: Worrying about not writing. Not worrying about what to write?
>
> DFW: Right. Worrying about not writing.[14]

The central challenge of the contemporary world, Wallace seems to think, is not just that we don't know how to live meaningful lives; it's that we don't even seem to be able to focus for very long on the question.

INFINITE JEST IS in part an exploration of society's increasing devotion to the perfection of distraction. At the center of the novel is a film so "fatally entertaining,"[15] so "terminally compelling,"[16] that those who watch it are reduced to a state of drooling anomie. One such unfortunate, a medical attaché, watches the fatal "entertainment cartridge" by accident one evening. Hours later:

> The medical attaché . . . is still viewing the unlabelled cartridge, which he has rewound to the beginning several times and then configured for a recursive loop. He sits there, attached to a congealed supper, watching, at 0020h., having now wet both his pants and the special recliner.[17]

The film, like the book in which it appears, is called *Infinite Jest.*

The book and the film both take their title from a well-known scene in *Hamlet*. In the graveyard behind a church Hamlet discovers the skull of Yorick, the court jester of his youth. Upon taking it up he cries:

> Alas, poor Yorick! I knew him, Horatio, a fellow of infinite jest, of most excellent fancy. He hath born me on his back a thousand times.[18]

In Shakespeare's rendering Yorick, the fellow of infinite jest, is drawn in stark contrast with the melancholy Dane. Wallace's contemporary treatment offers us a whole culture taken over by Hamlet's heavy disposition. The flight to distraction, however, ends no longer in the arms of a man of most excellent fancy, a court jester who bears you on his back and lifts your spirits. Instead, the power of infinite jest is sedating; it leaves you congealed, in your special recliner, having wet your pants. Entertainment of this perfect sort takes away our humanity instead of restoring it to us.

Because the false happiness of this perfect entertainment is merely a ruse, because the pursuit of it eviscerates us, collapses our world into "one small bright point,"[19] and because in its perfect version it is impossible to resist, Wallace's earlier novel is essentially a sad one.[20] It depicts our world as devoted to the perfection of an entertainment in the face of which we will necessarily annihilate ourselves.

The goal of *The Pale King*, as it might be imagined, is to show us how to avoid this fate.

Crushing, crushing boredom turns out to be the key. In a typed note discovered with the papers he left at his death, Wallace describes the premise of the book:

> Bliss—a-second-by-second joy and gratitude at the gift of being alive, conscious—lies on the other side of crushing, crushing boredom. Pay close attention to the most tedious thing you can find (Tax Returns, Televised Golf) and, in waves, a boredom like you've never known will wash over you and just

about kill you. Ride these out, and it's like stepping from black and white into color. Like water after days in the desert. Instant bliss in every atom.[21]

The Pale King was incomplete at Wallace's death, though excerpts from it have been published in several places.[22] The publishing house Little, Brown has announced plans to bring out the manuscript in some form or another. From the excerpts that have appeared so far, however, it seems clear that Wallace had moved beyond his earlier pre-occupations. The new novel is not so much interested in the transformation of our distractions, in the way they sedate us, even annihilate us, instead of bringing us back to ourselves. Rather, the new work is interested in the various states that precede and precipitate the flight to distraction: the boredom, the anxiety, the frustration, and the anger that propel us toward any distracting entertainment that offers relief. The spiritual journey of Wallace's IRS examiners consists in learning to live in these prior states—especially the state of boredom—and to find in them redemption and spiritual value.

This is no mean feat. One employee, Lane Dean, Jr., has particular difficulty sticking to his task. The description of his struggle seems to come from deep personal experience, and one cannot help but recall Wallace's own struggle with writing:

Lane Dean, Jr. . . . did two more returns, then another one, then flexed his buttocks and held to a count of ten and imagined a warm pretty beach with mellow surf, as instructed in orientation the previous month. Then he did two more returns, checked the clock real quick, then two more, then bore down and did three in a row, then flexed and visualized and bore way down and did four without looking up once . . . After just an hour the beach was a winter beach, cold and gray and the dead kelp like the hair of the drowned, and it stayed that way despite all attempts.[23]

There is no indication that Wallace was bored by the process of writing, but he struggled to stay on task, to keep at it to avoid distraction. He too bore down on his task, over and over again one must imagine, perhaps counting lines or pages—instead of forms—completed. How much greater must such a struggle be for those heroic characters who battle eight hours a day with a task so boring it literally drives you to distraction? Consider Lane Dean, Jr., later that same morning:

> His buttocks already ached from flexing, and the mere thought of envisioning the desolate beach unmanned him. He shut his eyes but, . . . when he opened his eyes, the In tray's stack of files looked to be still mainly the height it had been at 7:14, when he'd logged in in the chalk leader's notebook . . . and he refused once more to stand up to check how many of them there were, for he knew that would make it worse. He had the sensation of a great type of hole or emptiness falling through him and continuing to fall and never hitting the floor. Never before in his life up to now had he once thought of suicide.[24]

Dean's struggle is a spiritual one, a battle against the Hell of terminal boredom. And yet, Dean's point of view is not ultimate. His struggle is common, familiar—we all recognize it—but with the proper approach, Wallace seems to think, it is a struggle that can be won. That is what is suggested by the calmer and more peaceful world that is inhabited by the spiritually advanced adepts of IRS tax return examination. One room of these is described by Wallace as a kind of monastery, "each of the IRS examiners work[ing] in a small tight circle of light." And in this monastery we find all manner of spiritually accomplished agents. Atkins, who sits next to Dean, is one. He never seems to fidget or move at all while filling forms, and he claims the nigh-magical power of examining and cross-checking two files at once. Another agent can reportedly, by reciting a sequence of numbers, enter a state of exalted concentration. And then there is Mitchell

Drinion. "Drinion is *Happy,*" Wallace wrote in one of his notebooks.[25] He is so centered and calm, so at peace with the boredom of his task, that he has broken through to the bliss beyond. Drinion literally levitates as he works.

How does one achieve this state of bliss, in Wallace's view? Perhaps there is a clue in the experience of Don Gately. Gately is probably the central hero of *Infinite Jest;* he is a former Demerol addict and current residential counselor at Ennett House, the drug and alcohol recovery center down the hill from the Enfield Tennis Academy. Gately's heroism consists at least partly in his struggle to resist the various temptations and distractions of modern existence—the television, the loneliness, and especially the drugs. His description of what it is like to go through the pain of withdrawal, and later the physical pain of a gunshot wound, could well be a precursor to Drinion's approach to boredom. According to Gately, it all depends on living in the present moment. Toward the end of the novel he recalls various "evil fucking personal detoxes," some of them cold turkey and enforced by incarceration:

A Revere Holding cage for 92 days. Feeling the edge of every second that went by. Taking it a second at a time. Drawing the time in around him real tight. Withdrawing. Any one second: he remembered: the thought of feeling like he'd be feeling this second for 60 more of these seconds—he couldn't deal. He could not fucking deal. He had to build a wall around each second just to take it. The whole first two weeks of it are telescoped in his memory down into like one second—less: the space between two heartbeats. A breath and a second, the pause and gather between each cramp. An endless Now stretching its gull-wings out on either side of his heartbeat. And he'd never before or since felt so excruciatingly alive. Living in the Present between pulses.[26]

Perhaps the bliss that Drinion feels in his boredom is like the aliveness that Gately experiences when he is forced to live in the present moment. The pain of detox, like the hell of boredom, is sustainable only if one builds a wall around each moment. But the experience of doing so gives each moment a kind of vividness, of brilliance and sheen—indeed, a kind of "second-by-second joy and gratitude at the gift of being alive"—that cannot be felt if we step outside the moment. This is such a difficult experience to achieve that most normal people can find it only when they need it in order to survive:

> [T]his inter-beat Present, this sense of endless Now—it had vanished in Revere Holding along with the heaves and chills. He'd returned to himself, moved to sit on the bunk's edge, and ceased to Abide because he no longer had to.[27]

Gately's experience with detox seems to help him toward the end of the novel when he is dealing with the pain of a gunshot wound to his right shoulder. The pain is agonizing, all the more so since the recovering addict refuses to take narcotic painkillers, but his earlier experience with detox is a guide:

> He could do the dextral pain the same way: Abiding. No one single instant of it was unendurable. Here was a second right here: he endured it. What was undealable-with was the thought of all the instants all lined up and stretching ahead, glittering. . . . It's too much to think about. To Abide there. . . . He could just hunker down in the space between each heartbeat and make each heartbeat a wall and live in there. Not let his head look over.[28]

Gately's struggle not to look over the wall of each second recalls Dean's struggle not to look up at his stack of files; both recall the eight hours a day Wallace spends worrying about not writing, worrying about having given in to the temptation to look beyond the moment in which one is writing and think about it from somewhere else. The challenge is to build the wall around that moment so the distractions and temptations to look beyond it are mute. Dean hasn't learned how to build this wall yet, but the adepts have. That's why Dean's experience of boredom is an unendurable hell, while Drinion's is an eternal bliss. "What's unendurable," Gately tells us,

> is what his own head could make of it all. What his head could report to him, looking over and ahead and reporting. But he could choose not to listen. . . . He hadn't quite gotten this before now, how it wasn't just the matter of riding out the cravings for a Substance: everything unendurable was in the head, was the head not Abiding in the Present but hopping the wall and doing a recon and then returning with unendurable news you then somehow believed.[29]

Gately's aliveness, then, and Drinion's bliss are achievable precisely from within what is most unendurable. When the pain or the boredom or the anger or the angst is so overwhelming that it seems as though one cannot live through it for even a second longer, when it is so unendurable that it seems to have transformed itself into the definition of a living hell, then that is the moment when one has no other choice but to build a wall around the present and live entirely in the Now. That is why crushing, crushing boredom is the key. For riding it out forces a choice, in Wallace's view, the choice of total misery or to turn all distractions mute and abide in the joy and gratitude of the eternal Present.

WALLACE WAS AWARDED AN honorary degree from Kenyon College in 2005, and he gave the commencement speech at graduation that year. The address was published posthumously under a title only slightly shorter than the speech itself: *This Is Water: Some Thoughts, Delivered on a Significant Occasion, about Living a Compassionate Life.*

The central premise of the commencement speech, like much of Wallace's later work, is that simple, apparently uninteresting clichés often hide a deeper truth. According to Wallace, this fact gets covered over by the postmodern tendency to favor highly intellectualized, complex, and aestheticized principles over simple and aesthetically uninteresting ones that are nevertheless deeply true. The postmodern aversion to simplicity is "one of the things that's gutted our generation."[30]

Wallace's principle goal as a writer, it might be said, is to resuscitate the truths living within these clichés, to revivify them and make them vitally relevant again. Gately's experience of building a wall around each second, for example, is an enriched version of a famous slogan from Alcoholics Anonymous:

> Something as banal and reductive as "One Day at a Time" enabled these people to walk through hell, which from what I could see the first six months of detox is. That struck me.[31]

Wallace shows why the cliché holds a literal truth. "The most obvious, important realities," he says in the commencement speech, "are often the ones that are hardest to see and talk about."

The speech has become most famous for three macabre sentences that appear near the middle. "It is not the least bit coincidental," Wallace reported, to the assembled crowd of eager, scrub-faced graduates and the proud, smiling families gathered to celebrate their achievement,

> that adults who commit suicide with firearms almost always shoot themselves in: the head. They shoot the terrible master.

And the truth is that most of these suicides are actually dead long before they pull the trigger.

Not exactly typical fare for a graduation speech.

These sentences have become famous in retrospect, of course, because they seem now to have foreshadowed Wallace's imminent demise. And there is no doubt, of course, that Wallace was speaking even at the time from personal experience. This was a man, after all, who had attempted suicide at least once already, would try again less than three years hence, and would finally succeed in the effort six months after that.

But it is not the poignancy of these lines that we want to focus on here. Instead we see in them, and in the speech as a whole, a clue to precisely what was untenable in the position that Wallace had taken up. A clue, in other words, to why crushing, crushing boredom is not the key. At least not the key that Wallace thought it was.

THE CLICHÉ THAT WALLACE attempts to revivify in the Kenyon speech is the old pedagogical cliché that a liberal arts education teaches you how to think.

Twenty years after my own graduation, I have come gradually to understand that [this] cliché . . . is actually shorthand for a much deeper, more serious idea: learning how to think really means learning how to exercise some control over how and what you think. It means being conscious and aware enough to choose what you pay attention to and to choose how you construct meaning from experience. Because if you cannot exercise this kind of choice in adult life, you will be totally hosed.

The skill of exercising control over how and what you think is precisely the skill that Lane Dean, Jr., is struggling to master; it is the skill of choosing to think about the tax return you are now completing—and only that—instead of losing control and hopping the wall.

The bizarre genius of the commencement speech is that it finds this struggle everywhere in life: in traffic jams and crowded supermarket aisles, in soul-killing muzak and corporate pop; in the "stupid and cow-like and dead-eyed and nonhuman" faces that stand as obstacles to our daily chore; even in "Have a nice day" from the checkout girl, said "in a voice that is the absolute voice of death." Indeed, Wallace finds the struggle against banality, boredom, anger, and frustration in all the "dreary, annoying, seemingly meaningless routines" that make up our lives "day after week after month after year." This is the existence from which Wallace offers us reprieve.

Perhaps it is a caricature. We have all had days like this, of course, but surely it is an exaggeration to claim, as Wallace does, that these dreadful experiences are the essence of the contemporary world; that growing up and coming to know "the day-to-day trenches of adult life"—as these innocent graduates have yet to do—consist primarily in discovering that existence is unendurable.

But whether these kinds of frustrations are manifold or merely intermittent, whether they plague us incessantly, as they seem to have plagued Wallace, or visit us only in an off-ish hour, whether they are familiar and regular enemies or distant and exotic foes, we all recognize them. We recognize them as unhappy moments in life, the ones our lives would be better without; we rue them, bemoan them, perhaps even decry them. And we would happily have them gone.

The key to this, Wallace claims, lies in controlling our thoughts. Sure, the "fat, dead-eyed, over-made-up lady" ahead of me in the checkout line is screaming at her kid. Naturally, I find myself brimming with anger at her. But it doesn't have to be this way. All I need to do, according to Wallace, is to control what I think about her; to construct a different and happier meaning for the experience I now find welling up within me.

Maybe she's been up three straight nights holding the hand of a husband who is dying of bone cancer. Or maybe this very lady is the low-wage clerk at the motor vehicle department, who just yesterday helped your spouse resolve a horrific, infuriating, red-tape problem through some small act of bureaucratic kindness. Of course, none of this is likely, but it's also not impossible. It just depends what you want to consider.

It's hard to do, of course, and Wallace insists he is not giving moral advice. To control your thoughts about others, about the unpleasant features of the situation you are now in, about whatever it is at this very moment that is causing you unhappiness—to do this is difficult. It takes effort and will, and sometimes you simply can't manage.

But it is a possibility, according to Wallace. And not just any possibility but *the* possibility; the *saving* possibility for modern life. "[M]ost days, if you're aware enough to give yourself a choice, you can choose to look differently" at the situation, he tells us.

If you really learn how to pay attention . . . [i]t will actually be within your power to experience a crowded, hot, slow, consumer-hell type situation as not only meaningful, but sacred, on fire with the same force that made the stars: love, fellowship, the mystical oneness of all things deep down.

That is the real lesson Wallace wants to get across: that the choice to experience the world as sacred and meaningful—to do so by dint of effort and will—is a choice that is within our power to make. It is a choice that takes strength and courage and persistence, of course; perhaps it takes even a kind of heroism. But it is possible, Wallace thinks. And more than that, it is necessary in the modern world.

WALLACE WORRIED THAT he was "not the kind of person who could write the novel he wanted to write."[32] Perhaps, he reflected, he was simply not strong enough or dedicated enough or willful enough to get it done. "Maybe the answer," he wrote in that letter to Franzen, "is simply that to do what I want to do would take more effort than I am willing to put in."

But this was not simply an observation about Wallace's writing—it was an observation about his life as a whole. To write the character of Mitchell Drinion—a character who is *"Happy"*—Wallace would have to learn Drinion's trick. And that trick, it seems, was not just a trick for how to stay on task in his writing. It was a trick that turned unhappiness into happiness everywhere in life. It was the trick of taking something that he automatically experiences as annoying and miserable and nevertheless finding a way to control his thoughts about the thing, to force himself to think about it differently; literally to give it a happier meaning by the sheer force of his individual will. If he could not do this himself then he could not write the character. And if he couldn't write the character of Drinion, then he couldn't be the kind of writer required by the times.

This is pure speculation on our part, of course. The name *Mitchell Drinion* receives exactly four hits from Google as we are writing this, and each of the four pages is a reprint of D. T. Max's article about Wallace in the March 9, 2009, issue of *The New Yorker*. Wallace published precisely nothing about Drinion in his lifetime, and according to Max he even left out the story of the levitating Drinion in a stack of manuscript pages for *The Pale King* that he sent to his editor in 2007. Were it not for Max's access to the Wallace estate, and his detailed and insightful article, we would not know about Drinion at all.

So yes, this is speculation. But it is not completely ungrounded speculation, for all that. Drinion was the hardest character for Wallace to write, in our view, the character with whom he was terminally unsatisfied, because he could never be sure whether he had gotten Drinion's *Happiness* right. Wallace's project, after all, was not just the postmodern project of finding more literary conventions to break. It was instead the very traditional—some might call it existential—project of writing characters in order to explore the possibilities (and impossibilities) for living well in the modern world. In his final major interview, given to *Le Nouvel Observateur* in August 2007, Wallace talked about the writers whom he admired most and what he admired about them. Included in the list are St. Paul, Rousseau, and Dostoyevsky, among others. "[W]hat are envied and coveted here," Wallace says, "seem to me to be qualities of human beings—capacities of spirit—rather than technical abilities or special talents."[33]

Wallace thought he had discovered the capacities of spirit necessary for the modern world—he found them in Dean's struggle and Gately's success and especially in the character of the blissful, levitating Mitchell Drinion. But unfortunately, he was realizing once and for all that he did not have these capacities himself. He had located "what's human and magical that still live(s) and glow(s) despite the times' darkness," and he was desperately trying to apply CPR to it. But he himself was already dead inside.

PERHAPS THE SADDEST PART of Wallace's story is that the human qualities he aspired to, the capacities of spirit that he revered and coveted, are a mirage. Indeed the entire mode of existence that he castigated himself for not being strong enough to achieve, far from being the saving possibility for our culture, is in fact a human impossibility. Wallace's inability to achieve it was not a weakness, but the deep and abiding humanness in his spirit.

We can see this most clearly if we think back to the case of Martin Luther. The possibly autobiographical spiritual struggle that Wallace describes in Lane Dean, Jr., is formally similar to Luther's internal battle, the battle that led him to reorient completely the medieval metaphysical picture of God and man.

Consider the young, devout, and extremely pious monk Luther. So dedicated was he to eradicating all trace of sin in his soul that he worked constantly to purify himself. Indeed, he became obsessed with the identification and confession of personal sin. No doubt at least some of the traditional stories about the young Luther are false. But they are telling nevertheless. They describe Luther as a pious, innocent young monk who was so obsessed with the purity of his soul that he once kept his confessor for *six hours* to hear the full recitation of his sins. A monk who—at least once after a long and satisfying confession—rushed back to the booth to confess the hint of pride that had crept into his mind at the thought of the lengthy confession he had just offered! They describe a frustrated Johann von Staupitz, Luther's wise and patient confessor, who finally rebuked Luther for his incessant visits to the confessional, complaining, "You must get a hold of yourself, Martin. Every time you fart you want to make confession of your sins." Apparently Staupitz did finally reach the end of his rope: "Quit coming to me with these puppy confessions, Luther," he shouted. "Go kill your father or something—then we'll have a sin to talk about!"

The battle that Luther fought to eradicate sin in his soul mirrors the crusade against encroaching boredom, anger, frustration, and distraction that seems to have directed all of Wallace's life. One imagines Wallace the writer, like the young Luther, noticing himself not attending to his writing, rebuking himself for his weakness, returning to his task with renewed vigor and purpose, becoming momentarily satisfied with his newfound focus, rebuking himself for his momentary satisfaction, becoming disgusted with himself for not being stronger, and finally giving up in despair. The eight hours a day Wallace worried about not writing were like the eight hours a day Luther worried about not being pure: the harder each tried to attain his purpose, the more distant and unachievable seemed the goal.

Indeed, it was St. Paul himself—one of Wallace's favorites—who diagnosed the psychological conflict at issue. In his Letter to the Ro-

mans, Paul describes the inverse relation between one's attention to
the commandment *not* to covet and one's ability to achieve that end.
"Indeed I would not have known what sin was except through the
law," Paul writes.

> For I would not have known what coveting really was if the law
> had not said, "Do not covet." But sin, seizing the opportunity
> afforded by the commandment, produced in me every kind
> of covetous desire. . . . [W]hen the commandment came, sin
> sprang to life and I died. I found that the very commandment
> that was intended to bring life actually brought death.[34]

It's like that old party trick when someone tells you *not* to think of a
pink flamingo standing on top of a '57 Chevy leering at the giant red
turtle on the other side of the road.

Sure you didn't.

Luther's story reminds us that not every kind of mental, spiritual,
or psychological effect can be achieved by dint of hard work and control. Like falling asleep, some spiritual tasks require a more glancing approach. But Wallace is not alone in thinking that self-control is the key.

Western culture in the twentieth century can be read, in part, as a
series of responses to the death of God—to the death in the culture,
in other words, of a grounded, public, and shared sense that there is
a single, unquestioned set of virtues—Judeo-Christian virtues—in
accordance with which one's life is properly led. As the background
assumption of God's existence receded and atheism and agnosticism
grew more common, it became less obvious that Judeo-Christian principles held true for all. Of course, as Dostoyevsky suggested in *The
Brothers Karamazov,* if there is no God then everything is permitted.

Nietzsche welcomed this freedom, but others saw the death of
God as a great loss. Samuel Beckett's *Waiting for Godot,* for example,
can be read as a story about the continually unsatisfied hope for God's
return. His later play *Endgame* chronicles an even further stage in the

history of the West; there the culture is finally resigned to the loss of all meaning, to the continued and ever-continuing absence of God. The characters of *Endgame* are consumed not with the question of how one should go on in such desperate times, but rather with how one can finally bring existence to a close.

This sounds like a desperate state to be in, but Wallace's vision is a step further still. For one finds in Wallace no hope for salvation by God, nor even any resignation to the loss of this hope. Indeed, hope and resignation of this sort are moods almost completely absent in Wallace. He seems to have lost even the memory for the sacred as it was traditionally understood; any notion, that is, of an external source of meaning for the return of which one could legitimately hope or to the loss of which one could properly be resigned. "[U]nless you're Charlton Heston, or unhinged, or both," Wallace writes, "[God] speaks and acts entirely through the vehicle of human beings."[35] The sole possibility for meaning, according to Wallace, is found in the strength of the individual's will.

This is the sense in which Wallace's vision is a Nietzschean one. Nietzsche appeared, of course, like Beckett, at an earlier stage in the history of the West. He believed, for example, that it would be a long time before God's grounding role in the culture was no longer obvious or taken for granted. "God is dead," wrote Nietzsche,

> but given the way of men, there may still be caves for thousands of years in which his shadow will be shown.[36]

If there are such caves in Wallace's world, then he gives no indication of knowing about them. God casts no shadow at all in the world of *Infinite Jest*.[37]

Nietzsche's world had not declined so far. Nineteenth-century European culture on the whole still took for granted that the Judeo-Christian virtues were not only proper but sanctioned by God. Nietzsche could see that this was changing, that the background practices of the culture were pulling away from their supports, but he believed that the full transformation of the culture was still far in the future. Even so, he shared with Wallace the nihilistic idea that, once that transformation had finally occurred—as it has in Wallace's world—the lone source of meaning in human existence would be the strong individual's force of will.

The "free spirit" is Nietzsche's name for the individual who lives properly after the death of God. This free spirit is no longer constrained by any external norms at all for what it is appropriate or permissible to do. It is literally true for the free spirit, as Dostoyevsky worried it would be, that since there is no God, everything is permitted. Nietzsche—perhaps wriggling free from the overbearing constraint of a father and two grandfathers who held important positions in the Lutheran church—saw this as a joyous possibility indeed.

But there is no joy in Wallace's world. It is as if the true burden of this responsibility—the responsibility to escape from the meaninglessness and drudgery of a godless world by constructing a happier meaning for it out of nothing, literally ex nihilo as God himself once had done—was too much for any human spirit to achieve. It is a possibility that requires us to become gods ourselves.

WALLACE SAW, at least subliminally, what his view would cost. Look again at a key passage from the commencement speech. What is required, Wallace writes, is incredibly difficult; nobody will fault you if you can't manage it yourself. But choosing to look differently at the miserable and annoying and frustrating moments of existence, choosing to experience them nevertheless as happy, meaningful, sacred, perhaps even full of bliss—that is what we must learn to do.

[I]f you really learn how to pay attention, then you will know there are other options. It will actually be within your power to experience a crowded, hot, slow, consumer-hell type situation

as not only meaningful, but sacred, on fire with the same force
that made the stars: love, fellowship, the mystical oneness of all
things deep down.

Not only as meaningful, he says, but sacred. On fire with the same
force that made the stars. That is a reference, as it turns out, though
whether Wallace knows it explicitly or not is unclear from the context.
It is an echo, in fact, from the last lines of Dante's *Divine Comedy,* the
lines in which Dante describes what it is to feel ecstatic bliss in the
mystical union with God, to give up your entire identity and subsume
it beneath the sacred power of God's divine love, the love that moves
the sun and the other stars. Wallace demands nothing less than this.

And yet, the experience of the sacred that Wallace hopes for is so
transformed from its traditional state, so radically uprooted from its
traditional soil, that it can hardly be counted as a notion of the sacred
at all. No longer is the sacred moment of existence a gift from God as,
we shall see, it was in the medieval Christian culture; no longer is it
something we nourish and cultivate and safeguard with our sacrifices
and our rites, as it was for the polytheistic Greeks. The sacred is not
even found in moody sensitivity to a communal squeeze of the hand,
as it sometimes is in Melville. Rather, the sacred in Wallace—insofar
as he can see such a phenomenon at all—is something *we impose*
upon experience; there is nothing *given* about it at all. For Wallace
anything—even some type of "consumer-hell"—can be experienced
as sacred if I choose to make it so.

Wallace's saving possibility, therefore, is the most demanding and
the most impoverished all at once. It is the most demanding for at least
two reasons. First, it has raised the stakes, so to speak, when it comes
to happiness. As we shall see, only Dante's extreme kind of bliss—a
bliss so powerful that it supersedes any kind of human commitment
or attachment or project whatsoever, a bliss so overwhelming that it
reveals earth and all earthly goods as completely insignificant, so ecstatic that it takes you out of this world and into an infinitely better

one—only this kind of experience of the sacred will do. If this is the goal that Wallace seeks, then nothing available on earth can achieve it. The joy of a crowd rising as one in the spontaneous celebration of a feat of human greatness, the cozy warmth of the fireside, the comfort and gratitude of a family meal—none of these human kinds of happiness will do. Only in the ecstatic bliss of a levitating Mitchell Drinion does salvation lie.

But Wallace's vision is demanding in a second sense as well. For it demands that this bliss be experienced constantly, without cease, through even the most banal and frustrating and painful and awful aspects of existence. Indeed it demands that Hell itself be experienced as fully paradisiacal bliss.

There is some question whether this radically demanding picture of salvation is actually attractive. For it seems to level all possible experiences, leaving no room for the idea that any experience is better than any other. One wonders whether bliss of this eternal sort is even desirable at all. Is bliss—when there is nothing to contrast it with—actually enjoyable for human beings? Or is it rather that the full range of human emotions is required for any one of them to take on significance? We will see that this is Melville's view. The Catskill eagle that he admires can soar to the highest heights and descend into the blackest gorges, and by way of this variety sees the true meaning in all our states.

Finally, however, Wallace's vision of the sacred is also deeply impoverished. As we have seen, there is no sense whatsoever in Wallace that the "sacred" moments of existence are gifts, so there is no place for gratitude. The bliss that Wallace seeks is not only ecstatic and unworldly—extreme in a sense known only to Dante's medieval Christian monotheism—it is in addition generated solely by the individual will.[38] This divorces Wallace's notion of the sacred completely from its traditional support in some external notion of the divine. In Dante's world, by contrast, ecstatic bliss is possible only when one gives up one's individual will completely and releases it into the will of

God. "But mine were not the wings for such a flight," Dante writes, in the very lines from which Wallace was quoting:

> Here my powers rest from their high fantasy
> But already I could feel my being turned . . .
> By the Love that moves the Sun and the other stars.[39]

No wonder Wallace worried he was not strong enough to write the story he wanted. Only inhuman, divine strength would have been sufficient for the task.

Nietzsche thought we were strong enough for a project like this, that the true free spirits could live this way with joy. Indeed, Nietzsche believed that the only possibility for existence was for each of us to become gods ourselves. Nietzsche is thinking of this kind of infinite freedom when he describes the free spirits as living forever upon the open sea, the stable but constraining land to be discarded like a crutch. "We have left the land and have embarked," Nietzsche writes.

> We have burned our bridges behind us—indeed, we have gone
> farther and destroyed the land behind us. . . . Woe, when you
> feel homesick for the land as if it had offered more *freedom*—
> and there is no longer any "land."[40]

The person who feels homesick for land, in other words, who wishes for some stable ground to stand upon, some externally imposed constraint to guide him in his choice, this person is simply not strong enough, in Nietzsche's view, to experience the joy of infinite freedom.

To see what extraordinary strength this requires, we need to keep in mind the radical freedom that Wallace is aiming for. It is a freedom of will so complete that by its force one can experience searing pain as overwhelming joy; crushing, crushing boredom as instant bliss; hell itself as the sacred, mystical oneness of all things deep down. There are literally no constraints whatsoever to the meaning we can construct for our experiences. In the context of this infinite freedom any restriction whatsoever—even of the land beneath our feet—is woeful, deplorable; it chafes and burns.

But what if this is impossible for human beings? What if our very humanness sets limitations to the way we can experience ourselves and our world? What if it isn't possible to create meaning or find a sense of the sacred ex nihilo without some kind of constraints? In such a world, as Melville understood, grim perseverance is possible for a while; but in the end suicide is the only choice.

Melville too considers a character—Bulkington is his name—who is at home only in the infinite openness of the sea, for whom land "seemed scorching to his feet." And he thinks there is something serious and terrifying and wonderful about such a character.

> I looked with sympathetic awe and fearfulness upon the man, who in midwinter just landed from a four years' dangerous voyage, could so unrestingly push off again for still another tempestuous term.[41]

But there is no happiness in Melville's Bulkington: "in the deep shadows of his eyes floated some reminiscences that did not seem to give him much joy."[42] Indeed, by contrast with Nietzsche's joyful free spirit, Melville sees in Bulkington a grim, dangerous existence—one that is wonderful and awe-full, to be sure; indeed one that is devoted to the highest truth—but an existence, for all that, that is not livable for a mortal man. Bulkington himself is a "mortally intolerable truth."[43]

Bulkington reveals a deep tension, perhaps even a paradox, of human existence, in Melville's view. As a human being Bulkington has to work hard to keep his freedom; the seduction of the shore's safety is a constant danger. For upon the land is where all normal human comfort and vulnerability lies. And though these comforts and vulnerabilities are not true realities but only seeming ones, although they are not as stable as they seem to be and grounded in God, and although Bulkington himself recognizes this, nevertheless their comfort appeals to every human being.

> The port would fain give succor; the port is pitiful; in the port is safety, comfort, hearthstone, supper, warm blankets, friends, all that's kind to our mortalities.[44]

For Bulkington these human comforts and vulnerabilities must be resisted. Sure, the happiness of friendship seems a joy to normal folks, but Bulkington knows this joy is sanctioned by no God, and therefore in it lies no eternal truth; he knows that boredom, and anger, and frustration, and melancholy—yes, even the "damp, drizzly November in the soul" that we shall see is so important to Melville's central character Ishmael—all these are a mirage, a nothing, and so can properly have no effect. He is not driven to the sea by melancholy, like Ishmael is. Rather, the "slavishness" of the land can only be counteracted by the complete lack of constraint one finds at sea. In Wallace this is the freedom to treat melancholy as happiness, boredom as bliss, to make a comfort of even the stormiest waters.

But this kind of infinite freedom, according to Melville, is not a human freedom at all. The freedom to gaze at the eternal chaos of the universe and impose an arbitrary meaning upon it, to live eternally upon this open sea, that is the freedom of a god, a freedom no mortal life can sustain. Perhaps we should think of Wallace himself, therefore, as we read the description of Bulkington's last hour. When he is absent one morning, presumably having jumped from the ship, Melville describes Bulkington as a demigod.

> But as in landlessness alone resides the highest truth, shoreless, indefinite as God—so, better is it to perish in that howling infinite, than be ingloriously dashed upon the lee, even if that were safety! For worm-like, then, oh! who would craven crawl to land! Terrors of the terrible! is all this agony so vain? Take

heart, take heart, O Bulkington! Bear thee grimly, demigod! Up from the spray of thy ocean-perishing—straight up, leaps thy apotheosis![45]

Bear thee grimly, demigod. Indeed.

WALLACE SUFFERED FROM the burden of his perceived genius. About the MacArthur Fellowship he received in 1997, his friend Jonathan Franzen said:

> I don't think it did him any favors. It conferred the mantle of "genius" on him, which he had of course craved and sought and thought was his due. But I think he felt, "Now I have to be even smarter."[46]

This effect is well known in all walks of life: the pressure that success creates to be even more successful the next time round. It is the pressure on the CEO to maintain and even increase earnings, on the track athlete to defend his title; it is the pressure on Michael Phelps to win that eighth gold medal in the 2008 Olympics. Doing something that verifies one's genius can involve significantly more pressure—and therefore more difficulty—when it is meant to verify one's genius *again*. The burden of this pressure to re-perform is another thing that Elizabeth Gilbert and David Foster Wallace have in common.

When we last saw Gilbert she was sobbing on the bathroom floor of her big house in the suburbs of New York, deeply unsettled by the thought of facial tattoos. But that was Elizabeth Gilbert the imminent divorcée, the everywoman of modern American life. The figure we have in mind now is someone different—or at least it is a different aspect of the person we considered earlier. Elizabeth Gilbert the successful writer—that is the person who interests us now; in particular, the writer who has recently produced such a phenomenally successful book that it is, as she says, likely that everything she will write afterward will be judged in terms of it.

Gilbert spoke about the peculiar difficulty of prior success, and about creative genius more generally, at a TED conference in February 2009. "This kind of concern puts enormous pressure on an author," she says.[47]

You know that's the kind of thought that could lead a person to start drinking gin at nine o'clock in the morning.

Gilbert is strongly against this dark path—"I don't want to go there," she says. But the question is, How can she avoid it? How should she think of herself, and her task as a writer, so that it doesn't drive her to start drinking gin? And what conception of the writer, and the writer's task, should be avoided precisely because it encourages such a descent?

She places the blame squarely on Wallace's shoulders. Well, that's not quite fair—she doesn't herself mention Wallace, and it's very unlikely she has him in mind either. But she does think that the idea of the writer as someone who is personally and individually responsible for her work, who by dint of extreme effort and self-control can determine the outcome of her product—she does think that this essentially Renaissance notion of the writer as genius is a very bad start.

It wasn't always this way, she reminds us. Indeed, she recalls, the Greeks had a very different notion of the relation between writers and writing. But "then the Renaissance came and everything changed, and we had this big idea," she says.

[A]nd the big idea was let's put the individual human being at the center of the universe above all gods and mysteries. . . . And it's the beginning of rational humanism, and people started to believe that creativity came completely from the self of the individual. And for the first time in history, you start to hear people referring to this or that artist as being a genius.

This is the real problem, she says. Because if it is the writer's individual genius that is fully responsible for the character of the work, then the pressure to re-perform is immense and constant. Not only is one's entire worth and identity at stake in the outcome, but no individual success can ever assure it either: it is always possible that the next book will show the earlier success to have been a fluke.

This conception of the writer as genius only encourages a certain personality to focus even harder on how to succeed. It is like the young Luther rushing back to confess the pride he felt in his original confession. Purity of heart, like the purity of the writer's devotion, is not to be found—according to Gilbert—by trying hard to eradicate all impure thoughts.

Gilbert has an essentially Lutheran view of genius. Not the young Luther, who thought he could purify his soul by confessing properly and well and often, but Luther after his revelation, Luther after he has come to believe that good works on their own are irrelevant, for only by the grace of God can one achieve salvation. That's sort of what Gilbert thinks about writing. It doesn't involve the Christian God in particular for her, of course, and this is an obvious distinction from Luther. But Gilbert does think that one writes well only when the god of writing shines upon her, only by the grace of the attendant spirit— the genius—who comes to tell her what to write.

One can see the appeal of such a view; it does a lot to ease the pressure of creative performance by taking the responsibility for success out of the hands of the writer, just as it did a lot to ease the pressure of the demand to achieve purity for the early Luther. If one could convince oneself of the truth of this properly Lutheran vision, and really manage to live it, then perhaps one could avoid Wallace's fate.

Luther's actual revelation—the vision that switched his focus from works to faith, from the idea that salvation comes through the good work of confession and other hard-won indications of purity to the idea that God's grace alone can do the trick—this revelation is often described as turning on the interpretation of a biblical phrase about the "righteousness of God." God is not righteous in the sense that he gazes into your soul and passes a just judgment upon you, seeing clearly how much purity you have achieved, as the medieval Catholic view held. God is righteous instead, in Luther's mature view, in the sense that he justifies your existence through His love, a love he may offer no matter how sinful you have been. In this mature Lutheran view, God's grace is literally nothing over which the individual has control. We are pure, passive recipients of it, in just the way that Gilbert imagines the writer is a pure, passive recipient of her genius's inspiration.

Gilbert exemplifies this receptive view of creative genius in a story from the American poet Ruth Stone. Stone is in her nineties now but in reminiscences about her childhood, Gilbert reports, she vividly recalls her early encounters with the force of poetry.

> When she was growing up in rural Virginia, [Stone] would be out working in the fields, and . . . she would feel and hear a poem coming at her from over the landscape. . . . It was like a thunderous train of air. And it would come barreling down at her . . . And she would run like hell to the house and she would be getting chased by this poem, and the whole deal was that she had to get to a piece of paper and a pencil fast enough so that when it thundered through her, she could collect it and grab it on the page.

This idea of the poem as an external force, something wandering the world looking for a receptacle, a place to reside, is Gilbert's Lutheran ideal; it is what she thinks can save great artists from the destructive force and the dark times, from drinking gin at nine o'clock in the morning. As in the case of Luther, to get this understanding of the human being as writer requires a Gestalt shift, a shift that turns what was an onerous, pressure-filled, probably inachievable task into something that is entirely outside the artist's realm of responsibility.

It is not clear that this is a reason for the truth of the view, but it is at least Gilbert's instrumental reason for wanting to believe it. About Wallace's Nietzschean-type approach she says:

> I got to tell you, I think that was a huge error. You know, I think that allowing somebody . . . to believe that he or she is . . . the source of all divine, creative, unknowable, eternal mystery is just a smidge too much responsibility to put on one fragile, human psyche. It's like asking somebody to swallow the sun. It just completely warps and distorts egos, and it creates all these unmanageable expectations about performance. And I think the pressure of that has been killing off our artists for the last 500 years.

The idea that we must "become gods ourselves" as Nietzsche says,[48] that we must become the source of all "divine, creative, unknowable, eternal mystery," this dramatically self-aggrandizing view was indeed prefigured by the Renaissance notion of genius—and of rational humanism more generally. And we think Gilbert is right to resist it. It's not just too much responsibility for the human psyche, as she points out, but it's probably inconsistent with what are deeply human kinds of comfort and happiness too, as we will see in Melville. So on this issue we side with Gilbert over Wallace.

But there are disadvantages to Gilbert's pure receptivity view as well. For if the poem is a purely external force that rumbles through us—if the sacred and the divine and the meaningful can't be earned but depend on God's inscrutable grace—then this receptive view is just as incapacitating as Wallace's kind of Nietzschean nihilism. Whereas Wallace gives us an unachievable task, Gilbert gives us no task at all. We can pray for inspiration from the genius, of course, just as the mature Luther can pray for the grace of God. But what really matters in the end has nothing to do with how we live our lives.[49] What matters is only whether we happen to be near a pencil at the moment the poem rumbles through. Perhaps this is good news for pencil companies, but the rest of us can feel little joy in such a vision.

The question that remains is whether Gilbert and Wallace between them have completely covered the terrain. In Wallace's Nietzschean view, we are the sole active agents in the universe, responsible for generating out of nothing whatever notion of the sacred and divine there can ever be. Gilbert, by contrast, takes a kind of mature Lutheran view. On her account we are purely passive recipients of God's divine will, nothing but receptacles for the grace he may choose to offer. Is there anything in between? We think there is, and we will try to develop it in the final chapter of the book.

3

Homer's Polytheism

ALICE [to her husband]: One night in the dining room, there was a young Naval officer sitting near us. . . . Just the sight of him stirred me deeply and I thought if he wanted me, I could not have resisted.

I thought I was ready to give up you, [our] child, my whole future. (Stanley Kubrick, script for *Eyes Wide Shut*)

A T A LAVISH dinner party to honor their guest, Telemachus, before her husband King Menelaus and the full complement of his Spartan aristocrats, Helen tells a sensational story. It is not a story of heroism. Rather, the most beautiful woman in the world describes how, long ago, she left Menelaus and their young child to run off with an irresistible houseguest named Paris. Yes, that Paris. The one whose dalliance with Helen began the Trojan War.

An odd choice, you might have thought, for dinner party conversation in the Menelaus household.

Perhaps the most shocking feature of the scene, however—at least to us moderns—is that nobody at the party is shocked. Indeed, there is a stunning lack of moral outrage on display. Moreover, Homer's unqualified admiration for Helen is apparent. In his version of the story not only is Helen back with her husband playing the part of the perfect hostess and wife, but Menelaus himself even congratulates her: "An excellent tale, my dear, and most becoming."[1]

A similar erotic triangle could occur today, but Stanley Kubrick's exploration of the husband's shocked response couldn't differ more. What accounts for Homer's treatment of the scene? One might try to attribute the whole scandalous episode to the fact that Helen has slipped drugs into everyone's drinks (which she has). This might explain Helen's magical effect on her guests while nevertheless allowing them to remain recognizable moral agents. But this explanation would leave us unable to account for Homer's own later comment on the situation. When Menelaus went to bed that night, according to Homer, "beside him lay Helen of the light robes, shining among women."[2]

Homer's admiring characterization of Helen, daughter of Zeus, suggests that his understanding of human action and existence is radically different from our own. It ought to inspire us to delve deeply into Homer's understanding of what it is to be a human being. Rather than trying sympathetically to understand his admiration for Helen, however, readers and commentators since ancient times have taken it to reveal some deficiency in Homer's view of morality and moral responsibility. Helen seems both to deny that it was wrong to abandon her family and run off with Paris, and also to refuse responsibility for the act, suggesting that Aphrodite, the goddess of erotic attraction, made her do it. Concerned by the possibility of such a twofold dodge even ancient readers of Homer, though they admired him, sometimes felt compelled to "correct" his account of Helen's role in the Trojan War. On some alternative versions of the story, for example, Helen is made to pay a debt to society.[3]

Contemporary scholars have been equally unable to take seriously Homer's treatment of Helen. Either they fail to discuss her case at all, or else they take it as further proof that Homer had a primitive grasp of moral concepts. Indeed, perhaps the three most influential interpreters of Homer in the twentieth century—Bruno Snell, E. R. Dodds, and Bernard Williams—argue that Homer failed to understand the great moral insights, respectively, of Kant, Hume, and Nietzsche.[4] But what if they are wrong? What if Homer's understanding of human existence is in fact more profound than ours, rather than less? And what if Homer's admiration for Helen is the entering wedge into this profound world, the episode that, sympathetically understood, opens up Homer's whole understanding of the sacred and its importance in human life?

Indeed, Homer's world should neither be patronized as primitive with respect to our modern philosophical and psychological notions of moral agency, nor be celebrated as somehow standing at the origin of our now more fully developed Western culture. Rather, we must recognize that our modern attitudes and philosophical theories have concealed the real attractiveness of Homer's view. Instead of smugly interpreting him using our modern conceptions of human being, we must read him as an artist sensitive to positive phenomena of existence that we have long since lost the ability to see.

The Homeric Greeks were open to the world in a way that we, who are skilled at introspection and who think of moods as private experiences, can barely comprehend. Instead of understanding themselves in terms of their inner experiences and beliefs, they saw themselves as beings swept up into public and shareable moods. For Homer, moods are important because they illuminate a shared situation: they manifest what matters most in the moment and in doing so draw people to perform heroic and passionate deeds. The gods are crucial to setting these moods, and different gods illuminate different, and even incompatible, ways a situation can matter. The goddess to whom Helen was most attuned was Aphrodite; she illuminates a situation's erotic possibilities and draws one to bring these out at their best. Achilles, by contrast, is sensitive to Ares' mood—an aggressive mood in which opportunities to shine as a ferocious warrior become the most important aspects of the situation at hand. Other gods call forth other attunements. The best kind of life in Homer's world is to be in sync with the gods. As Martin Heidegger puts it:

[W]e are thinking the essence of the [Homeric] Greek gods . . . if we call them the attuning ones.[5]

At the center of Homer's world, then, is the sense that what matters is already given to us, and that the best life is the one that manages to get in sync with it. This vision speaks eloquently to our own modern needs. Homer's Olympian gods give his Greeks a sense of the sacred that underwrites the joys and sorrows of a truly meaningful existence. To lure back these Homeric gods is a saving possibility after the death of God: it would allow us to survive the breakdown of monotheism while resisting the descent into a nihilistic existence.

Homer's epic poems brought into focus a notion of *arete,* or excellence in life, that was at the center of the Greek understanding of human being.[6] Many admirers of Greek culture have attempted to define this notion, but success here requires avoiding two prominent temptations. There is the temptation to patronize that we have already mentioned. But there is also a temptation to read a modern sensibility into Homer's time. One standard translation of the Greek word *arete* as "virtue" runs the risk of this kind of retroactive reading: for any attempt to interpret the Homeric Greek notion of human excellence in terms of "virtue"—especially if one hears in this word its typical Christian or even Roman overtones—is bound to go astray. Excellence in the Greek sense involves neither the Christian notion of humility and love nor the Roman ideal of stoic adherence to one's duty.[7] Instead, excellence in the Homeric world depends crucially on one's sense of gratitude and wonder.

Nietzsche was one of the first to understand that Homeric excellence bears little resemblance to modern moral agency. His view was that the Homeric world understood nobility in terms of the overpowering strength of noble warriors. The effect of the ensuing Judeo-Christian tradition, on this Nietzschean reading, was to enfeeble the Homeric understanding of excellence by substituting the meekness of the lamb for the strength and power of the noble warrior.[8]

Nietzsche was certainly right that the Homeric tradition valorizes the strong, noble hero; and he was right, too, that in some important sense the Homeric account of excellence is foreign to our basic moralizing assumptions. But there is something that the Nietzschean account leaves out. As Bernard Knox emphasizes, the Greek word *arete* is etymologically related to the Greek verb "to pray" (*araomai*).[9] It follows that Homer's basic account of human excellence involves the necessity of being in an appropriate relationship to whatever is understood to be sacred in the culture. Helen's greatness, on this interpretation, is not properly measured in terms of the degree to which she is morally responsible for her actions.

What makes Helen great in Homer's world is her ability to live a life that is constantly responsive to golden Aphrodite, the shining example of the sacred erotic dimension of existence. Likewise, Achilles had a special kind of receptivity to Ares and his warlike way of life; Odysseus had Athena, with her wisdom and cultural adaptability, to look out for him. Presumably, the master craftsmen of Homer's world worked in the light of Hephaestus's shining. In order to engage with this understanding of human excellence, we will have to think clearly about how the Homeric Greeks understood themselves. Why would it make sense to describe their lives in relation to the presence and absence of the gods?

Several questions focus this kind of approach. What is the phenomenon that Homer is responding to when he says that a god intervened or in some way took part in an action or event? Is this phenomenon recognizable to us, even if only marginally? And if Homer's reference to the gods is something other than an attempt to pass off moral responsibility for one's actions, then what exactly is it? Only by facing these questions head on can we understand whether it is possible—or desirable—to lure back Homer's polytheistic gods.

The gods are essential to the Homeric Greek understanding of what it is to be a human being at all. As Peisistratus—the son of wise old Nestor—says toward the beginning of the *Odyssey*, "All men need the gods."[10] The Greeks were deeply aware of the ways in which our successes and our failures—indeed, our very actions themselves—are never completely under our control. They were constantly sensitive to, amazed by, and grateful for those actions that one cannot perform on one's own simply by trying harder: going to sleep, waking up, fitting in, standing out, gathering crowds together, holding their attention with a speech, changing their mood, or indeed being filled with longing, desire, courage, wisdom, and so on. Homer sees each of these achievements as a particular god's gift. To say that all men need the gods therefore is to say, in part at least, that we are the kinds of beings who are at our best when we find ourselves acting in ways that we cannot—and ought not—entirely take credit for.

There are many cautionary tales in Homer involving characters who try to take credit for favorable events that would properly have been experienced as beyond their control. Consider the case of Ajax, for example. After fighting valiantly for the Greeks in the Trojan War he met with difficulty on his voyage home. In the treacherous sea his ships were dashed against the giant rocks of Gyrae, though Ajax himself somehow managed to escape:

> [A]nd he indeed would have evaded fate . . . had he not bragged with blinded heart. He said that he'd escaped the sea's abyss despite the gods: Poseidon heard Ajax rave; at once he gripped his trident in giant hands; he struck the rock of Gyrae and cracked it. One half stayed in place, but one split off, plunged down into the sea; that part was where the maddened blustering Ajax sat; it bore him down into the boundless tide. And there, when he had drunk much brine, he died.[11]

What are we supposed to make of such a story? Not that some theological entity named Poseidon played a genuine causal role in

Ajax's death. That is not what we should hope to retrieve from the Greeks. Presumably what happened to Ajax, after all, is that once his ship had been wrecked and he had climbed onto an enormous rock, an earthquake split the rock in two and sent him to his death. Whatever we retrieve from the Greeks, it must be consistent with our understanding of the physical makeup of the universe.

The Greek position becomes interesting not when it is thought of as an alternative to our causal explanation of events, but rather when it offers a fresh account of our particular human kind of excellence. Indeed, eloquently articulated in the Ajax story is a view of what we ought to aspire to as human beings. At its heart is the idea that there is something deeply wrong about Ajax's attitude in this situation—so wrong that it is an affront to our self-conception, and that in some sense it explains and justifies his death. Instead of blindly and selfishly taking credit for his escape, in such a view, Ajax should have been grateful that things turned out as favorably as they did. Gratitude, not braggadocio, is the appropriate response to a happy event.

Indeed, gratitude is more than simply the appropriate response in Homer's world; it is essential to a well-lived life. After all, to explain Ajax's demise in terms of his self-conceit, as Homer does, is to insist that his reaction was an affront to everything the Greeks held sacred. That's what it means to say that Poseidon struck him down: for Homer the death of Ajax made sense only in the context of Ajax's utter rejection of anything sacred.

So a certain kind of gratitude becomes an essential component in the Homeric understanding of the best possible life. In one sense, then, the gods are whatever stands beyond us that requires our gratitude. The demand for this kind of gratitude is rather marginal in the modern world. But the basic phenomenon that motivates this idea is nevertheless recognizable to us. Imagine an Ajax-like character who survives the sinking of the Titanic: he's the guy who sees evidence of his own greatness in the fact that he was picked up by the rescue boat. Something in this rankles, even now.

ALTHOUGH IT IS NOT at the center of our conception of ourselves, the idea that we should recognize and be grateful for favorable events when they occur is not entirely alien to us. The Greeks experienced this phenomenon in a particular way, however. It was not just that they felt lucky when something they experienced to be beyond their control turned out well for them. It was that they experienced these favorable events as meaningful for, and directed at, them.

To see this point, consider the difference between the Homeric Greeks and the Romans living in the second and first centuries BC. The Romans took very seriously the importance of luck in their lives, and they personified this force in the goddess Fortuna. Often represented as blind—indicating that her choices are indifferent to those whom they affect—Fortuna has no natural precursor in the Homeric world. The goddess Tyche, who is typically considered the Greek equivalent of Fortuna, doesn't begin to play an important role in Greek mythology until the Hellenistic age, at least five hundred years after Homer.[12]

The distinction between Fortuna and the Homeric Greek gods is important: if Fortune shines upon a Roman citizen then the proper sentiment is not gratitude, since Fortune didn't have him in view at all. Rather, to experience one's life as ruled by Fortune is, at best, to cultivate a kind of stoicism and reserve. The Roman Stoic stalwartly endures the vicissitudes of life, inoculating himself against fortunes and misfortunes alike. This kind of reserve, of willfully enforced detachment, could not be further from the Homeric conception of excellence in a life. And yet, there is something familiar about it in our secular age. The notion that blind luck determines the course of our lives leads quickly to the nihilistic idea that our lives have no meaning. Roman Stoicism is grandfather to the nihilism of the secular age.

The connection between luck and meaninglessness is a theme tailor-made for the contemporary world. Woody Allen seems to be exploring this connection in his 2005 movie *Match Point*. In the film Chris Wilton is a social-climbing tennis instructor at a high-end London club. The opening scene of the movie shows a static image of a tennis ball suspended just above the net, as Wilton explains his philosophy of life in voice-over:

> The man who said "I'd rather be lucky than good" saw deeply into life. People are afraid to face how great a part of life is dependent on luck. It's scary to think so much is out of one's control. There are moments in a match when the ball hits the top of the net, and for a split second, it can either go forward or fall back. With a little luck, it goes forward, and you win. Or maybe it doesn't, and you lose.

As the movie proceeds, Wilton becomes involved in a love triangle that he escapes by murdering the less convenient of his two girlfriends. The question that motivates the story is whether he will be caught. Wilton himself recognizes what is at stake:

> It would be fitting if I were apprehended . . . and punished. At least there would be some small sign of justice—some small measure of hope for the possibility of meaning.

The possibility of meaning, however, is cut short. By sheer luck—of the sort exemplified by the chance event of a tennis ball on the top of the net—another man is arrested for Wilton's crime. It follows, with the force of a syllogism, that there is no hope for the possibility of meaning in our lives. By emphasizing life's dependence on luck, Allen is committed to nihilism.

Being lucky and being cared for are radically different phenomena. If we experience blind luck to be the source of whatever is beyond our control, as the Romans did, then it makes no sense to feel grateful for the favorable things that happen; the cost, however, is a kind of detachment from the world that makes it impossible to experience meaning in our lives. The Greeks, by contrast, held the world in constant wonder. They could not help but be amazed and grateful whenever anything favorable happened in their lives. This kind of amazement and wonder, and the gratitude that follows naturally from it, is the key to everything sacred in the world of the Greeks.

To UNDERSTAND BETTER the Greek sense of the sacred, let us consider an example in which it seems natural to Homer to invoke the presence of the gods. In a representative scene toward the end of the *Odyssey*, the suitors throw a host of spears at Odysseus from point-blank range. Homer describes the event:

Again six suitors cast their shafts with force; but each shot missed its mark—Athena's work.[13]

The idea here is that it must not have seemed merely arbitrary or fortunate to Odysseus that these enemy spears missed their mark. It must have seemed to him, rather, that there was some meaning or purpose in this fact, that *he* was being cared for in the event. Homer's way of expressing this is to insist that the spears missed Odysseus *because* Athena was protecting him from the enemy attack.

There is something one can retrieve from this description and something one cannot. Obviously we cannot believe that some supernatural entity named Athena actually *caused* the spears to turn aside. Even if we replace Athena with the Judeo-Christian God, our secular age typically rebels at the thought (though some, of course, will admit this possibility). But whatever the precise metaphysical and theological facts, let us focus on the phenomenology of the situation. Imagine yourself, for the moment, in Odysseus's place. Six of your enemies have amassed before you at close range; each picks up a spear and together they hurl them at you all at once. You are prepared, as the great warrior always is, to die a heroic death in the following instant. Indeed, it looks inevitable. But instead:

> One spearhead struck the sturdy hall's doorpost, and one, the tightly-fitted door itself; two other ash-wood shafts, tipped with stout bronze, just struck the wall. And though two shafts drew close, they leveled nothing more than glancing blows.[14]

What relief, what amazement, what gratitude one must feel! And can it possibly have been blind chance? By any natural measure, it must seem to Odysseus, things should have gone the other way. One experiences this—or at least Homer's character experienced it—not just as mere luck or good fortune, but as an event that tells him he is well cared for. Athena's work indeed.

ALTHOUGH WE ARE NOT likely to attribute events like this to the work of a god, there is nevertheless something familiar in Odysseus's way of experiencing the situation. Those who escape natural disasters or other dangerous situations, for example, often do feel that it was not a mere accident that they were saved. Indeed, it is sometimes difficult—when one is the target of a statistically unlikely event—to feel otherwise.

Consider a scene from the movie *Pulp Fiction*, which provides a contemporary version of the Odysseus event. Jules and Vincent, played by Samuel L. Jackson and John Travolta, are hit men sent to retrieve a package for their boss. At an apartment they find three of the men who have stolen the package, but are surprised by a fourth man hiding in the bathroom. The fourth man "charges out, silver Magnum raised, firing six booming shots from his hand cannon." Amazingly, none of them hits the mark. Jules, obviously shaken by the event, sits down in a chair.

JULES (to himself): We should be fuckin' dead right now.
(pause) Did you see that gun he fired at us? It was bigger
than him. We should be fuckin' dead!

VINCENT: Yeah, we were lucky.

Jules rises, moving toward Vincent.

JULES: That shit wasn't luck. That shit was something else.

Vincent prepares to leave.

VINCENT: Yeah, maybe.

JULES: That was . . . divine intervention. You know what divine
intervention is?

VINCENT: Yeah, I think so. That means God came down from
Heaven and stopped the bullets.

JULES: Yeah, man, that's what it means. That's exactly what it
means! God came down from Heaven and stopped the
bullets.

VINCENT: I think we should be going now.

JULES: Don't do that! Don't you fuckin' do that! Don't blow this
shit off! What just happened was a fuckin' miracle!

VINCENT: Chill the fuck out, Jules, this shit happens.

JULES: Wrong, wrong, this shit doesn't just happen.

VINCENT: Do you wanna continue this theological discussion
in the car, or at the jailhouse with the cops?

JULES: We should be fuckin' dead now, my friend! We just witnessed a miracle, and I want you to fuckin' acknowledge it!

VINCENT: Okay man, it was a miracle, can we leave now?[15]

The events of this scene are strikingly similar to those in Homer, right
down to the number of projectiles launched. And Jules's understanding of the situation is very much like Odysseus's: neither can help
but experience his survival as something more than blind chance.
But there are some differences. For one thing, in the contemporary
version of the scene there is another explanation possible. Vincent
provides the modern counterpoint to the story, seeing the event as

nothing more than a statistical fluke: "Chill the fuck out, Jules," he says, "this shit happens." Like the Roman citizen invoking blind Fortuna, Vincent can see no motivation for Jules's gratitude. After all, he must be thinking, the flip of a fair coin plays no favorites. Sometimes things just work out well.

It is probably fair to say that Vincent's experience of the situation is canonical for our secular age. Having rejected the metaphysical notion that a superordinary being can have any kind of causal effect, it can seem obvious to the contemporary agent that gratitude in such a situation is superfluous. Indeed, the feeling of gratitude can even seem metaphysically irresponsible. Nevertheless, it does sometimes happen, even in our secular age, that one is overwhelmed by such a feeling. When this happens, as it does for Jules, another difference between us and the Greeks stands out. It is a kind of revelation for him that changes the way he understands himself and the world. For Odysseus, by contrast, it is the only explanation possible. Further comment is otiose; a simple "Athena's work" will do.

IF OUR MODERN AGE has two possible interpretations of the event, it is natural for us to want to know which is right. "Why did the bullets miss their mark?" we want to know. Was Vincent right that it was a mere statistical aberration, or was Jules right that it was an act of grace? The answer to this question is crucial for determining how seriously we can relate to Homer's world.

One way of hearing the question is metaphysical: Is there an entity, it seems to be asking—like the Judeo-Christian God, for example— who is the source of such a providential act? If there is then Jules is right to have the reaction he does; if not then Vincent has the upper hand. This version of the question is a distraction. For the real issue is not primarily metaphysical—it is not, in other words, about whether God or gods exist as supernatural entities, or what their various properties are. Rather, the real question is phenomenological: it is about what ways of experiencing the world and of understanding ourselves have underwritten those further metaphysical and theological claims. The question that really matters, in other words, is not whether God was the causal agent but whether gratitude was an appropriate response.

Why is this the relevant question? Well, it helps to keep in mind the issue that we are trying to address. The nihilism of our secular age leaves us with the awful sense that nothing matters in the world at all. If nothing matters then there is no basis for doing any one thing over any other, and the contemporary burden of choice weighs heavily. The main question for the secular age is how to relieve ourselves of this burden. Now, Odysseus lived in a world in which this burden had no place. The Homeric conception of a human being—and especially of excellence in a human life—did not allow for it. So the real question is what that notion of excellence amounts to, and whether any version of it is livable today.

This might seem a dodge. After all, we have claimed already that the Homeric notion of *arete* involves getting in the right relation to the gods. Isn't such a project predicated on the belief that the gods exist? Well, yes and no. It might be natural to say that the Greeks themselves believed in the gods. This is a historical question about which we make no commitments. But what is truly important is that the Greeks felt that excellence in a life requires highlighting a central fact of existence: wonderful things outside your control are constantly happening for you. That background sense of human existence is what justified and reinforced the feeling of gratitude that was so central to the Homeric understanding of what is admirable in a life. Whether that gratitude is directed toward Athena, Jesus, Vishnu, or nobody at all is almost irrelevant.

So let us return to Vincent and Jules. Each of them has escaped death in a quite astonishing way. The question is what the appropriate response to this astonishing event should be. Vincent is unmoved, explaining it as a mere statistical aberration; Jules, by contrast, sees

some meaning in the event, and is overwhelmed by a sense of gratitude. Which of these responses is more attractive, more in tune with
our aspirations as human beings? When put this way we can see that
the question is trickier. It amounts to something like the following: Is
it better to be completely indifferent when events beyond my control
turn out favorably for me? Or is it rather that the gratitude many
people spontaneously feel in such situations is not only appropriate
but somehow to be cultivated and valorized? Which conception of
ourselves is the one we are called to cultivate?

Our claim is that gratitude is the more fitting response.

IN HOMER'S WORLD, lack of gratitude is one of the surest signs that
a character is deficient. We have seen already that Homer explains
Ajax's death in terms of his self-satisfaction and lack of gratitude,
but this theme returns several times in the Homeric works. Perhaps
the most important example is found in the behavior of Penelope's
suitors.

While Odysseus is away from home, a number of the Ithacan
princes grow determined to marry his wife Penelope and thereby
come into possession of Odysseus's estate. At the beginning of the
Odyssey a large group of these men, collectively called the suitors, has
descended upon Odysseus's household to court his wife. Homer describes the suitors in a range of unflattering ways, making it clear that
they act with no respect for the laws and customs of the land. Abusive
guests at Odysseus's home, they voraciously consume his food, drink
his wine, and generally make a nuisance of themselves. Furthermore,
they do all this while attempting to usurp his kingdom, seduce his ser-
vants . . . and steal his wife. The suitors are in no way admirable men.

If Odysseus is a paradigm of excellence in Homer's world, therefore, the suitors are something like its opposite. For this reason it is
interesting to see how Homer describes their faults. Eumaeus, Odysseus's loyal swineherd, begins the story:

All they want is to prey on [my master's] estate, proud dogs:
they stop at nothing. . . . They make butchery of our beves and
swine . . . As for swilling down wine, they drink us dry. Only a
great domain like his could stand it. [Hom. Od. 14.92, Fitzgerald translation 14.111]

Eumaeus is clearly outraged by the suitors, and sure enough we moderns recognize their behavior as outrageous too. To us it seems outrageous not least because it is unfair, ungenerous, and lacking in respect
for the property of others. No doubt we have other explanations as
well. But what justifies the outrage in Homer's view is not any of
these things, or even anything like them. Rather, the suitors' behavior
is despicable in Homer's world because it shows a lack of respect for
the gods. In Eumaeus's description, it shows that the suitors are "cold-
hearted men, who never spare a thought for how they stand in the
sight of Zeus" (Hom. Od. 14.81, Fitzgerald translation 14.99).

One feature of the suitors' lack of respect for the gods is found
in their "arrogant" or "unconstrained" bearing. "The blessed gods
are fond of no wrongdoing but honor discipline and right behavior," according to Eumaeus (Hom. Od. 14.83, Fitzgerald translation
14.100). So failing to act in accordance with the "laws and customs"
of Ithaca, as the suitors do in their arrogance, is itself an affront to
the gods.

A further indication of their lack of respect, however, is that the
suitors are almost never shown making sacrifices to the gods. At a psychological level the ritual act of sacrificing the fattest cow or the choic-
est goat was probably motivated by the idea that some supernatural
being would enjoy the feast. Perhaps there was even some thought of
a quid pro quo: if we give you this nice tasty cow, oh superbeing, will
you please treat us well? Obviously none of these psychological motivations is recoverable by us today. But there is a deeper significance
to the ritual sacrifice as well, one that is tied to the importance of
wonder and gratitude in Homer's world. The Greeks themselves prob-

ably didn't understand this deep connection, but it was built into the practices of the culture in which they lived.

Ritual sacrifice is so important in Homer's world not just because it is a way of *communicating* the sense of gratitude that the best people already naturally and appropriately feel. It is, moreover, a way of *bringing about* that sense of gratitude in people who don't already have it, or don't have it enough, and *reinforcing it* in those who do. If performed properly and regularly, in other words, ritual sacrifice of this sort not only *expresses* gratitude, it *induces* it. The proper performance of the ritual is therefore motivated by, but also reinforces and strengthens, a deep commitment to the basic Homeric sense of the sacred: that it is the highest form of human excellence to recognize, be amazed by, and be grateful for whatever it is that draws you to act at your best.

In Homer's world, of course, the ritual sacrifice was literally a sacrifice *of* something: it typically involved the slaying or burning of a valuable animal, and in extreme cases the slaying of many animals. (The sacrifice of a "hecatomb," which Homer mentions over a dozen times in the *Odyssey*, is literally and properly the slaying of one hundred oxen.) But perhaps more important, the ritual sacrifice was a sacrifice *for* the participants: in sacrificing they offer up something deeply valuable to them. To make such a sacrifice willingly, and to do so motivated by the idea that such an act is noble and good, is not just a nice thing to do; it is essential for human excellence in Homer's world. We understand this mood of gratitude better in its absence, and that is why the suitors are a helpful case. The gratitude that motivates the ritual act of sacrifice, and that is reinforced by it, is incompatible with the kind of self-satisfaction and arrogance the suitors display.

THE PHENOMENA OF GRATITUDE and wonder form the background to Homer's entire understanding of human existence: Homer finds things to wonder at and be grateful for that our modern theories almost necessarily cover up. Take one of the simplest examples: sleep. In the *Iliad* Sleep is himself a god—at least once addressed as the "lord of all gods and of all men" (Hom. Il. 14.230ff).[16] In the *Odyssey,* however, as we have seen sleep is primarily a power that other gods have to give. In the opening book of the *Odyssey,* Penelope weeps and weeps "for her husband Odysseus, until Athena, gray-eyed goddess, shed sweet sleep upon her eyelids" (Hom. Od. 1.363). And later in the poem the messenger god Hermes is revealed to carry a wand "wherewith he lulls to sleep the eyes of whom he will, while others again he awakens even out of slumber" (Hom. Od. 5.46).

Even when the gods are not explicitly responsible for someone's going to sleep, however, Homer's way of describing the event is deeply informed by his understanding of human beings as not fully in control of central aspects of their existence. We have seen already the extraordinary range of ways Homer has to describe the phenomena of being drawn into and awakened from sleep. In Homer people do not just go to sleep, as if that was something one could *do;* sleep itself is a sacred gift.

The variety of ways Homer has of describing sleep indicates what an important role it plays in his conception of human existence. For us sleep is the blank episode that separates our moments of activity; when we are sleeping we are no longer quite ourselves. By contrast, in Homer's world sleep is an event that epitomizes the human condition. It is often in sleep that the gods visit humans, give them direction and purpose, formulate their plans for them, quell their anxieties and refresh their desires. Sleep is a canonical human event in Homer because it is the paradigm of an activity at which one cannot succeed by trying harder. And yet, one is not completely powerless in the face of it either. One can prepare oneself for sleep, be grateful that it comes, wonder at the transformation it brings about. And all these, for Homer, are characteristic of us at our best.

Homer finds this particular kind of human excellence almost everywhere he looks. Sometimes it occurs in the context of heroic activity. In one episode, after a shipwreck, Odysseus has been tossed about for two days and two nights, alone on a single plank of wood in the middle of the sea. Finally he spies a shoreline, but the situation is treacherous:

> There were no harbors where a ship might ride, no havens and no coves, just jagged reefs and jutting crags. Odysseus' knees went weak; his heart was hesitant. [Hom. Od. 5.408]

It is not difficult to imagine the dismay one might feel in such a situation. To stay at sea is to perish of starvation or drowning or exposure; to seek land is to risk being dashed upon the jagged rocks. No wonder Homer has Odysseus talking to himself, his "mind and spirit pondering." And yet, while he is busy despairing of his options:

> a heavy surge was taking him, in fact, straight on the rocks. He had been flayed there, and his bones broken, had not gray-eyed Athena instructed him: both hands were put in motion to grab a rock-ledge as it was passing, and he held on, groaning, as the surge went by. [Hom. Od. 5.425, Fitzgerald translation, slightly modified.]

Homer has a sterling grasp of what it is to be in a situation like this. In particular Homer's Odysseus, like the modern-day heroes we saw in the opening chapter, refuses to take credit for the action performed. After all, *he* was busy pondering and despairing of his fate. His hands did reach out for the rock and grab it, to be sure. But from Odysseus's point of view they were "put in motion," motivated by a force outside himself, gray-eyed Athena.[17]

HOMER DESCRIBES AN ARRAY of situations in which something outside our control evokes, or ought properly to evoke, a kind of amazement and gratitude from us. When a stranger offers assistance, on Homer's account, it is almost always a god or goddess in disguise;[18] when, in a particularly critical instance, someone's speech moves the public to your side, that, too, is a god or goddess looking over you.[19] Even when men are gathered at a council—if it really matters and everyone shows up—Homer cannot resist the idea that a god or goddess did the job.[20] To say this is not to engage in any fancy metaphysical claims. After all, in each of these cases a real person—the stranger, the public speaker, the herald—is involved as well. Rather, to say that a god is behind each event is to emphasize that gratitude and amazement are the appropriate response.

The gods play other roles as well. Sometimes the presence of a god, in Homer, is simply an indication that human existence at its best is on display. We have already seen the case of heroic action in this regard. But there are simpler cases too. Sometimes a god is involved, for example, when a person simply stands out—shines, as we sometimes say—in the way that a truly charismatic person might. Consider the scene in which Odysseus is preparing to visit the king of the Phaeacians:

> Athena, the gray-eyed goddess, made him more robust and taller; and she gave him thicker hair, which flowed down from his head in curls and clusters that seemed much like the hyacinth in flower. Just as a craftsman who has learned his secrets from both the gray-eyed goddess and Hephaestus frames silver with fine gold and thus creates a work with greater plenitude and grace, so did the goddess now enhance with grace the head and shoulders of Odysseus. Then by the sea he sat apart, a man handsome and radiant. [Hom. Od. 6.225]

The Greek word for grace here is *charis,* which is the root for our word *charismatic*. Literally a charismatic person is one who has been favored by the gods with a gift of grace or talent. The charismatic person lights up a room, as, for instance, the great Russian ballet dancer Nureyev was said to do. In his description of a scene at Andy Warhol's Factory, Stephen Holder describes Nureyev's effect:

> I remember watching the dancer strut out of the elevator, the quintessence of princely hauteur, with an entourage of handsome young men. Under the blaze of his charisma, the party's three other star guests—Montgomery Clift, Judy Garland and Tennessee Williams—seemed to wilt, as they huddled together on the couch, looking intimidated and rather wrecked.[21]

The three other guests were no shrinking violets: beautiful and famous alike, at the height of their careers and with plenty of star power among them, they might easily have held center court in some other situation. But like Odysseus under the favor of Athena, Nureyev's charisma was palpable; he stood taller, smelt better, walked prouder, and simply outshone all the others around him. If Homer had written this scene then the facts would have been the same; but to emphasize Nureyev's effortless charisma—something given to rather than manufactured by him—Homer would no doubt have said that grace was showered upon him as the gift of a god.

That description highlights something crucial about the scene. For what is essential in all these examples is that one cannot achieve the result by trying harder. The person who *tries* to be charismatic inevitably comes off as a preening oaf; the person who deliberately reaches for the rock is likely to shred himself to bits; the person who tries desperately to go to sleep is guaranteed to have a long night of sleeplessness before him. Homer says Athena enhanced Odysseus with grace because it is something Odysseus could not have done for himself.

ONE DOES NOT have to believe that the Greek gods actually exist in order to gain something deep and important from Homer's sense of the sacred. One does, however, have to reject the modern idea that to be a human agent is to be the sole source of one's actions. Because this modern notion of human agency is so pervasive, it can lead us to act in ways that hide the phenomena that Homer was sensitive to. To see this let us explore briefly the modern view.

It is natural and intuitive to us—indeed, almost an axiomatic truth of our modern existence—to think that a person should be criticized if he fails to take responsibility for his actions. Human actions just are, in the modern conception, behaviors for which the human agent is responsible. In the middle of the twentieth century the French philosopher Jean-Paul Sartre worked out the logical extension of this view in his existentialist philosophy. "The first effect of existentialism," Sartre writes, "is that it puts every man in possession of himself as he is . . ."[22]

The modern view that we are entirely responsible for our existence stands in radical contrast with the Homeric idea that we act at our best when we open ourselves to the world, allowing ourselves to be drawn from without. Indeed, once we see the force of this contrast it becomes obvious why the central Homeric phenomena are hard to find in our modern world. What Homer considers to be the paradigm of excellence seems to us hardly to count as human action at all.

IF WE ARE to take seriously the Homeric notion of excellence then we will have to give up the modern notion that we are fully responsible for our actions. There are reasons to think this is a good idea.

Consider Chuck Knoblauch, the infamous second baseman for the New York Yankees. Once considered one of the game's best fielders, Knoblauch developed severe and inexplicable throwing problems in 1999. He became incapable of accurately making the short throw from second to first; once an errant throw sailed into the stands, hitting sportscaster Keith Olbermann's mother in the face. Knoblauch worked desperately on his throwing, but the more attention he paid to it the worse the problem got. In Homer's terminology, as we shall see, Knoblauch was interfering with the gods.

The phenomenon is more common than you think—it occurs in sports like baseball, golf, tennis; football quarterbacks are not immune—and it is commonly called "the yips." The standard explanation is that the athlete begins to get in the way of his body's finely honed ability to act of its own accord. Instead of letting the activity be drawn out of him, Knoblauch was attempting to generate the throw deliberately. Dr. Shawn Harvey, a psychiatrist who has worked with pro athletes and is considered an expert in the area of sports psychology, comments on this phenomenon:

> They start to overthink something that should be really reflex-
> ive. They begin to take too much time to consider all the mach-
> inations that go with that. It destroys their ability to do what
> they have been practicing so long.[23]

The idea is that when you have a highly honed skill, when you are in the zone, when your actions flow out of you rather than being generated by you, then you are acting at your best; the worst thing you can do in this kind of situation is to get in the way of whatever is going on.

If we think of ourselves as the sole and self-sufficient source of our activity, as we tend to do in the contemporary world, then it is difficult to imagine any response to Knoblauch's situation other than the one he chose: to focus more clearly and more deliberately on the action he is performing in order to perform it better. Indeed, the psychologist's analysis that this amounts to overthinking can sound almost paradoxical: how can thinking more, and more clearly, about what one is doing ever lead to anything but an improvement? But if one thinks, as Homer does, that human action at its finest belongs to the domain of the gods—a domain that is necessarily beyond our ken—then it will seem obvious that trying to get clear about the situation will lead to an unattractive result.

This is the aspect of the phenomenon that Homer has squarely in focus. Let us take a look at his version of the story. When Odysseus finally returns to his home island of Ithaca, he is reunited with his son Telemachus. Together, with Athena's help, they devise a plan to defeat the suitors: remove all the weapons from the great hall and store them in a locked closet to which only they have access. In the dark of night Odysseus and Telemachus set about their task:

> The two—Odysseus and his noble son—sprang up to gather helmets, shields embossed, and spears with beech-wood shafts. Then they went off; Athena lit the way. She held up high a golden lamp: she shed entrancing light.
>
> At that, Telemachus cried suddenly: "My eyes, dear father, see a prodigy: the walls, the handsome panels, fir crossbeams, the towering pillars are so bright—they seem as if they had been lit by blazing flames. Some god—of those who rule high heaven—must have come to us."
>
> Odysseus stopped his son: "Be silent; curb your thoughts; do not ask questions. This is the work of the Olympians."
> [Hom. Od. 19.30]

Perhaps this is a lesson about the sacred that we are now in a position to appreciate: when things are going at their best, when we are the most excellent version of ourselves that we can be, when we are, for instance, working together with others as one, then our activity seems to be drawn out of us by an external force. These are shining moments in life, wondrous moments that require our gratitude. In those episodes of excellence, no matter the domain, Odysseus's voice should ring through our heads: "Be silent; curb your thoughts; do not ask questions. This is the work of the Olympians."[24]

THE HOMERIC GREEKS were open to the world in a way that we can barely understand. With all our modern skill for introspecting our inner states, we tend to think of the best human activities as those that are thought through internally, completely, and well. We even tend to think of our moods as private, inner experiences to which others have no access. The Greeks, by contrast, experienced themselves as empty heads turned toward the world. The very idea of an inner experience was surprising and bizarre to them. Homer, for example, was amazed that Odysseus could keep his feelings hidden from others. At one point in the *Odyssey* Odysseus has returned home to Ithaca and met with his wife Penelope. Because he is not ready to reveal his identity to her yet, he pretends to be an old friend of Odysseus's, and tells her of their last encounter. Hearing the stories of her husband, Penelope bursts into tears. It is hard for Odysseus to see his dear wife in such a state, but he cannot show her how much he is moved for fear of giving away his identity. Homer marvels at his ability to conceal his sadness in this situation. He speaks with awe of that "master of invention" who has the trick of weeping inwardly while his eyes remain as dry as bone:

> Imagine how his heart ached for his lady,
> His wife in tears; and yet he never blinked;
> His eyes might have been made of horn or iron
> For all that she could see. He had this trick—
> Wept, if he willed to, inwardly.[25]

The idea of an inner experience was so peculiar to the Greeks that they even experienced their dreams as occurring out in the world. When a god visits someone in a dream, for example, she is experienced as slipping through a crack in the doorway, gliding through the room, standing at the bedside of the dreamer, and speaking to him there.[26] In general, the Homeric Greeks had almost no sense of an inner life of the sort that seems so obvious to us. Dreams, feelings, and especially moods, for the Homeric Greeks, were not experienced as occurring *in individual minds* at all. Rather, moods were public and shared, and people felt themselves swept up *in a shared mood* like drops of water in a hurricane.

For Homer moods were important because they illuminated a shared situation; that is, they manifested what currently mattered and they thereby drew people to perform heroic and passionate deeds. Aphrodite, as we have seen, established a mood that attuned those in a shared situation exclusively to its erotic possibilities. Other gods established other moods. To say the gods are the attuning ones is to say they are whatever it is that is responsible for there being a way that things already matter to us, and whatever it is that calls us to get in tune with that.

If the gods are the attuning ones, then the essence of human greatness, for Homer, was to let oneself be attuned to the moods a god set for a situation. But moods do not last forever: they well up, hold one for a while, and finally let one go. *Physis* is the Greek name for this transient character of moods and mattering, and the idea that moods are transient in this way is crucial for Homer's kind of polytheism. Perhaps the most notable fact about Homer's world is that it comprises an entire pantheon of gods. Each of these gods focuses a mood and a set of practices that sustains it, and each is a shining exemplar of the most excellent way of life in his or her domain. Human beings at their best are open to being swept up and held for a while by one or another of these world-defining moods. But the fact that there is a pantheon of gods, rather than a single one, indicates that there is no underlying principle that unifies their different ways of life. Excellence in the erotic domain of Aphrodite, for example, is simply incommensurate with excellence in Hera's domestic world. Because the Greeks understood human excellence in terms of being open to divine moods, and because these moods are transient, there is no motivation in Greek existence to reconcile the meanings that the various gods illuminate. This polytheistic plurality of incommensurate gods makes sense of Helen's ability to move seamlessly between her domestic life with Menelaus and her erotic life with Paris. She feels no call to reconcile or rank these understandings of herself, but instead remains open to being swept into each. In this, Homer says, she is shining among women.

WE BEGAN THIS CHAPTER with Helen's dinner party tale of running off with Paris. Though it seems shocking to us that she would recite such a story, even Menelaus found it wonderful. The disparity between our reaction and Homer's to such an event brings into focus the ancient Greek receptivity to a plurality of incompatible gods. It led to our asking what phenomenon Homer is responding to when he says that a god took part in an action or event. No doubt there are many possible answers to this question; and there are no doubt also many cases in which no real phenomenon is playing a role at all. There is a whole soap opera of events that occurs on Mt. Olympus, for example, that is irrelevant to what we can hope to retrieve from Homer's work.[27] But it is clear that Homer invokes the gods in order to account for the observation that a central form of human excellence must be drawn from without. A god, in Homer's terminology, is a mood that attunes us to what matters most in a situation, allowing us to respond appropriately without thinking.

This Homeric conception of the gods puts other demands on the well-lived life. For if the best kind of human life requires the presence of the gods, then the best kinds of human beings must invite the gods by expressing wonder and gratitude in their presence. To develop an appreciation, therefore, for those situations in life when favorable things occur out of our control, and to develop a sense of wonder and gratitude in the face of such situations—this too is required for a life well-lived. When we develop in ourselves the ability for this kind of wonder and gratitude then we become a standing invitation to the gods.

With this account of excellence in mind let us return to the question of why Helen was such a revered figure in the Homeric texts.

Homer's Greeks were brought to a state of reverential awe when they were in the presence of anything that was beautiful in the highest degree. Standing in the presence even of beautiful, well-crafted things inspired in them sacred wonder. Consider, for example, Telemachus's description of Menelaus's extraordinary palace:

> My dear friend, can you believe your eyes?—the murmuring hall, how luminous it is with bronze, gold, amber, silver, and ivory! This is the way the court of Zeus must be, inside, upon Olympos. What a wonder! [Hom. Od. 4.75]

The word that is translated "wonder" here—*sebas* in the Greek— literally implies the sacred phenomena of reverence, worship, and honor, as well. It is used in Homer to indicate that one cannot help but to stand in awe before something sacred. Indeed, the literal translation of the phrase is something like "Wonder holds me as I look upon this."

Our word *beautiful,* therefore, does not properly convey the kind of sacred feeling that the Greeks felt before the finest things. In fact it is trivializing merely to say that Helen was the most beautiful woman in the world. Indeed, her standard epithet is *dia gunaikon,* which literally means a goddess among women. But really we have to say something even more than that: Helen is the embodiment of eros. Indeed, she is so above all others in this sacred domain that she is considered a daughter of Zeus himself.

To say that the erotic dimension of existence is sacred in Homer's world is to say that it immediately inspires gratitude and wonder in all the noblest human beings. Eros is not just physical or sexual pleasure in Homer's Greece. Rather, it is an entire way of being that draws the best kinds of people naturally to one another: a way of being that is overseen by golden Aphrodite herself. And Helen is the epitome of that sacred dimension of life. In this domain, all other women in Homer's world are measured against her.[28]

Helen is a site of erotic attractiveness in the effortless way that Nureyev was a charismatic force. Noble people are drawn to her inexorably, beautiful things gather round her naturally, and everything about her—from her way of talking to her way of carrying herself to her way of interacting with others—manifests the paradigm of excellence in this erotic domain. This is the Helen who is "shining among women."

Homer understands this at the deepest level. Consider, for example, the description of Helen's initial entrance in Book 4 of the *Odyssey*. Homer emphasizes not only how beautiful Helen is, but how beautiful the things surrounding her are; extraordinary gifts from mystical places that others have been inspired to give her, like everything in her presence, seem to shimmer and glow. She, like Nureyev, travels with an entourage of beautiful attendants who add to the sense that she is the shining center of eros. Notice the attention to detail in Homer's description:

> Helen came out of her scented chamber, a moving grace like
> Artemis, straight as a shaft of gold. Beside her came Adrastê,
> to place her armchair, Alkippê, with a rug of downy wool, and
> Phylo, bringing a silver basket, once given by Alkandrê, the
> wife of Pólybos, in the treasure city, Thebes of distant Egypt.
> He gave two silver bathtubs to Menelaus and a pair of tripods,
> with ten pure gold bars, and she, then, made these beautiful
> gifts to Helen: a golden distaff, and the silver basket rimmed
> in hammered gold, with wheels to run on. So Phylo rolled it
> in to stand beside her, heaped with fine spun stuff, and cradled
> on it the distaff swathed in dusky violet wool. Reclining in her
> light chair with its footrest, Helen gazed at her husband and
> spoke . . . [Hom. Od. 4.120, Fitzgerald translation 4.131–48]

Helen is beautiful, yes. But, more than that she allows everyone else in the culture to understand what beauty is. To measure Helen's action, therefore, by some distinct standard of moral responsibility is not just wrong—in Homer's world it is completely anathema. It reduces Helen's beauty to a subsidiary fact about her, inessential in comparison to the moral value of her action. If Helen's running off with Paris is an attunement to eros in Homer's world, it would have been understood as a sacred act of the most excellent kind, holding oneself open to being drawn by Aphrodite's call.

Furthermore, it is clear that the Greeks understood it that way. It is true that running off with Paris caused the Trojan War. But that is not lamentable in Homer's world; it is just the way life is. Indeed, it even creates opportunities for other kinds of excellence and nobility. The great Greek warrior Achilles, for example, was so heroic in battle that even when he was alive he was "honored as a deity" (Hom. Od. 11.480). His heroic feats were so extraordinary that they set the standard for excellence in the domain of the heroic warrior, another sacred dimension in Homeric Greece. And even though he died while still young, these feats justified his life as among the best conceivable in Homer's world. As Odysseus tells him, when they meet in the underworld: "Achilles, neither past nor future holds a man more blessed than you" (Hom. Od. 11.478). Indeed, the very sorrows of existence have their meaning in Homer's world precisely because of the kinds of excellence they bring about. Odysseus himself—a great hero of the age—is a "man who has endured much suffering" (Hom. Od. 7.212 et passim[29]). And as the great Phaeacian King Alcinous says about Odysseus's sorrows, "The gods brought this about: for men they wove the web of suffering, that men to come might have a theme to sing" (Hom. Od. 8.580).

Helen's running away with Paris, therefore, was regrettable, but it was not an irresponsible moral act. Indeed it was not an act in the moral dimension at all. Rather, it was an act of sacred eros, weaving together both wonder and woe, that men to come might have a theme to sing.

4

From Aeschylus to Augustine:
Monotheism on the Rise

THE GREEKS OF Homer's era lived intense and meaningful lives, constantly open to being overwhelmed by the shining presence of the Olympian gods. As happy polytheists, their world was the opposite of our contemporary nihilistic age. How did the West descend from Homer's enchanted world, filled as it was with wonder and gratitude, to the disenchanted world we now inhabit?

To pose the question this way is to mock the traditional story of the West. At least since Hegel, in the early nineteenth century, the narrative of Western history has been one of progress. We have learned to think of the Enlightenment, or some more recent period, as the pinnacle of this steady advance. The self-sufficiency of freedom, the lucidity of reason, and the security of a world completely explained and controlled: all these indicate history's advance.

There is, to be sure, a traditional counterstory as well, a story that sees our current disenchanted state as the result of accumulating decline and loss. Nostalgia pervades this counterview: it rejects the contemporary, disenchanted world in favor of an earlier, enchanted age. The burden of standing as one's own free ground; the arid, ruthless path of reason's march; the sad inertness of a world explained and controlled: all these indicate history's decline.

But what if neither story is right? What if the idea that both stories share—that wonder and enchantment have been left behind—is instead a misunderstanding of the contemporary world? What if we haven't lost the sacred, shining gods, but have simply lost touch with the meanings they offer?

Indeed, both smug celebration of our progress and nostalgic regret at our loss are misguided. The nihilistic burden of our secular age undermines the idea of progress, while the meaningful possibilities on the margins of our secular world cast doubt upon the idea of loss.

The story of how we lost touch with these sacred practices is the hidden history of the West. Rather than a catalogue of unrecognized historical facts, this history can be described as a series of stages by which we obscured the worldly wonders that people in the Homeric Age saw everywhere. It is the history of the way the gods were ignored, not lost; of the way we closed ourselves off to their beckoning call. To understand this hidden history is to see that this type of engagement with the world is still available to us. It has been marginalized in our culture, to be sure, but it stands ready to be cultivated and revivified. The hidden history of the West will be a guide to rediscovering the practices that reveal the sacred enchantments of the world.

To write an account of this hidden history would be impossible within the scope of this book, so what follows instead is a series of glimpses, each considering a high point in the literature of the West. From Aeschylus to the Gospel of John, from Paul and Augustine to Dante and Luther, and finally to Descartes and Kant, we will see both what kind of meaning was smothered and what kind of meaning emerges through the organizing force of these great works that have focused our culture. The following two chapters, therefore, take us at breakneck speed from Aeschylus's Classical Athenian culture in the fifth century BC to Kant's High Modernity at the end of the eighteenth century.

The reader may rebel at our steadfast refusal to explain any transition from one epoch to the next. But whereas the brief engagement with each work is a narrative choice, our inability to explain the transition between epochs is imposed from without. True, in the traditional narratives of both progress and loss one expects a rational account of the process of history. In Hegel's view, for example, the transition points in history are not chance occurrences but rational events: each movement of history is a solution to the contradictions in the period before. But the movement from Homer's understanding of human excellence to Aeschylus's is no more rational than the movement from Aristotle's understanding of science to Galileo's. As Thomas Kuhn points out, the transition from one scientific paradigm to the next is a complete Gestalt shift that is inexplicable precisely because it leaves nothing by means of which to explain it. There is no rational relation between Aristotle's account of motion and Galileo's; the two are simply incommensurate. And so it is with Homer and Aeschylus. We can say something about what each has that the other does not, but we cannot tell a story about why and how history made the transition from one to the next.

Still, the fact that each work is a part of our history, the history of the West, is crucial for the contemporary age. For something of these past practices is preserved in the margins of our contemporary world. By attuning ourselves to the senses of the sacred that animate each of the following works of art, we will be able to recognize and bring back to life those practices that can sustain a sense of the sacred in our secular age.

AESCHYLUS, WHO LIVED in Athens in the fifth century BC, is recognized as the father of tragedy. He conveyed in his plays both intense elation and terror. At times Aeschylus's plays were so frightening, it is said that pregnant women watching them gave birth prematurely. But the joyous mood they brought about was equally vivid: simply by viewing his trilogy, the *Oresteia,* one became a proud participant in the greatness of the Athenian Golden Age.

Aeschylus wrote several hundred years after Homer, at the beginning of the Classical period in ancient Greece, and his gods, though the same Olympian gods in name, were not Homer's diverse collection of moods. Instead, Aeschylus's gods were radically different. They had become the forces underlying the Athenian world. In Aeschylus's writings the gods govern what matters and determine what it makes sense to do in every situation. They demand a kind of unity to all one's actions, and cannot rest content with the happy diversity that Homer allowed.

Despite the demand for unity, there is a competing group of gods in Aeschylus's age. In the *Odyssey,* Homer's gods were a diverse but tolerant family. They cooperated in guiding and protecting human beings at home, at war, in lovers' beds. But Homer and his worshipers of the Olympian gods achieved their happy state only by repressing an older group of gods—the ancient gods of family loyalty, who stood for fertility, blood relations, and revenge. These ancient moods of vengeance and blood loyalty—amazingly!—are simply not a part of Homer's world. But according to Aeschylus, there was a price to repressing these ancient moods. What mattered most in his world was not the happy diversity of Homer's Olympian gods, but the opposition between two total and uncompromising senses of what is right: the new Olympian gods represent one, the ancient, primitive Furies the other.

Although each group of gods has many members, neither has any real diversity within it. The ancient gods of the *Oresteia,* for instance, are presented monolithically as old hags devoted to a single way of life: they protect families and local clans and drink the blood of those who don't carry out the bloody revenge they demand. The new gods, by contrast, find their expression in Apollo. His fanatical and single-minded belief in detached universal reason has replaced the diversity of Homer's Olympian gods. Moreover, not only is each group a unity, each claims to be universally right. Both the old gods and the new, in other words, claim to have the one right understanding of justice, and each claims the privilege of punishing those who transgress their standards.

The drama of the *Oresteia* consists in the fact that the old and new accounts of justice are completely opposed. The old gods of revenge, the Furies, who are all women, put the family ahead of all other values; the new gods, mostly men, are for detached universal law that makes no exception for particular individuals, families, or cities. Apollo articulates the new, detached conception of justice when he proclaims:

> Never, for man, woman, nor city . . . have I spoken a word, except that which Zeus, father of the Olympians, might command. This is justice.[1]

In contrast with this, the Furies care only about family, and think of justice in terms of exacting revenge upon those who harm a blood relative:

> We drive from home those who have shed the blood of kin.[2]

The Furies' mafia-like conception of justice had no place in Homer's world; Homeric culture repressed the natural tendency toward blood loyalty. According to Aeschylus, the Furies are outraged at having been treated this way; they are furious at having been "set apart" and "driven under the ground" by the sky gods on Olympus. They respond:

> [W]e are strong and skilled;
> we have authority; we hold
> memory of evil; we are stern
> nor can men's pleadings bend us.[3]

The conflict between the old and new gods is central to Aeschylus's conception of classical Athenian culture. This conflict plays itself out in ever increasing and subtle ways. The first and most straightforward of these takes place in *Agamemnon,* the first play of the trilogy.

Agamemnon is the great general who led the Greeks in the ten-year campaign against the city of Troy. His brother Menelaus is the cuckold on behalf of whom the war was waged. A tragic episode at the start of the war stands in the background of the *Oresteia*. To appease the gods on the way to Troy, Agamemnon made a sacrificial offering of his beloved daughter Iphigenia. The chorus reminds us of this episode, right at the opening of the play. They recount Agamemnon's distress at the prophet's devastating demand:

> My fate is angry if I disobey these,
> but angry if I slaughter
> this child, the beauty of my house,
> with maiden bloodshed staining
> these father's hands beside the altar.
> What of these things goes now without disaster?[4]

Right away, Agamemnon's conflict focuses the battle between the old and new gods. As both father to Iphigenia and king to his people, Agamemnon is caught between two conflicting sets of demands, and it is this tragic conflict that sets the play in motion. In contrast with this, think of the way Homer presents Odysseus. He is, by turns, father, king, and adventurer, each at the appropriate time. He is never in a situation in which he has to choose one world over another. Indeed, Homer's polytheism allows these multiple roles to coexist in one individual, without any sense that the conflicts among them must be reconciled. Aeschylus's monotheistic tendency to seek unity, by contrast, highlights the conflict that multiple roles can engender, and requires a satisfactory resolution of it in the culture.

The death of Iphigenia is retold as a flashback, but the events of the *Oresteia* proper begin with Agamemnon's return home after the Trojan War. Clytemnestra, Agamemnon's wife, is angry with her husband. Naturally, she is angry about the loss of her daughter Iphigenia. But she has other reasons for hating Agamemnon as well. She is jealous that he has come home with a beautiful Trojan slave named Cassandra, for instance, though this jealousy is somewhat misplaced since Clytemnestra herself has begun a love affair with Aegisthus, Agamemnon's cousin, during her husband's long absence. As always, the Greek tragedy is filled with complicated, incestuous, and salacious details, and in this case a generations-long curse that we need not go into here. What matters for our purposes, though, is that when Agamemnon returns home from the war, Clytemnestra kills him and his girlfriend in cold blood, right within the walls of the king's own royal house.

Clytemnestra's action is overdetermined by the situation. Still, she recognizes that the culture will see the act as appropriate if it is done in the name of Iphigenia's Furies. She states her case this way:

No shame, I think, in the death given
This man. And did he not
First of all in this house wreak death
by treachery?
The flower of this man's love and mine,
Iphigeneia of the tears
He dealt with even as he has suffered.[5]

The problem is that, in addition to having exacted revenge upon the murderer of her child, which the Furies see as appropriate, Clytemnestra has also murdered her king, which is the kind of abrogation of universal law that the new gods abhor. The chorus, which stands for Athenian common sense, is caught between these two interpretations of the event. On the one hand, it is right for a mother to have exacted revenge for the death of her child:

Here is anger for anger. Between them
Who shall judge lightly?
The spoiler is robbed; he killed, he has paid.[6]

But on the other hand, it is a treacherous act of regicide:

> O king, my king
> How shall I weep for you?
> What can I say out of my heart of pity?
> Caught in this spider's web you lie,
> Your life gasped out in indecent death,
> struck prone to this shameful bed
> by your lady's hand of treachery . . . [7]

Whether Clytemnestra's action was justified or not depends upon whether it was an act of vengeance directed at the murderer of her daughter or an act of regicide directed at the rightful king: whether it was done in the name of the old gods or the new.

The question of how to understand Agamemnon's murder becomes even more pointed in the second play of the trilogy, *The Libation Bearers.* This play centers on the return of Orestes, the son of Agamemnon and Clytemnestra and the brother of Iphigenia. Orestes feels that justice must be served for the death of Agamemnon, his father and king. The question he confronts is whether he should perform an act of vengeance upon Clytemnestra in the name of the Furies or an act of just retribution in the name of the new gods and their universal law. Should he kill her in an act of furious revenge as the murderer of his beloved father, or should he kill her coolly and dispassionately, as the murderer of his rightful king?

The Chorus recognizes that the Furies' notion of blood vengeance, creating an unending cycle of revenge, will destroy any culture that adheres to it.

> The truth stands ever beside God's throne
> Eternal: he who has wrought shall pay; that is law.
> Then who shall tear the curse from their blood?
> The seed is stiffened to ruin.[8]

In order to end this cycle of revenge in the culture, therefore, Orestes needs to kill his mother in the name of Apollo and universal justice, not in the name of the Furies and their blood vengeance. He needs to do it coolly, rationally, and deliberately, in other words; he needs to do it as if it follows necessarily from an unimpeachable argument. That seems to be the only way to end the violence that threatens to bring the culture to civil war.

The problem is that you can't just slit your mother's throat because rational argument requires it. The Furies are the basic motivational force in the culture. The Furies can whip people up into an emotional frenzy, and can spur them to do things that they otherwise wouldn't; but without this kind of anger it is hard to imagine how reason alone can motivate a person to act. As David Hume said, many centuries later, reason is the slave of the passions.

In the end Aeschylus dreams up an ingenious solution to the problem. Read the *Oresteia* yourself to see the trick he employs. But even though Orestes manages to do the deed coolly and dispassionately, in the name of the Olympian commitment to reason and law, the culture is not saved by this reasonable act. Clytemnestra's Furies hound Orestes, demanding that she be avenged. The conflict in the culture is not just an individual one, Aeschylus seems to be telling us, and no individual act can bring it to an end. Instead Athenian culture as a whole needs a set of practices that can find a way of reconciling the old and new gods.

This is the amazing feat that Aeschylus manages in the final play of the trilogy, but at the beginning of *The Eumenides,* the situation looks hopeless; the culture seems doomed to civil war. It is at this point that Athena comes up with a plan. Athena is one of the new, Olympian gods. As a woman, though, she favors local forms of persuasion to either Apollo's universal reason or the Furies' violent confrontation. Athena understands that when the Furies protest being

spurred, outcast . . .
driven apart[9]

they are right. Homer repressed the goddesses of earth and blood and privileged the Olympians. Thanks to him, the dangerous side of human emotions was vilified rather than confronted. Indeed, Homer calls the Furies "loathsome," and mentions them only five times in the whole of the *Odyssey.*[10]

Athena understands that it is repression itself that has made the Furies dark and dangerous. Like a therapist she suggests that the Athenian culture acknowledge and find a place for the Furies. Aeschylus sees that passions such as moral outrage enforce morality and that forces such as sexuality are necessary to motivate actions. Such motivations are more universal than the blood loyalty of families and clans that the Furies champion; but they are not so general as to be impotent, like the abstract universal rules of reason that Apollo and most of the Olympian gods endorse.

Athena persuades the old goddesses that they can gain respect from the new gods, and reverse the repression and exclusion they have suffered, if they take on the important role of primal and motivating passions in the culture. Thanks to Athena's recognition of this legitimate role, the Furies' anger is transformed into goodwill. They give up family vengeance and become the Eumenides, the Kindly Ones, who promise to use their motivating passions to care for Athens and the Athenian way of life, rather than instigating family strife. As Athena says:

> Let our wars range outward hard against the man
> Who has fallen horribly in love with high renown.
> No true fighter I call the bird that fights at home.[11]

In addition to transforming the Furies, Athena transforms the Olympian gods as well. In particular, she replaces the tendency of the new gods to follow detached universal rules and denigrate the emotions with a jury system responsive to the local sensitivities of the involved Athenian citizens. This, in turn, becomes essential to the special practices of the Athenian way of life, the practices that the Eumenides can care for and protect. In this way, then, Athena transforms both the old and the new gods and unites them in an ideal city-state of which all Athenians can be proud.

At the end of the play Athena affirms the new way of life she has established in Athens. "I myself," she says, "shall not endure this city's eclipse in the estimation of mankind."[12] The former Furies, now the Kindly Ones, and the Olympian gods then march out of the theater together singing the glory of Athens, inviting the audience—the citizens of Athens themselves—to join them saying: "Singing all follow our footsteps."[13] Thus both groups of gods together with the citizens of Athens walk right out of the play into the streets of Athens chanting the city's praise.

Through this ritual the Athenians are able to see that they have left Homeric polytheism behind by virtue of a new mood—the mood of love of Athens—that has been produced by participating in the play itself. The citizens are united in the pride they feel in being the preservers of that god-given mood. What they are proud of is how *all* Athenians are united in the mood of patriotism produced by the play. The play itself, then, becomes a glamorized example—indeed a genuine paradigm—of what the Athenians have accomplished and what they are justifiably proud of. It shows them how, by being receptive to the new mood of love of Athens, they have reconciled the old gods—the angry, bloody emotions of outrage and revenge—and the new gods, with their tendency toward detachment and moral fanaticism.

In this way the play itself functions like a god. It is not a situation-specific god of the sort found in Homer, however, a god that draws you to act in the here and now. Rather, it is a more universal god, a more monotheistic god; it is a god that shows the whole Athenian culture what it is up to as a people. The *Oresteia* draws all Athenians to participate in the unfolding of their shining new world by involving them in a celebration of the Athenian way of life and instilling in them a particular Athenian kind of pride. This sacred and paradigmatic importance of Aeschylus's play was clear even to the Athenians themselves. Each year the citizens of Athens selected a new prize-winning tragedy to be performed at the expense of the city for just that year. The *Oresteia* was the only play that was performed at the city's expense year after year.

With civic pride as the society's most overpowering emotion, and Athens as the locus of this total devotion, Aeschylus's conception of the sacred moves away from Homer's polytheism toward a more unified, monotheistic conception of the universe. This poses a peculiar problem for Aeschylus's conception of the Olympian gods. In particular, without Homer's polytheism there is no place for Zeus in Aeschylus's Athens; no place, in other words, for the father of the polytheistic Olympian family of gods. Aeschylus recognizes this problem and has an amazing, if only barely articulated, solution to it.

For Aeschylus, Zeus is no longer a personified god presiding over the pantheon. But he isn't a cultural force like the Furies and the Olympian gods in the *Oresteia* either. Instead, Zeus has become the taken-for-granted way of acting that sustains all these forces. As the pervasive background, he cannot be described, but he underlies all significant events. The chorus, for example, refers to "Zeus: whatever he may be"[14] and adds: "For what thing without Zeus is done among mortals."[15]

Zeus, in other words, is the *hidden and unrepresentable background* that sustains all the meaningful practices of the culture. This is such a deep and powerful conception of the sacred that it will figure centrally in the Judeo-Christian account of God the father, but it will not be evoked as the possible poetical achievement of Western culture until Melville's *Moby Dick*.

Aeschylus's *Oresteia* doesn't just describe a solution to the tensions in Athenian culture; it actually brings that solution about. As the Athenians march together out of the theater, singing their praise of Athens, they not only see what is great about their city, the pride for Athens wells up around them. But Aeschylus is such a deep thinker that he even has a sense for the dangers internal to the patriotic mood he establishes. In particular, he recognizes that overpowering emotions such as patriotism cannot so easily be made constructive. Once all the citizens have been led by Athena to share an identity that gives them an overwhelming mood of patriotism, the feeling is so powerful that they desperately desire to hold onto it forever. This temptation goes against the transience of *physis,* however. Homer understood that moods, insofar as they make things matter, necessarily run a transient course: they well up, dominate everything for a while, and finally fade away. Aeschylus could see this about the mood of patriotism as well. When the Furies anxiously ask Athena whether she will "guarantee such honor for the rest of time?" Athena answers honestly: "I have no need to promise what I can not do."[16] But the desire for permanence was built into the patriotic mood of Athenian culture nevertheless. The seed of Athens's undoing was planted with it at its inception.

In the years following Aeschylus's triumphant play, the Athenians set out to establish the universality and permanence of Athens by force. They attempted to guarantee that their city-state would last forever by annexing all neighboring states into an Athenian empire. Colonies that did not acknowledge the Athenian gods and pay a yearly tribute to Athens were destroyed—the men killed and the woman and children sold into slavery. But rather than securing the empire, this ruthless rule led to rebellion in the colonies and factionalism and even civil war at home. In the end, the Golden Age of Athens lasted only fifty years.

THE *ORESTEIA* MANIFESTED and focused for all Athenians what they were up to as Athenians. Heidegger calls anything that performs this focusing function a work of art. The Greek temple is his primary example of an artwork working. The temple, Heidegger says, held up to and focused for fifth-century BC Greeks everything that was important and meaningful in their world. As he puts it:

It is the temple work that first fits together and at the same time gathers around itself the unity of those paths and relations in which birth and death, disaster and blessing, victory and disgrace, endurance and decline acquire the shape of destiny for human being.[17]

Like the temple, the *Odyssey* was a work of art for the Homeric Greeks. It was the sacred work, in other words, that manifested and focused the practices paradigmatic for the Homeric world. The *Odyssey* disclosed the existential space in which shining heroes like Odysseus and Achilles and shining examples of the erotic like Helen, as well as bad guys like the suitors, made sense as possible ways of life. When sung about, these figures gave direction and meaning to the lives of the ordinary Greeks in Homer's world. The medieval cathedral and Dante's *Divine Comedy* played a similar role in the Middle Ages: they showed Christians the dimensions of damnation and salvation, and thereby made possible sinners and saints.[18] And so too for the other epochs in the history of the West: thanks to works of art paradigmatic for the age, one knew where one stood and what one had to do.

The paradigms from different epochs are fundamentally incommensurate. They literally have no common measure on the basis of which they can be compared. What makes sense as a life worth aspiring to in one age might well be reviled in another. There could not have been saints in Homeric Greece, for example. At best there could have been weak people who let others walk all over them. Likewise, there could not have been Greek-style heroes in the Middle Ages. Such people would have been regarded as impulsive and irresponsible sinners. To be a saint or a hero is not just to behave a certain way; it is to be held up as worthy for doing so. The paradigmatic works of art for an age let certain ways of life shine forth. But in doing so they cover up what is worthy in other—radically different—ways of life.

Temples, cathedrals, epics, plays, and other works of art focus and hold up to a culture what counts as a life worth aspiring to. Works of art in this sense do not *represent* something else—the way a photograph of one's children represents them. Indeed, Heidegger says explicitly that the temple "portrays nothing."[19] Rather, works of art *work;* they gather practices together to focus and manifest a way of life. When works of art shine, they illuminate and glamorize a way of life, and all other things shine in their light. A work of art embodies the truth of its world.

Of course the temple or the tragedy can only shine in this way when it exists in the context of a living community organized around it. The same Greek temple today, decaying in a desolate rock-cleft valley, cannot be organizing a culture; it cannot focus, glamorize, and stabilize a whole understanding of being for the people whose lives are organized around it. It no longer "gives to things their look and to men their outlook on themselves."[20] The temple today can, of course, be an object of aesthetic appreciation. It can elicit "oohs" and "aahs" from the tourists who are standing beside it. But when a Greek temple or a medieval cathedral plays this role, it is no longer "working" as a work of art.

The job of a work of art is to disclose a world, give meaning, and reveal truth. In this sense, works of art working can be thought of as sacred. They give meaning to people's lives and people guide their lives by them, so people treat them as divine. They venerate them like gods and make shrines dedicated to them. That is what happened to the *Odyssey,* the *Oresteia,* and *The Divine Comedy.* Each of these texts was venerated as sacred by those in the world it illuminated. In this way artworks can play the traditional role of a god. They are a nonhuman authority that gives meaning and purpose to those whose lives are illuminated by them.

To bring out a culture in its best light, we can say, is to *articulate* the culture. A poet like Aeschylus articulated the Athenian world in which he lived. But it is not only poets who do this job. Statesmen like Pericles in Athens, Lincoln at Gettysburg, and Martin Luther King Jr. at the Lincoln Memorial each articulated what mattered for the culture at the time. A philosopher like Kant or a theologian like Aquinas might also be said to have articulated his culture. Articulators focus and so renew what is meaningful in a culture; they bring out a shared-background understanding of what matters, and therefore of what it makes sense to do.

Since articulators focus a shared background, their audience understands them immediately. This was certainly the case for Aeschylus, as it was for Dante, Lincoln, and King. But articulation is the lesser role for a god. A god at its best doesn't just renew a world by glamorizing and focusing it; the most potent gods actually transform the world, turning an old world into a new one. We can call that transformation—the most powerful thing a god can bring about—*reconfiguring* a culture instead of merely articulating it.[21]

Reconfigurers change a culture so radically that they cannot count on an already established language and shared practices to make themselves intelligible. As a result, reconfigurers are essentially incomprehensible to the people of their culture. Indeed, they are barely intelligible to themselves.

Reconfigurers are either gods or madmen. But which of these is only determined in retrospect. If the new god actually works to reconfigure the world, and the practices organize themselves around its way of life, then the god becomes an exemplar of a whole new understanding of everything that matters and of how to act. The chances are strongly against this, however. There are always powerful conservative forces in the culture that tend to destroy the new understanding or to take it over and mobilize it for the current order. If the new world fails, therefore, it is necessarily measured by the current understanding, and against this norm it can look ridiculous.

A hint of what such a reconfiguring paradigm might look like is offered by the music of the sixties. Bob Dylan, the Beatles, and other musicians seemed to offer a new understanding of what really mattered. This new understanding almost coalesced into a cultural paradigm in the Woodstock Music Festival of 1969. There people lived for a few days in an understanding of being in which mainline contemporary concerns with willful activity, order, sobriety, and efficient control of oneself and others as well as nature were marginalized while a new mood of openness, enjoyment of nature, dancing, and Dionysian ecstasy became central. Technology was not smashed or denigrated; rather the power of electronic communications was put at the service of the music that focused this transformed mood.

If a sufficient number of people had recognized in Woodstock what they most cared about and had recognized that many others shared this recognition, then a new world might have come into being. But Woodstock failed to be a new god. In retrospect it is bound to seem to us who are still in the grip of our current world that the concerns of the Woodstock generation were not widespread and serious enough to reconfigure our culture; worse, it can seem like a foolish, juvenile experiment. Still, we are left with a hint of how a reconfiguring cultural paradigm might work.

A reconfiguring work that opens a new world would have to have a threefold structure.

First, there would have to be background practices in place on the basis of which things made sense, and sacred things shone. To do their job of revealing a world, such practices would have to remain in the background, like the illumination that Athena gives to the shared work of Odysseus and Telemachus when they are hiding weapons in the storeroom, or like Aeschylus's Zeus, "whatever he may be." The background practices would be transparent to the people who simply lived in them, followed them, and passed them on through socialization from generation to generation. Such self-concealing practices are crucial. Without them there would be nothing to reconfigure—nothing showing up *as* anything at all.

Second, a reconfiguring person, thing, or event would have to do more than an *articulating* work of art like the *Oresteia*. The *Oresteia* focused the current practices and mood so they were clear and coherent; it led people to appreciate the shining of the cultural style they already shared. The reconfigurer, by contrast, would introduce new practices and a new mood that transformed people's understanding of themselves and their world by showing a radically new way of life.

Finally, the work of the reconfigurer would be so radical that people could not understand what it called them to do. People would need an articulator—something or someone that made sense of what the reconfigurer was up to and spelled it out as a paradigm incarnating their new world.

In the history of the West we have only two figures who do such a threefold reconfiguring job. They are an odd pair: Jesus and Descartes. Jesus as presented in the Gospels is a successful reconfigurer who sets up the Christian World in which there can be a savior as well as saints and sinners; Descartes sets up our Modern World in which people and things become subjects and objects. To see how reconfiguring actually works, we need to look at the purest example of successful reconfiguring we have—the work ascribed to Jesus.

WHETHER OR NOT a person named Jesus actually existed—and if so, whether he did what Jesus is supposed to have done—is no doubt a fascinating historical question. But it is not our concern here. What is relevant for us instead is the phenomenon of reconfiguring itself. As he is described in the Gospels, Jesus totally transforms people's understanding of what it is to be a human being. This is a superhuman thing to do. Like a god the biblical Jesus reveals a new Christian World. So Jesus' work as reconfigurer must have a threefold structure.

First, there have to be some background practices already in place. There was, of course, the Hebrew understanding of being. These background practices were behind everything. They had to withdraw from notice so that people could live on the basis of them. The Hebrews understood that for God to perform this background function of grounding all intelligibility, he would have to be *unrepresentable*.

We will have to wait until we get to *Moby Dick* before we can spell out this unrepresentable background function further.

Second, there must be an exemplar that embodies the new way of life—the new understanding of being—and lets it shine. In the Gospel of John, Jesus tries to express this role when he says: "Anyone who has seen me has seen the Father" (John 14:9). That is, Jesus sees himself as a shining example of a new background understanding of what it is to be a human being. Philosopher Søren Kierkegaard calls him "The Paradigm" and drives the point home by saying that after God's Incarnation in Jesus all direct access to God the Father is cut off.

The paradigm is more than the background since it makes the style of the background practices visible. Yet the paradigm is dependent on the invisible background that it manifests. So Jesus says: "the Father is greater than I" (John 14:28). But he also says: "the Father and I are one" (John 10:30). He adds: "you will know for certain that the Father is in me and I in the Father" (John 10:38). Of course, the disciples do not understand any of this; they just write down what Jesus says.

Almost one hundred years later St. John is still trying to find the right words to make sense of the phenomenon of being a paradigm. One of the most difficult things John says of Jesus is: "He was in the world that had come into being through him" (John 1:10). That sounds impossible, yet there is no better way to describe the phenomenon. Being a paradigm has to be described in just that paradoxical way. The reconfigurer must be something or someone *in* the new world and so it depends on that world, yet it *discloses* the world and so the world depends on it.

Finally, Jesus' message must be so radical that it is essentially unintelligible to those in whose midst he is living. This is a near paradox for any reconfigurer. If Jesus' way of life is really radically different from that of his contemporaries, then he must seem completely unintelligible, and so raving mad. By contrast, if he doesn't seem raving mad then it must be because his way of life is not so different from the current one after all. To reconfigure a culture in the genuine sense, one must somehow steer between these options. We will see how Jesus manages to do this in a moment. But first, notice that the Gospels do present him as a reconfigurer with precisely these characteristics.

The Gospel of John makes it clear that Jesus' life totally transforms the Hebrew understanding of what constitutes a life worth living. But Jesus has no concepts to express his new understanding and so has to speak in parables—parables his followers can't understand even when he tries to explain them. It's not even clear that, according to John, Jesus can understand his own actions and parables. How could he if the only way of thinking and acting available is the way of life he feels called to overturn.

Furthermore, according to the Gospel of John Jesus knows he is a reconfigurer and so he knows that he needs articulators to convey his message. As he says:

> [W]hen the Spirit of Truth [the Paraclete or Holy Spirit] comes he will lwead you to the complete truth, since he will not be speaking of his own accord, but will say only what he has been told . . . [John 16:13]

Jesus' articulators, in other words, will have to come after he is gone to make sense of what Jesus said and did. Shining through the articulators, The Holy Spirit will manifest Jesus' joyful, loving mood, remind people of what Jesus said, and spell it out in its relation to specific situations, so as to reveal to people how to act in the light of Jesus' life and parables. As Jesus puts it:

> I have said these things to you while still with you; but the Paraclete, the Holy Spirit, . . . will teach you everything and remind you of all I have said to you. [John 14:25–26]

Jesus himself understands, therefore, that his reconfiguring activity requires the threefold structure laid out above. To put the phenomenon in Christian terms we could say: God the father, with his mood of righteousness, is the Hebrew background practices on the basis of which anything makes sense; God the Son is the paradigm who shows a life that gathers the practices in a new way and manifests the new mood of agape love;[22] and the Holy Spirit is the shining new style of life that draws John and Paul, among others, to articulate the Christian way of life. The central movements of the next nearly two thousand years of history in the West can be understood as attempts to spell out Jesus' understanding of human existence.

THE FIRST AND MOST important Christian articulator is St. Paul, who, before any of the gospel writers had written down their memoirs, writes his letters to the early Christian communities, telling them how to act. Paul does not try, like John and later theologians, to appropriate philosophical concepts in order to articulate Jesus' message. Theologians like St. Augustine and St. Thomas Aquinas do their best to explain Jesus' teachings by using Greek concepts. But, as we shall see, the Greek concepts only get in the way. Rather, St. Paul, simply by reporting on his own experience, does a much better job of articulating how a Christian should live than do the theologians. Indeed, later articulators such as Martin Luther sweep the theologians out of the way and take up where Paul left off.

Jesus, as described in the Gospels, does not provide a worked-out view of how to live. Rather, as a reconfiguring exemplar, the Jesus figure offers lots of examples. He is not articulate, but he shows luminously the new way of life. Paul, in turn, channeling the Holy Spirit, articulates what it was that Jesus was showing. He spells out how, in the light of the new Paradigm, the Hebrews must radically change their behavior.

But how could the Holy Spirit ever make Jesus intelligible? As we have just seen, if Jesus really revealed a radically new way of life there could be no current language for expressing it. So, if one tried, one would either be unintelligible, and so seem to be crazy, or one would make sense and then the transformation wouldn't be radical. How can there be a middle ground? In the New Testament, thanks to Paul, we get to see before our very eyes an example of how to manage this seemingly impossible task.

First we need to go back and look at the Hebrew world Jesus was called to transform. The Hebrew practices were focused on the law. The Ten Commandments and the whole book of Leviticus are largely about actions—what to do and what not to do—six hundred and thirteen laws in all. What you could and couldn't do on the Sabbath, what you could and couldn't eat, and so on. According to the Hebrews, if you followed the Ten Commandments and the detailed law you led a *righteous* life; if not, you led a *wicked* one.

Jesus transforms radically the whole Hebrew understanding of human being and of what counts as a life worth living. Instead of outward actions, Jesus organizes the worthy life around private, personal, inward desires. In the Sermon on the Mount, for example, Jesus says: "[You] were told, 'Do not commit adultery.' But what I tell you is this: If a man looks on a woman with a lustful eye, he has already committed adultery with her in his heart."[23] This makes the inner desires of the heart more important than outward actions. From a Hebrew point of view it is a crazy idea. My desires are private. The law can't prohibit looking on a woman with a lustful eye. There can't be witnesses who take someone to court because he was caught lusting. I can't control my desires, and after all why should I? They don't hurt anyone.

In general, then, the idea that one is guilty for one's desires must seem crazy to the Hebrews. For Jesus to make sense at all, the idea that one is guilty for one's desires requires that the culture must have some marginal understanding of private desires, and even think that some are condemnable. Otherwise no one could have understood Jesus' condemnation of a lustful eye. Imagine someone in Homeric Greece preaching: "He commits adultery who lusts after a woman in his heart." People would not have understood a thing. If you can't cry or dream inwardly, how could you lust inwardly? Even if the Hebrews experienced private desires, for a law-culture such desires shouldn't have even marginal importance. So how could the Jews understand the prohibition of lusting in one's heart?

The answer must be that the Hebrews understood and condemned a few desires. They just didn't consider it that important. And indeed that is exactly what we find. Among the Ten Commandments, exactly one prohibits an inner desire. In particular, the tenth and final commandment prohibits coveting your neighbor's things, including his slaves, donkeys, house, and wife. Paul saw the connection between Jesus' prohibition of adultery and the commandment prohibiting coveting. He says:

> I had not known sin, but by the Law: for I had not known lust, except the Law had said, Thou shalt not covet.[24]

For the Hebrews the coveting prohibition was marginal. It is only one commandment out of ten, and the last commandment at that. But Jesus singles out all private inner experience and makes it central. Happily, we can use the Ten Commandments to quantify the difference between the marginal and the central here. We can see that for Jesus and Paul desire goes from 10 percent of the things we need to be concerned about, to something closer to 100 percent.

Jesus changes the prohibition of all the outward actions mentioned in the Hebrew Law into the prohibition of the inner thoughts of those actions. Paul emphasizes what was later put down by Matthew, that "thoughts [of] murder, adultery, fornication, theft, perjury, slander— these all proceed from the heart; and these are the things that defile a man" (Matthew 15:19). In so doing, he switches private inner feelings in general from the margin of one's life to one's central concern.

And what about the law? For the Jews, keeping the Sabbath was an immensely important practice. As the New Testament writers tell it, it looks like the Jews were so concerned about not breaking the law, and were so busy catching lawbreakers and denouncing them to the priests, that they didn't even notice the miracles Jesus was performing. Take, for example, the miracle of the cripple whom Jesus tells to walk. When Jesus told him to stand up, the man recovered instantly; "he took up his stretcher and began to walk. [However], that day was the Sabbath. So the Jews said to the man who had been cured, 'It is the Sabbath. You are not allowed to carry your bed on the Sabbath'" (John 5:8–10). John continues:

> It was works of this kind done on the Sabbath that stirred the Jews to persecute Jesus. He defended himself by saying, "My father has never ceased his work, and I am working too." This made the Jews still more determined to kill him. [John 5:16–18]

Undeterred, Jesus dismisses even the dietary laws in Leviticus simply by saying: "A man is not defiled by what goes into his mouth, but by what comes out of it" (Matthew 15:18).

In his new vocabulary Jesus describes his marginalizing of the law by saying that, rather than obeying the law, he "fulfills" it. That means one does not take the Law and its prohibitions *literally*, but one is drawn to act in a way that manifests the *spirit* of the law. Jesus thus brings the purity of one's desires from the margins of the Hebrew sense of what counts as a worthy life to the center of his Christian sensibility; at the same time he moves the law from the center to the margins. In this way he completely transforms the Hebrew world. The Christian no longer aims to be righteous instead of wicked. Instead, he aims to be a saint rather than a sinner. His task in life becomes not righteous actions but the purification of his desires.

Moreover, purification is not something you can do on your own. You need a savior to transform you, the Gospels tell us. When you are reborn then Jesus lives in you; you put on his body. But what does that mean? It might well mean that Christian salvation occurs by catching Jesus' contagious new mood of agape love. The term *agape* in the Gospels, usually translated "charity," means a joyful, overflowing care for every human being within reach to the point of being ready to die for them. Your desires are still out of your control, but entering this mood by hanging out with Jesus and his disciples, you are reborn a joyful new being with pure desires.

As described in the Gospels, Jesus is a successful reconfigurer. Like a god, he let a new world be. In that new world people are defined by their inner desires and intentions, not their external actions. This is an important move away from Homeric responsiveness to the power of the shining gods, and also away from the Athenian sense of the importance of a culture's background practices dramatized by Aeschylus. We must now follow the way in which the emphasis on inner experience rather than overt action combines with Greek philosophy and leads step by step from St. Augustine to St. Thomas Aquinas, to Luther, to Descartes, to Kant, to the death of God and Nietzschean nihilism.

To MAKE SENSE OF the new Christian world, Christian thinkers had to conceptualize the Christian revelation. For more than a thousand years they tried valiantly to grasp the Judeo-Christian *religious experience* using a variety of Greek *philosophical concepts*. This turns out to have been a bad idea.

The mismatch should have been obvious. Without thinking yet about the turn to Christianity, consider the relation between the traditional Hebrew culture and the Classical Greek. For the Greeks of Plato's era, in the fifth century BC, human beings had one, single, universal essence: at their best they were rational agents who, through disinterested philosophical argument, could discover objective, universal, timeless truths of nature and human ethical excellence. They could contemplate the supreme being Plato called the Good.

For the Hebrews around Plato's time, by contrast, things looked very different. For one thing, what gave the Hebrews their essence and identity was not their rationality, but the special covenant they had with God. That covenant was anything but a universal feature of human beings: after all, it distinguished the Hebrews from everyone else. Furthermore, this understanding of their essence had repercussions elsewhere. For example, the Hebrews felt they grasped the truth not by detached contemplation of the Good but by total commitment, by being true to their God and keeping his covenant. And the truths that were revealed to them were therefore of a different character as well: they were local and historical, rather than universal and timeless; they needed to be preserved by tradition rather than standing independent of us as objective and eternal.

Ours is a uniquely conflicted culture, the product of two powerful and opposed traditions. Other cultures have multiple traditions too: China has Buddhism and Confucianism, for example. But these traditions normally complement each other or ignore each other. No culture but ours has two traditions so inclusive and at the same time so opposed. The Greek discovery of detached, disembodied access to timeless, universal truth contradicts the Hebrew commitment to an involved, historical God. One side sees as essential our ability to think; the other our sense of the sacred. For the monotheistic inheritors of this conflicted tradition, it was very natural to try to bring its two most fundamental ways of life together.

This conflict becomes even more apparent when we consider the importance of the incarnation in the Christian tradition. As a paradigm of existence, Jesus' life cannot be reduced to a set of eternal truths. It really matters to the Christian tradition that Jesus came into the world at a certain time and place and that by living in the way he did he illuminated possibilities of existence for his followers. It matters that he exemplified the mood of agape love, which others could catch just by being around him. This mood could not be captured in universal principles that one can discern by philosophical contemplation. It is a way of being attuned to what matters that one can get in touch with only by being around those who exemplify it. This embodied aspect of Christianity is essential to its understanding of the saving mood of agape love, and therefore essential to the notion of salvation itself. It is precisely the part of Christianity that resists conceptualization in Greek philosophical terms.

But that did not stop St. Augustine. Augustine was the first important Christian to interpret Christianity using the categories of Greek philosophy. He lived from AD 354 to 430, and his account of Christianity draws heavily on his understanding of Plato's account of the nature of human beings and of the Good.

According to Plato, every soul desires the eternal Good outside space and time. Augustine followed Plato in embracing eternity over time, and he agreed too that only the eternal is ultimately real. Moreover, Plato held that human beings could get in touch with this reality by using their minds to contemplate it. To learn about the abstract and eternal form of Beauty, for instance, one might start by considering a particular beautiful person, then ask what that beautiful person has in common with all other beautiful people; this will lead you to ask about beautiful souls, and then the beauty of laws and knowledge, and finally to the nature of beauty itself. A Platonic ascent of this sort leads ultimately to contemplation of abstract, eternal truths.

But Augustine found something spiritually unfulfilling about this pure Platonic account. He tells us in his *Confessions* how, before he became a Christian, he experienced a Platonic ascent to contemplation of the Platonic Good. But the Platonic Good was too abstract to satisfy Augustine's longing for a divine being, and too inert to be a saving power. He tells God:

> *I caught sight of your invisible nature, as it is known through your creatures.* But I had no strength to fix my gaze upon them. In my weakness I recoiled and fell back into my old ways, carry-

ing with me nothing but the memory of something that I loved and longed for, as though I had sensed the fragrance of the fare but was not yet able to eat it.[25]

Notice that what Augustine loves and longs for is not something abstract and eternal, but something that has a delicious fragrance and that he wishes to eat. This in a word is the confusion of Greek abstraction and Christian embodiment. Augustine recognizes that he needs not just the abstract word, which one can contemplate rationally, but the "word made flesh":

I began to search for a means of gaining the strength I needed to enjoy you, but I could not find this means until I embraced the *mediator between God and men, Jesus Christ, who is a man, like them,* and also *rules as God over all things, blessed for ever.*[26]

Later, when he has converted to Christianity, Augustine has a much more concrete experience of the divine. He says to God:

You shed your fragrance about me; I drew breath and now I gasp for your sweet odor. I tasted you, and now I hunger and thirst for you. You touched me, and I am inflamed with love of your peace.[27]

This is precisely the kind of sensuous experience of agape love that one would expect from an early Christian, an experience that takes seriously Jesus' incarnation and the importance of His bodily presence in one's salvation.

And yet. At the same time that Augustine is craving the sensuous, embodied presence of God, he cannot resist the Platonic pull to the abstract, disembodied, and theoretical account of the universe. Immediately after describing his unslaked thirst for God's embodied presence, he describes the incarnate God as one "enfeebled by sharing this garment of our mortality."[28] Indeed, he goes on later to say that God gave Jesus a body in order to enforce his humility, as if to endorse Plato's idea that the ultimate and true reality is not the one here on earth but the one in some abstract, Platonic heaven.[29] And ultimately it becomes clear that the body was literally an embarrassment for Augustine. He complains that men can't control their erections at will, for example, and he promises that this unfortunate condition will be corrected when, on the Day of Judgment, all people get back their bodies.[30] In the meantime, however, the Platonic pull toward the abstract and theoretical wiped out what was essentially Christian in Augustine's experience.

Indeed, this wipeout of the body begins even earlier in Augustine's account. For although he craves a sensuous relation with God, he finds a way to interpret this experience so that it involves no bodily presence whatsoever. Augustine pulls off this marvelous trick by treating sensuous, bodily experiences entirely in terms of the inner states they bring about. As we have seen already, for the Greeks from Homer through Plato inner experiences were almost entirely ignored, at best a curiosity. Homer marveled at Odysseus's ability to weep inwardly, but in his view that was not an important accomplishment, just an unusual one. Likewise for Plato, desire (*eros* in Greek) was not an inner experience, but the soul's attraction to a truth outside the self.

It was Jesus as interpreted by St. Paul who first put the emphasis on one's desires as the truth about one's inner self. As we have seen, saints and sinners were distinguished not by their public actions, or by their access to eternal truth, but rather by their private impulses. Either one's desires were pure or, as in the case of desiring adultery, they made one a sinner.

But apparently by the time of Augustine, three hundred years after Jesus, the idea of a special inner mode of access to the truth had still not caught on. Augustine had to get the culture to recognize the importance of an inner life. So, in his *Confessions,* Augustine calls attention to the fact that people came to watch St. Ambrose read. Why? Because he read to himself! As Augustine puts it:

When St. Ambrose read, his eyes scanned the page and his heart explored the meaning, but his voice was silent and his tongue was still. [*Confessions,* Book VI:3, 114]

Apparently, in Augustine's time everyone read aloud. That St. Ambrose had direct access to the meaning of the text showed that the inner was not merely the locus of desires but could be a storehouse of experiences of the truth. What was new for Augustine—not found in Plato's philosophy nor in Jesus' contagious love—was that the saving truth was accessible in one's heart. St. Ambrose's reading habits showed that the inner was not merely the locus of desires but a receptacle of truth about the world and about God. Augustine notes:

[W]hen I love [God], it is true that I love a light of a certain kind, a voice, a perfume, a food, an embrace; but they are of the kind that I love in my inner self. [*Confessions,* Book X:6, 211]

We end here stressing the importance of the inner in Augustine because there is a direct path from Paul's emphasis on the purification of our inner desires to Augustine finding God's truth in his heart. This valorization of the human being as an essentially inner domain lay dormant through much of the next twelve hundred years. But Descartes picks up the Augustinian thread when he emphasizes the self-sufficient "cogito"[31] whose inner experiences are cut off from "the external world." And one hundred fifty years after that Kant finally brings the idea to fruition when he articulates his conception of human beings as fully autonomous selves. But before we move on to Descartes and Kant we will have to take a detour by way of St. Thomas Aquinas and Dante, who draw on Aristotle rather than Plato to make Christianity intelligible in Greek terms. And whose failure to do so is dramatized by Luther.

5

From Dante to Kant: The Attractions and Dangers of Autonomy

THE GUIDING THEME of our book can be stated in a series of questions. First, what understanding of being human has shaped the various epochs in the history of the West? In particular, how did the various accounts of human existence show us who we are in relation to a source of meaning outside of us; in relation, in short, to what we have held sacred in our various ways. Second, how did these accounts of human being, and of the sacred, keep the problem of nihilism at bay? And finally, is there anything in these self-understandings from our history that we can use to combat the nihilism of our secular age?

These are the questions that direct a phenomenological, rather than humanist or Hegelian, reading of the history of the West. A phenomenological account of this sort focuses on the way people experienced themselves and the sacred rather than on the rational conceptions they had of themselves and their world. It sees in our history not unidirectional change—neither forward nor backward—but a series of different paradigms of cultural practice each of which highlights some aspects of human experience and covers up others. In our reading of the great texts that focused the epochs of Western history we ought, then, to look for whatever it was about those epochs that allowed them to avoid the problems we have, though it led to our problems eventually.

We begin this chapter with Dante Alighieri's *Divine Comedy,* the pinnacle of and paradigm for the High Middle Ages. The central feature of Dante's world is his sense that the universe is created by God, and therefore that its moral and spiritual meaning is written on its face. Medieval Christendom, in other words, was a world in which absolutely everything had its place. This is about as anti-nihilistic a universe as one can imagine. Far from there being no intrinsic meanings, the Medieval World is absolutely replete with them. We need to ask: Are there experiences at the margins of our own world that reflect the anti-nihilistic aspect of this medieval understanding?

The medieval understanding of Creation is no longer accessible to the West in its original form. Even most believing Christians don't understand our world today as a created world in which every aspect of the universe has a God-given meaning that it wears on its face. Still, Dante's general idea, that we are free to retrain our desires so that they are directed toward what ultimately sustains and fulfills them— so that they become attuned, in other words, to the meanings that are already out there in the world—will turn out to hold an important clue for our nihilistic age.

As we follow the stages by which our culture lost touch with the gods, and with them all mattering and meaning, Dante offers several other important insights. Within his work is a warning about the attraction of hell that we have yet to heed; a promising way to find meaning in our earthly lives, though he himself finally failed to appreciate it; and a stunning demonstration of how in the end the Greek understanding of reality undermines the Judeo-Christian revelation it was introduced to articulate.

CHRISTIANITY WAS VERY RADICAL, and it needed a lot of articulating. For almost a thousand years the Western world tried unsuccessfully to articulate Christianity in Platonic Greek terms. Augustine and other church fathers tried, in particular, to give a central place to an incarnate god while accepting Plato's adoration of an abstract eternity and his resulting denigration of the body. Then, a surprising breakthrough occurred. A bunch of lecture notes that had been decaying in a cellar for years were rediscovered, translated into Arabic, eventually translated into Latin, and brought to the West.

The author, Aristotle, turned out to be a brilliant critic of Plato's philosophy. He held that enduring, material things like trees and tables—not eternal, abstract ideas as in Plato—were the most real. He also contended that being embodied was not enfeebling or humiliating, as Plato and Augustine had held. Rather, bodies were empowering, according to Aristotle; indeed, embodied individuals were more perfect than disembodied souls.

Christian philosophers and theologians soon recognized that Aristotle, rather than Plato, was their man. They devoted themselves to making Christianity intelligible in Aristotelian terms. Greatest among these articulators was St. Thomas Aquinas, who lived from 1225 until 1274 and who took on the huge task of writing a *Summa Theologica*, which reconciled in detail the Greek and Christian understandings of reality. And the great popularizer of St. Thomas's theology was Dante Alighieri, who lived a generation after St. Thomas.

Dante laid out Thomas's achievement in a poem he called *The Comedy*. It was written in the vernacular, Italian, instead of scholarly Latin, and it focused and held up to the people of the day their medieval understanding of everything that is. In this way it was a work of art that functioned like a god. The "Historical Introduction" to *The Inferno* by Archibald MacAllister tells us that before [Dante's] death in 1321 the first two parts [of *The Comedy*] had already . . . achieved a reputation tinged with supernatural awe.[1]

No wonder that by the sixteenth century Dante's poem was recognized as sacred and thereafter called *The Divine Comedy.*

Aristotle held that the world is hierarchically organized. That means not only that it is unified, but also that things are ranked within it with respect to how perfect they are. At the top of all this order is a being Aristotle called The Prime Mover. The Prime Mover, in its absolute perfection, draws all beings to itself.

According to Aristotle, the hierarchical order is primarily manifest in the natural world. But the idea of a hierarchical universe in which *everything* has its place fit well with the Judeo-Christian belief in a creator God. In the Medieval World everything from lead to gold, from mice to elephants, and from sinners to saints was ranked. Even each type of sin was ranked. As Dante descends into Hell in the first part of *The Divine Comedy,* each type of sinful life he sees is worse than the one above it. Indeed, even the saints themselves are ranked! In the final part of the poem, as Dante is drawn upward toward Paradise, the saints he meets are more and more saintly. One could call all this monolithic monotheism. There is no place for the poly-worlds of Homer or for the tragically conflicting situations of Aeschylus.

Dante popularized St. Thomas's metaphysics and theology in his famous poem, but his initial motivation was much simpler than that. At the age of nine he had met an eight-year-old girl in Florence named Beatrice Portinari. He fell in love with her "at first sight." From that moment Dante took Beatrice to be his Lady, and he vowed to write a poem about her like nobody had ever written for his Lady before.

And he did.

The Divine Comedy is set in 1300, when Dante is thirty-five years old. He has gone "astray / from the straight road," he writes in the famous opening lines of the poem, and "woke to find myself alone in a dark wood." We know nothing of how Dante has gone astray, only that he has, and that he must undertake a journey, therefore, to save his soul. The journey itself, however, is clearer. It will take him through the entire Christian spiritual universe. First Dante must walk down through Hell itself, where he will see every type of sin that Christianity names, along with the punishments that are fit to each. Next he will ascend the mountain of Purgatory, where he will see the souls of those who sinned but repented, and the process of rehabilitation they must undergo. And finally, in Paradise, he will see the various types of saintly souls, and the increasingly blissful states they can achieve. In this way Dante will gain an understanding of precisely what a worthy life consists of and all the ways one can fail to achieve it.

Along this journey Dante will have two guides. Through Hell and most of Purgatory the great Roman poet Virgil will lead the way. Virgil, however, is a peculiar choice to guide Dante through the Christian universe. After all, he died before Jesus was born. Indeed, there are interesting ways in which Virgil's Roman Stoic philosophy leads him to misunderstand what matters in the Christian world. Finally, Virgil's understanding gives out altogether, since reason alone is not capable of comprehending Christian love. This is when Dante's second guide takes over. As he ascends through the various levels of Paradise, his Lady Beatrice leads the way.

THE GATES OF HELL through which Dante and Virgil pass are inscribed with a dedicatory poem that ends in the famous line: "Abandon all hope ye who enter here."[2] Hell is not only for those who have sinned but also for those who had the misfortune to live before or otherwise outside the influence of Christ. Of the nine circles in Hell, the least severe by far is the first circle, called Limbo, which is reserved for the virtuous pagans and unbaptized children. In Limbo Virgil finds his eternal home, along with the other great figures of the

Classical and Old Testament worlds: the poets like Homer and Ovid, the philosophers like Plato and Aristotle, and until they were later rescued by Jesus, the Hebrews like Abraham, Noah, and David. The virtuous pagans never had a chance to be Christians, so the lives they lived were the best they could manage under the circumstances. In Limbo they continue their virtuous lives, acting with moderation and dignity. But they can sense that they are missing something. As Virgil says, they are spared the suffering of Hell except for one affliction: "that without hope we live on in desire."[3]

Sighing fills the air of Limbo, as the virtuous pagans sense the absence of something they cannot quite understand or articulate. In Dante's Christian world, to be a human being of any epoch is to have been created by God to need the total fulfillment He makes possible. But God's universe offers that fulfillment only if one gets in the right relation to it by catching the Christian mood of agape love. The problem is that nobody knew this until Jesus came along and showed it, so the noble souls in Limbo have missed their chance.

In the next four circles of Hell a variety of sinful souls are described: lustful, gluttonous, avaricious, and wrathful souls, among many others. Unlike the souls in Limbo, these are Christians who have gone astray. Without going into the details, it is worth pointing out that their sins all have a certain structural similarity: they loved something that was not sufficient to fulfill their desires. The lustful, for example, loved the carnal delight of sex—they "sinned in the flesh."[4] Among these Dante counts not only Paolo and Francesca, whom we met in Chapter 1, but also Cleopatra, Tristan, and of course Helen and Paris. (Notice that Dante's interpretation of Helen is very different from Homer's.) The sin they share is to have wasted all their love on something that couldn't in the end offer spiritual fulfillment.

Without considering Dante's positive alternative, one can see what he thinks is wrong with lives like these. The way Dante understands these sinners, they are various kinds of sex and love addicts. (Or they are addicted to food, or money, or even their own anger.) The structure of addictions like these is uniquely unfulfilling. Consider an analogy with an addiction to cigarettes. The addict keeps coming back for more of the thing he thinks will fulfill him, make him happy, or give his life meaning. It looks desirable, and therefore it seems as if it should satisfy his desires to have it. But in fact when a smoker has finished one cigarette, he's left only with a craving for another. Ultimately such a sinner gets nothing but the desire for more of the unfulfilling thing.

Dante is certainly right that a life devoted to this kind of addiction is to be avoided. But his Aristotelian picture gives him a particular analysis of the case. In his view God's perfection, like the perfection of the Prime Mover in Aristotle, draws everything to Him. Human beings, in particular, are born to be fulfilled by the direct experience of God. To let your love be averted from Him and aimed at anything else—even the Lady Beatrice—is to have lived an unfulfilled life.

Whether it is possible to gain fulfillment through total commitment to another person or not, the souls deeper down in Hell have got a different problem. Within the fifth circle there is an enormous wall that separates upper from lower Hell. Within the wall is Hell proper, which Dante calls the City of Dis. (Dis is the Roman name for the Greek god of the underworld, Hades.) In order to get to the bottom of Hell, and from there up to Purgatory and then Paradise, Dante and Virgil will have to pass through the City of Dis.

Here is where Virgil's non-Christian background becomes a liability. In his capacity as tour guide, Virgil marches off to demand entrance through the imposing city gate. "Take heart," he tells his fearful charge.

> Nothing can take our passage from us
> when such a power has given warrant for it.[5]

When he reaches the gate, however, and presumably demands access in the name of God, the group of guards at the gate run behind the wall: "I couldn't hear my Lord's words," Dante reports,

> but the pack that gathered round him suddenly broke away
> howling and . . . slammed the towering gate hard in his face.[6]

Virgil is stunned. "Who has forbidden me the halls of sorrow?" he wonders.[7] But Virgil misunderstands the spiritual layout of Hell. He thinks that the lowest circles of Hell must be like a sturdy prison built to keep the worst offenders in. After all, that is certainly what Hell would be like in the Roman world. And true to this pagan conception Virgil says at one point in describing the souls of Dis, "I will explain how each is prisoned, and why."[8] But the City of Dis is not a prison to keep the most sinful souls in; it is a fortress built to keep God out. Dante, the Christian, understands this immediately. He talks about how he was

> . . . eager to learn what new estate
> of Hell those burning fortress walls enclosed.[9]

The City of Dis is a fortress instead of a prison because the souls who live within it have not just turned their love toward something less fulfilling than God; they have actively rejected Him. Saint Thomas distinguishes between carnal sin and spiritual sin, and that distinction is mirrored in the geography of Dante's Hell. Carnal sin is loving good things such as food, sex, and material goods, but loving them too much. Such overvaluation is punished outside the wall of Dis. Spiritual sin, by contrast, is rejecting God's creation. The spiritual sinners have barricaded themselves inside the walls of Dis, and use their energy to keep God out.

But why would anybody rebel against God? We can learn from Milton's *Paradise Lost.* There, Satan says he "would rather rule in Hell than serve in Heaven." He resents being created by God so that he, Satan, can find peace and fulfillment only in contemplating Him. He wants to make up his own mind about what to worship. Likewise, Dante's Satan, and the rebellious angels who follow him and defend the wall of the City of Dis, are dedicated to freely choosing what satisfies them. They reject God's creation in order to give things value as they see fit. Thus the sinners inside the City of Dis substitute for natural attractions willfully and actively chosen ones. For example, inside Dis Dante finds the homosexuals who cruise in packs. In Dante's world this is a rebellious rejection of a natural desire for monogamous heterosexual love.[10] An even more serious sin is the rejection of life itself, so suicides are punished even deeper inside the City of Dis.

As we shall soon see, the further Dante goes down in Hell, the less open the shades become to the appeal of things stemming from God's love and the more they close in on themselves. Moreover, the further away from God the shades are, the less moved they are by love of him. God is after all the Prime Mover. As a result, the deeper they go, the less they can move. At the bottom of Hell the most serious sinners are literally frozen in a pool of ice. Because they were unmoved by anything in God's creation, they can't move at all.

Milton's Protestant Hell is hot all the way down. We are used to an active, interventionist Satan at the head of armies of fallen angels. But Dante's Satan is so self-sufficient that he is not drawn to do anything. He is almost completely immobilized in the ice. All he can do is flap his wings, and indeed it is thanks to his flapping that Hell is frozen over.[11]

The Enlightenment admired all ways of life that strove for independence, so they praised the self-sufficiency that gave itself its own laws as autonomy. For the Medievals, however, to exclude oneself from bliss in order to save one's autonomy was the very essence of sin. Dante can thus be read as warning his contemporaries about the evils of autonomy. That warning could include those of our contemporaries tempted by Nietzschean willfulness—such as David Foster Wallace, whom we have already discussed. In a creation that draws us toward what is fulfilling, the attempt to set up one's own values and assign one's own meaning to things rather than cultivate their latent meaning can lead to a sad sort of nihilism in which there is no meaning and nothing moves us at all.

DANTE NEEDS A PLACE for free will in his system. If your will ultimately has nothing to do with the kind of life you lived—if that life
was preordained and there was nothing you could have done about
it—then what sense does it make to reward or punish you for that
life? But if Dante is against the kind of willful autonomy found in the
City of Dis, how can he have any notion of freedom of the will?

Dante does, indeed, have a place for free will in his system, but
it's not the kind of free will we're used to. For one thing, freedom for
Dante lies not in your ability to choose which life you're going to live or
what actions you're going to perform, as we might imagine. In particular, it doesn't involve freedom from some kind of external constraint
upon your action. That's the kind of freedom that most naturally goes
against a notion of determinism, and it's the kind of freedom we worry
about most. But it's not at all what Dante has in mind.

Rather, freedom according to Dante consists in being free to retrain your desires to focus on what will be fulfilling. In Dante's view
the job of training one's desires lies principally with the State and the
Church, and the problem with the modern world is that the State
and the Church have failed to do their job.[12] Indeed, if we were raised
properly and so had the right desires then each of us would go straight
to God like an arrow shot from a bow.[13] But even in Dante's world,
when the Church and State are failing to train us properly, we have
the freedom to retrain ourselves on our own if we so desire. That is
the phenomenon described in detail in Dante's account of Purgatory.

Dante's overall view is that the senses, and our desires, are bound
by what grabs them, but we have the freedom to form those senses by
means of our will and intellect so that the right things grab them. The
reforming glutton, for example, can retrain himself in such a way as
to no longer see food as the only object worthy of his desire. Former
gluttons in Purgatory are actively engaged in this type of retraining.
They agree to undergo the torture of Tantalus, a kind of forced diet-

ing. The main difference between Hell and Purgatory, then, is that those in Hell embraced their bad desires, while those in Purgatory repented them. The act of repenting is the free act of the will on the basis of which one can be judged. Repentance puts one on the path to salvation, and the "punishment" consists in freely going through the regime of reforming one's senses and desires so that they are directed in the right way.

All souls are naturally attracted to things in the world, according to Dante. How do we turn these attractions toward living a worthy life? Two options present themselves. The first says to try to withhold your desire, or even rid yourself of it. This is a typically Stoic type of approach, and it is the one that Virgil adopts. "Reason must guard the threshold of consent," he says.[14] The appetites, in other words, are to be kept in check; reason must keep us from giving in to our desires.

Dante has a different, Christian, view. All love is good in Dante's view as long as it is directed toward an appropriate object in an appropriate way. He counters Virgil's Stoic view that free will should *curb* love with the Christian view that free will should *direct* love. Dante thinks that you should intensify your love and be committed to whatever attracts you with total devotion, and then if it fails to satisfy you, which it surely will, you can learn from your mistakes until you finally find someone or something worthy of total passion and commitment. The last thing you should do is trim your desire. Free will allows you to train your desires in the right direction.

IT SEEMS AS THOUGH Dante admits a variety of desirable goals. At least that's what it looks like. The question is whether Dante can be consistent. In particular, the question is whether Dante thinks it is possible to find someone or something *here on earth* that is worthy of total passion and commitment. To the extent that he cannot, he runs the risk of recapitulating Augustine's error of giving an interpretation of Christianity that can't make sense of an embodied, incarnated Christ.

In his poem Dante does not neglect Jesus and seek access to an eternal disembodied God by way of his deepest inner self, as did Augustine. Dante was a totally outgoing person deeply involved in the politics of his city of Florence and also totally devoted to the woman who inspired his poem. Happily for him the early Christian mood of total devotion to Jesus had indirectly inspired a group of French poets called troubadours to develop a new understanding of love. It wasn't Greek *erotic* desire, but it wasn't Christian *agape* either. It was a new mood that came to be called courtly love. This new kind of love involved total devotion to a person who became the center of your life. Indeed, in the troubadour tradition your beloved actually gives you your identity. Without her you would cease to exist as the person you have become in loving her. You understand who you are entirely in relation to her, and therefore you are ready to die for her. In short, the troubadours invented romantic love and Dante was a romantic lover.

The depth of Dante's devotion to Beatrice is signaled in his poem. In the middle of *The Divine Comedy*, at the top of the mountain of Purgatory, Dante witnesses a pageant of the books of the Bible; the pageant portrays the history of the church. In the middle of the pageant a cart arrives pulled by a griffin. The griffin is a traditional symbol for Jesus: as a beast with two natures it mirrors Him who was both man and God. The procession comes to a halt, and the cart stops just in front of Dante. In the cart he notices a hooded figure. Something is happening which is the culmination of the history of the church. Angels fly overhead singing, "Blessed is he who comes." We are fully prepared for the hood to pull back and reveal Jesus Christ. But here is where Dante makes his most audacious move. For the figure in the cart isn't Jesus; it's Beatrice! Dante has put his girlfriend in Jesus' place! Dante has put Beatrice in the place of Christ. He has, indeed, written a poem about his beloved that glorifies her more than any poet before him has ever exalted his Lady.

There is something phenomenologically plausible about this as well. The phenomenon here is that love can draw one to another person so that she becomes the center of one's world. If one is blessed enough to be drawn into such a love, then everything in one's life makes sense in relation to her, and the sense it all makes is shining and glorious and completely satisfying. One understands oneself completely and happily in terms of the definition this love gives to one's life.

If this is the experience Dante had, then it is not crazy for him to see Beatrice in the role of Christ the Savior when he sees her in the pageant at the top of Purgatory. The mood of romantic love for another is not so far, after all, from the various forms of the sacred that we have seen up till now. For one thing, it is not a feeling that one can choose. Like being guided by Athena or catching the contagious mood of agape in the presence of Jesus, romantic love too is something that strikes one, takes one over. It demands a sense of gratitude. Finally, one understands exactly how to act on the basis of it. Romantic love gives one an attunement to a situation that makes everything matter in its appropriate degree. If Dante had stopped with Beatrice at the top of Purgatory, therefore, he'd have described a completely livable world that could bring joy and meaning into his life.

Moreover, the kind of devotion that he has to Beatrice is devotion to her as a physical, embodied being. He talks about her beautiful green eyes, her lovely mouth, and especially her legs, in characterizing his total devotion. In this way Dante captures an essential part of the Christian intuition that the saving mood is one that happens in the physical, embodied world. If he finds his fulfillment in his commitment to Beatrice, then he has found a way to resist the Augustinian mistake of trying to interpret Christianity in a completely abstract and disembodied way. This is the moment when Dante has the chance to give an interpretation of Christianity that frees it from the Greek abstractions with which it is incompatible.

Unfortunately, that is not the path Dante takes. The West will have to wait another five hundred years before Søren Kierkegaard develops the phenomenology of romantic love Dante began to describe. In Dante's case, although Beatrice does guide him through Paradise, he does not find his life's meaning through his commitment to her. Rather, having guided Dante through the circles of Heaven, Beatrice returns to her seat in the rose in which the saved souls sit when contemplating God. Having placed her in the position of Savior, putting her in the place of the one St. John says is the truth and the way, Dante treats her as a ladder he can leave behind when he reaches God. For Beatrice herself is not the ultimate object of love in Dante's final picture.[15] She is the way but not the truth.

When Beatrice returns to her seat, Dante can see her high up in the rose, right below St. Peter. She gives Dante one last smile, and then turns back to contemplate the radiance of God. Dante reports that: "Experiencing that radiance, it is impossible to think of ever turning from it."[16] Beatrice has led Dante to achieve the beatific vision—a direct contemplation of God. But the bliss of God's love is so overwhelming that far from organizing his life and providing the point of all his actions, it takes him out of his life altogether. Instead of returning to politics with renewed vigor, or trying to live as Beatrice would have him do, Dante seems to lose all sense of himself as an individual. According to St. Thomas the beatitude caused by the contemplation of God's radiance is the ultimate goal of human life. The bliss of contemplating God is so overwhelming, however, that it makes all other earthly joys irrelevant.

So Dante is never going to look back at Beatrice. What had been the most important commitment in his life on earth turns out to be irrelevant to his fulfillment. In effect, the single most important distinction—the distinction between his love for Beatrice and everything else in his life—gets leveled by the bliss of contemplating God.

Similarly, Dante's commitment to politics ends up looking irrelevant. From his place in Paradise Dante looks back toward the earth and reports: "I saw this globe so lost in space that I had to smile at such a sorry show."[17] He sees that everything earthly, even politics, is trivial and says: "I saw the dusty little threshing ground that makes us ravenous for our mad sins."[18] Like his love of Beatrice, everything political that was meaningful in his life has been trumped by God's radiance. Once Dante sees God, he is never going to turn away from God's radiance to take sides in politics or to gaze on Beatrice again.

ARISTOTLE'S DESCRIPTION OF the Prime Mover is that it moves all other beings by way of the attraction of its perfection. The last lines of *The Paradiso* describe the Christian version of the Greek Supreme Being taking control of Dante's desire and will:

> . . . I could feel my being turned . . . by the Love that moves the Sun and the other stars.[19]

The Dante who, thanks to the troubadours, found that the most important experience in his life was his love for an individual woman, has been drawn into the orbit of The Prime Mover. His individual will along with his love of Beatrice and his political commitments have been overwhelmed by the bliss of contemplating God. One might say Dante has been blissed out. While bliss wipes you out, joy makes you more intensely you. And in Dante's world every joy is meaningless compared to the bliss of the beatific vision. "Bliss beyond bliss, all other joys transcending," he says.[20] Dante is ultimately absorbed into the love of all creatures for their Creator.

But is this really the way to a fulfilled existence? It seems more like the way to avoid a meaningful life rather than the way to attain one. Indeed, it might be a medieval form of nihilism; for it says that there is nothing in this life that has any meaning whatsoever—even Beatrice's saving love or Dante's deep political motivations are trivial compared with the love of God. It is here that Dante inadvertently shows us that the Greek metaphysics Aquinas is working with undermines the agape love we saw in the early Christianity of John and Paul. On the early Christian model one lives in the world with Jesus in you, and that means you live in the mood of joy not bliss, a mood that guides you to definite and directed action in the world of the Word made Flesh. The concept of the love of God is therefore ambiguous. In Dante's world it turns out to mean the love of each of us for Aristotle's Supreme Being, whereas in the Gospel it means Jesus' love for each of us. In Dante's final mystical merging there is no place for Jesus as an embodied object and paradigm of agape love. Dante's final experience is merely that God's radiance is "painted with man's image."[21] Jesus is just a face, in Dante's view, with no body beneath it to hold it up.

In sum, the medieval attempt to articulate Christianity in Aristotelian terms must fail. The negative message of the *Inferno* is phenomenologically apt: autonomy really does lead to *active* nihilism, since when all meaning originates with us nothing has authority over us or the power to move us. But, if we try to put the Christian love of an incarnate Jesus into Aristotelian terms we end up with a Supreme Being and a love so overwhelming and *passive* that it wipes out individuality and all meaningful differences. Dante's unconditional commitment that has drawn him to Beatrice, and that might have offered him and his medieval Christian culture a new source of personal meaning, is wiped out by an impersonal, Greek, mystical experience. Indeed, it turns out that what has been called the Medieval Synthesis—Aquinas's and Dante's achievement of conceptualizing the Christian revelation in Aristotelian terms—is not the answer to nihilism but another step in its direction.

St. Thomas, following Aristotle, claimed that the highest goal in life was the beatific vision of the Prime Mover—renamed The Supreme Being. St. Thomas understood this as the bliss of directly contemplating God. But as we have just seen, in Dante's poem this leaves no place for Jesus and agape love, nor for a community of joyful Christians, nor, indeed, for individual selves.

Martin Luther, writing a century after Thomas and Dante, was determined to rescue Christianity from Aristotle and get back to the early Christianity expressed in the letters of Paul. Luther minces no words in stating his disgust at the disastrous influence of Aristotle:

> It grieves me to the quick that this damned, conceited, rascally heathen has deluded and made fools of so many of the best Christians with his misleading writings. God has plagued us thus for our sins.[22]

And he adds:

> The universities need a good, stiff reform. . . . It is my advice that the books of Aristotle, . . . which have hitherto been esteemed the best, be entirely removed from the curriculum.[23]

Luther thus decisively breaks with the attempt to bring together Greek philosophy and Judeo-Christian experience. He could be criticizing St. Augustine, St. Thomas, and Dante when he says: "It does [the sinner] no good to recognize God in his glory and majesty, unless he recognizes him in the humility and shame of the cross."[24] Or more succinctly: "The 'theologian of glory' calls the bad good and the good bad. The 'Theologian of the cross,' says what a thing is."[25] That is, Christians are not called to experience the Greek-type pure presence of the divine, but are called to relate to Jesus, the "Word made Flesh" as described by John and experienced by Paul.

In general, Luther had no use for mystics and monks. Both types were cut off from the world in which, according to Luther, communal joy—rather than blissed-out contemplation of God—is the contagious Christian mood. Luther is adamant that

> we . . . ought freely to help our neighbor through our body and its works, and each one should become as it were a Christ to the other that we may be Christians to one another.[26]

Rather than leave the world by contemplating God's truth in the depth of the self as Augustine did, or by merging with the love moving creation as Dante did, the Christian is reborn "a new man in a new world."[27]

A new world was, indeed, on the horizon. Thanks to Luther the Aristotelian/Thomistic/Dantian theology ceased to hold center stage in our cultural understanding of ourselves. The reborn Christian, whose mood is directly shared with Jesus and with all other Christians, does not need the mediation of popes and priests. According to Luther, every Christian is a Pope and "all they which faithfully believe in Christ are saints."[28]

This is not a way of being a self-sufficient or autonomous being, but it does open the possibility of thinking of oneself as at least self-sufficient vis à vis the church—up to then the most powerful institution in the West. In the new world of the Enlightenment that Luther ushers in, this can come to sound very self-sufficient, especially when he says:

> [A] Christian man, if ye define him rightly, is free from all laws, and is not subject unto any creature, either within or without. . . . For he hath such a gift, such a treasure in his heart, that although it seemeth to be but little, yet notwithstanding the smallness thereof, is greater than heaven and earth, because Christ, which is this gift, is greater.[29]

Luther's reformation, and the Protestant Reformation more generally, thus provided a corrective to the medieval passive nihilism of Dante. But its emphasis on individual freedom also prepared the way for the active nihilism associated with the death of God. Luther's corrective to medieval nihilism centers on his insistence that God's love embraces us despite our sins. The mood of Christianity in Luther, therefore, is joy and gratitude.[30] In Luther's own life this mood gave him a certainty about how to act. This certainty was manifest in his famous statement at the Diet of Worms in 1521: "Here I stand; I can do no other." Certainty about how to act in this world therefore—a certainty for which one would "die a thousand deaths," as Luther says in his commentary on Paul's Letter to the Romans—stands in stark contrast with the hope that a mood of bliss might lift one out of this world and its commitments, as in the medieval nihilism of Dante.

But the corrective came at the price of meaning. In order to emphasize the peculiarities of this mood of joy and gratitude, Luther stressed that it was experienced in terms of a personal and individual relation to Jesus. This personal and individual relation to Jesus is not the same as the Enlightenment celebration of the independent individual, but it was a step in that direction. Reform Christianity had the effect of emphasizing the individual as defined by his inner thoughts and desires at the expense of a God-given hierarchy of ordered, worldly meanings outside the individual.

Indeed, in Luther's account of Christianity the world in its political, religious, and environmental forms is entirely disenchanted. We have now traveled far from Dante's medieval hierarchy of meanings—in which the value of everything is written on its face. Rather, each individual is as a king, according to Luther, since one no longer follows the laws in service to the king and his state. One is indebted instead to the mood that Jesus' love and suffering instills in you, and it is this mood that determines what is lawful. That is to say, as Jesus said, love fulfills the Law. One is no longer dependent on the priests and their mediation or intercession in one's relations with God. Rather, Jesus justifies you as an individual by giving his grace and love to you directly.

This brings us a long way toward the Enlightenment understanding of the self as the self-sufficient source of meaning in the universe. But unlike the Enlightenment thinkers, especially Descartes and Kant, Luther still had a strong sense of the individual's dependence on a Savior. According to him, works of devotion offered by the church and by individuals are worthless, willful acts of pride, unless they are experienced in faith and humility. We can't give faith to ourselves any more than we can give ourselves our other moods:

> Faith is a living and unshakeable confidence . . . [it] makes us joyful, high-spirited, and eager in our relations with God and with all mankind. . . . Righteousness of this kind cannot be brought about in the ordinary course of nature, by our own free will, or by our own powers. No one can give faith to himself . . . [31]

Descartes took the next big step toward nihilism by denigrating receptivity entirely and focusing exclusively on what one can obtain by one's own willpower.

IT IS NOT UNTIL the early seventeenth century that we arrive at the French philosopher René Descartes, the only reconfigurer in the West besides the Jesus figure we have described. Just as Jesus established our Christian World with its saints and sinners, Descartes established our Modern World in which we understand ourselves as self-sufficient *subjects* standing over against self-sufficient *objects*. He does this by drawing on Augustine's emphasis on the inner depths of the soul and on Luther's emphasis on each Christian's independence. But Luther, with his understanding of moods—especially agape and gratitude—preserves a sense of the necessary receptivity of the Christian while Descartes claims that human subjects at their best are completely detached, self-contained, and, far from being passive, have a willpower so great that it rivals God's. He says:

> It is free-will alone . . . which I find to be so great in me that I can conceive no other idea to be more great; it is indeed the case that it is for the most part this will that causes me to know that in some manner I bear the image and likeness of God.[32]

ONE EXEMPLAR OF THE experience of the sacred that we have used consistently is the experience of moods. We described the gods of Homer in terms of the overpowering moods that they set and the actions that they draw out of people by virtue of those moods. But we have seen other moods as well: the mood of patriotism in Aeschylus, of agape in John and Paul, of bliss in Dante, and of joy and gratitude in Luther. A crucial feature of the Enlightenment is that moods— insofar as they are discussed at all—are stripped of the central features that have characterized them in earlier epochs. Typically moods were public and shareable—one could catch the mood of fierce courage from being in the presence of Ares or Achilles, or one could catch the mood of agape from being in the presence of Jesus. But in our current Cartesian characterization of the individual as a subject, moods become private, inner states that are essentially unavailable to others. We will see that the older, public notion of moods as the stand-in for the sacred is crucial to Melville's way of resisting all forms of will and all forms of monotheism.

It should be clear from what we have said that one does not have to believe that the Greek gods actually existed in order to gain something deep and important from Homer's sense of the sacred. (The same holds for Jesus the performer of physically impossible miracles.) One does, however, have to reject the modern idea that to be a human agent is to be the sole and self-sufficient source of the actions one performs. Because this modern notion of human agency is so pervasive, it can lead us to act in ways that cover up the phenomena that Homer was sensitive to. To see this we need to trace briefly the genesis of the modern view of the self.

Before Descartes the culture could hardly be said to have glorified the inner self. As we saw, St. Augustine had to work to get people to recognize its importance as a path to divinity. Even after Augustine, it seemed obvious that we are beings essentially open to all sorts of forces from without. And in Dante's world, the human soul was receptive both to God's divine love and to Satan's pull toward autonomy. Indeed, one thing the Homeric and the Medieval worlds have in common is the idea that we are at our best when we *don't* allow our own thoughts and ideas to get in the way of what we are directly drawn to do.

Descartes by contrast, building on Augustine, brought to the fore the idea that we are self-sufficient beings who stand on our own and are defined by our private thoughts and desires. If I want to know who I am, in this Cartesian view, I can do no better than to look within—to ask myself which thoughts I accept as mine.

Under Descartes' influence, then, we have come to understand ourselves as *subjects*—sites of *inner* thoughts, desires, and volitions— while "the *external* world," according to Descartes, consisted of meaningless *objects*—those nonsubjective entities that stand over against me. Before Descartes, people did not understand themselves as subjects and objects, but rather as God's creatures. After Descartes, we have come to see ourselves as almost infinitely free assigners of meaning who can give whatever meaning we choose to the meaningless objects around us.

This completely overthrows the more traditional idea that we are beings open to the world and its various forces upon us. For the first time in human history, therefore, people were confronted by the question: how ought we to live if we understand ourselves in this completely self-contained way?

Descartes thought he had the answer. He claimed that with his reason and experience he could find rules for figuring out rationally what in each situation was the right thing to do. He was determined to work out his ethics as soon as he finished his work in science and mathematics. He notes:

[L]est I should remain irresolute in my actions in the interval . . . I drew up for myself *a provisional code of morals,* consisting of some three or four maxims.[33]

To further work out his philosophy, he tells us, he retired to a warm room where he was free from passions.

But Descartes apparently found no way to base an ethics on the austere world of subjects and objects, so, while his contributions to science and mathematics are important breakthroughs, he never returned to developing his ethics. Still, he managed to reconfigure the Western world entirely, taking the willfulness that in Dante had been the defining feature of evil and making it the most fundamental and God-like aspect of human being. In this way he contributed a crucial step toward nihilism.

DESCARTES' UNDERSTANDING OF FREEDOM WAS so radical that it needed an articulator; this was the great eighteenth-century German philosopher Immanuel Kant. Kant argued that if we are self-sufficient subjects then there can be no law about how we should act other than the law we give to ourselves.

In Kant's view the subject replaces God as the orderer of the world. Kant argued famously that Enlightenment means learning finally to take responsibility for your own actions. In other words, the maturity that comes with Enlightenment requires me to obey the Pope or the King only if I freely choose to do so. Autonomy, or setting up one's own laws and choosing to act in accordance with them—the ultimate sinfulness of the souls in Dante's Dis—now becomes the highest human good.

This Kantian view owes a debt to Luther and is, at the same time, a deviation from his position. True, Luther emphasizes the importance of the individual. But it is essential to Luther's Christianity that the mood of joy and gratitude comes from the experience of *receiving* God's grace. It is only because I feel indebted to God that I am in a position to be certain about how I ought to act. So Luther can say: "Here I stand, I can do no other. *God help me.*" The certainty is an existential certainty in Luther—it is being joyfully committed to acting in the way I know I must.

By the time Kant turns it into a recipe for ethical activity, however, it has turned around completely—as Kant himself recognizes. Whereas in Luther the source of my existential certainty about how to act is my experience of Jesus' unfailing love for me, in Kant I alone take responsibility for all my acts. And indeed, according to Kant, this is a sign of my maturity.

There are lots of details in Kant about what features this self-given law ought to have, but the essential point here is that the moral law must be given to us by ourselves. In Kant's terminology, we are self-law-givers—"autonomous" agents who ought to act in accordance with the principles we set for ourselves. Nothing outside of us—no God or other force, no impulse, no revered text, no parental demand, custom, or state decree—can be that upon which we base our actions when we are acting at our best. All external forces are denigrated by Kant as "heteronymous determinations of the will."[34] That is, other-given causes of our actions. If we allow these external forces to influence us in our actions, then we are failing to live up to the demands placed upon us as the kind of free, self-sufficient beings we essentially are.[35]

Although the Kantian view is formulated in abstract language, its basic impulse is woven deeply into the modern world. It is natural and intuitive to us to think that a person is criticizable if he fails to take responsibility for his actions. Human actions just are, in the modern conception, behaviors for which the human agent is responsible. As we have seen, in the middle of the twentieth century the French philosopher Jean-Paul Sartre worked out the logical extension of this view in his existentialist philosophy. "Existentialism," Sartre writes, "places the entire responsibility for [man's] existence squarely upon his own shoulders."[36] We have come a long way from Homer's endorsement of Helen's sense that when she ran off with Paris Aphrodite drew her to do so.

The modern view that we are entirely responsible for our existence stands in radical contrast with the Homeric idea that we act at our best when we open ourselves to being drawn from without. Indeed, once we see the force of this contrast it becomes obvious why Homeric phenomena are covered up in our modern world. What Homer considers to be the paradigm of human excellence seems to Kant, and to most of us, hardly to count as human action at all. Homeric excellence, to the modern world, looks like heteronymous determination of the will—wrongful abandonment of our freedom. Helen's running off with Paris seems to us an addiction or a compulsion. She seems to us out of control—an eminently criticizable case of a woman who loves too much.

The danger of the Kantian position is that by making us entirely responsible for our actions we place in our own hands the question of what matters most. But the history of the last 150 years suggests that we are not the proper source for meaning in the world. Indeed, the step is very short from the Kantian notion of the human being as a fully autonomous self to the Nietzschean notion of the human being as a free spirit who makes up whatever meanings he likes. Precisely because they are freely made up, however, meanings can also be freely taken back. Therefore, they have no authority over the maker. And this is just the active nihilism that Dante already recognized could not sustain a meaningful conception of human existence.

Writing less than a century after Kant, and a generation before Nietzsche, Herman Melville could already see the threat of this nihilism looming. Even more amazing, though, is that he could envision the recovery of Homer's polytheistic gods as a way to surmount it. We thus bring our story full circle as we turn now to *Moby Dick*.

6

Fanaticism, Polytheism, and Melville's "Evil Art"

I HAVE WRITTEN A wicked book," wrote Herman Melville. "[A]nd feel spotless as the lamb."

It was November 1851, and Melville was writing to his friend and neighbor Nathaniel Hawthorne. The English edition of Melville's *Moby Dick* had appeared a month earlier and the American edition was just coming out. "It is a strange feeling," he continued.

> [N]o hopefulness is in it, no despair. Content—that is it; and irresponsibility; but without licentious inclination. I speak now of my profoundest sense of being, not of an incidental feeling.[1]

Melville saw in *Moby Dick* something deeper and more threatening— in a word, more wicked—than the scandalous tales of cannibalism and primitive, open sexuality that had already secured his reputation as the first and reigning American literary sex symbol.[2] His five earlier novels—sea adventures published at an extraordinary pace between 1846 and 1850—had created controversy, excitement, and a yen for unexpurgated editions. As the London *Times* wrote in a review of Melville's first novel, *Typee,* describing the home, provisions, and *enthusiastic* attentions he reports having received as a castaway on a

Polynesian island in the South Pacific: "Enviable Herman! A happier dog it is impossible to imagine than Herman in the Typee Valley."[3] His marriage to Elizabeth Shaw, in 1847, could not be held in a church—according to one source—"for fear his fans would crowd into it."[4]

But *Moby Dick,* although in some sense classifiable as a sea adventure like Melville's earlier books, is wicked in a darker and more penetrating sense. When the whaling ship *Ann Alexander* was rammed and sunk by a sperm whale off the coast of Chile, toward the end of August 1851,[5] Melville wondered whether his literary black magic had somehow provoked the beast. "It is really and truly a surprising coincidence—to say the least," he wrote about the similarity between the eponymous whale of his forthcoming novel and this newly reported Chilean one.

> I make no doubt it *is* Moby Dick himself for there is no account of his capture after the sad fate of the Pequod about fourteen years ago.—Ye Gods! What a Commentator is this *Ann Alexander* whale. What he has to say is short & pithy & very much to the point. I wonder if my evil art has raised this monster.[6]

If the *Ann Alexander* tragedy punctuated the dangerous powers of his new book, however, its underlying orientation had been clear for some time. Toward the end of June 1851, as Melville was putting the finishing touches on *Moby Dick,* he offered to send a copy of some of the manuscript to his friend Hawthorne:

> Shall I send you a fin of the *Whale* by way of a specimen mouthful? The tail is not yet cooked—though the hell-fire in which the whole book is broiled might not unreasonably have cooked it all ere this. This is the book's motto (the secret one),—Ego non baptiso te in nomine—but make out the rest yourself.[7]

The Latin passage that Melville leaves unfinished, the secret motto of *Moby Dick,* is traditionally completed as follows: Ego non baptiso te in nomine Patris et Filii et Spiritus Sancti—sed in nomine Diaboli. "I baptize you not in the name of the Father and the Son and the Holy Spirit," it says, "but rather in the name of the Devil."[8]

WHAT MAKES *MOBY DICK* such a wicked book? And if it is so wicked then how can Melville feel "spotless as the lamb" having written it? What hidden message does its secret motto conceal? And what, precisely, is Melville's evil art?

The table is not yet set for such a feast. Suffice it to say for the moment, however, that whatever the answer to these questions, the stakes are as high as they can possibly be. The book is not just wicked, according to Melville, not just licentious or even heinous; it is infused throughout with the fire of hell, thoroughly broiled and cooked within its oven. And Melville is not just innocent, either, as if some jury had acquitted him in trial. He is pure and guiltless in an infinitely deeper sense. "Spotless," he emphasizes, "as the lamb."

The lamb of God, that is.

Our Lord Jesus Christ.

The religious imagery here is complicated. It seems to combine a secret, hellish, and presumably therefore anti-Christian wickedness with some kind of radically pure innocence; innocence so pristine that it is assimilable in some way or another to the guiltlessness of Jesus Christ himself. In any traditional interpretation these images are diametrically opposed. What it means to combine them, as Melville does, is anything but clear.

The ambiguities are manifold. For one thing, it turns out that the secret motto that Melville mentions in his letter to Hawthorne may not be so secret after all. Captain Ahab himself—the fanatical, mad, monomaniacal whale hunter at the center of the book—invokes a version of this Satanic formula during a key episode in the narrative.

As his three pagan harpooners prepare for their final chase, Ahab solemnly intones the sacrilegious incantation to baptize, in their pagan blood, the harpoon that is meant to kill the great white sperm whale Moby Dick.

Moreover, it is not clear, after all, precisely what the secret motto is. In the one place outside the book where he publicly invokes the formula—the letter to Hawthorne that we have seen already—Melville leaves the phrasing incomplete. "Ego non baptiso te in nomine," he begins tantalizingly. But then he refuses to render satisfaction. "[M]ake out the rest yourself," is all he is willing to say. In what completed version then—if any—does this saying stand as the secret to the book? In whose name does the new kind of baptism occur?

Finally, the spotlessness is puzzling too. Does Melville think somehow that whatever anti-Christian wickedness the book entails, or seems to manifest, it is nevertheless ultimately a kind of salvation for our culture, the way Jesus in his innocence promised salvation to an earlier age? Does he see in *Moby Dick*—properly interpreted, of course, according to its secret motto—a new kind of hope, a new kind of sacred, perhaps even a saving possibility for the culture as a whole?

These questions offer a way into one of the most puzzling passages in Melville's profound and deeply puzzling book, a passage unexplored by most interpreters, misunderstood by most of the rest. But it is clearly a central passage in the book, probably even an essential one. For in it Melville seems to make a prophecy. "If hereafter any highly cultured, poetical nation," he writes,

> shall lure back to their birthright, the merry May-day gods of old; and livingly enthrone them again in the now egotistical sky; on the now unhaunted hill; then be sure, exalted to Jove's[9] high seat, the great Sperm Whale shall lord it.[10]

Listen to that.

MOBY DICK IS, of course, a story about the pursuit of The Whale. It is a story about mad monomaniac Captain Ahab's quest, and the quest too of all those whom he has enlisted for the voyage of his Nantucket-based whaling ship the *Pequod*.

But the whale is many things to many people. Perhaps this is suggested already by the higgledy-piggledy collection of extracts that stand as prelude to the book; extracts collected, as we are told, by a "mere painstaking burrower and grub-worm of a poor devil of a Sub-Sub"-Librarian.[11] This disordered jumble of a collection includes all the "random allusions to whales he could anyways find in any book whatsoever, sacred or profane."[12]

The rude juxtapositions and bizarre extrusions that one finds among these extracts are at least partly comedic. When the description of the whale's breath—"such an insupportable smell, as to bring on a disorder of the brain"—is followed by Pope's satirical characterization of a petticoat—constructed as though "armed with ribs of whale"—one can hardly fail to laugh. And the odd and apparently irrelevant non sequitur occasionally catches one as well, jutting out as it seems to, like some inexplicable natural event. One piece from the *Life of Samuel Comstock,* for example, reads in its entirety: "If you make the least damn bit of noise," replied Samuel, "I will send you to hell."

Not exactly clear what that has to do with whales.

But if the extracts are partly comedic, they seem to serve a deeper purpose as well. For they suggest—even if they don't actually demonstrate—that the whale has a possible infinity of meanings. He is "King of the boundless sea," as an old whaling song indicates, ruling over the infinite like God himself. But he is also Leviathan, at least once the great enemy of God—sometimes known as Satan—as a passage from Isaiah attests.[13] He is the swallower of Jonah, his mouth is a chaos, but King Henry (quoted by Melville) tells us that the spermaceti found within his head is "The sovereignest thing on earth . . . for an inward bruise." From his monstrous bulk, as Lord Bacon writes, "we have received nothing certain."[14]

The suggestion here, to be developed in detail throughout the course of *Moby Dick,* is that the whale is a mystery, so full of meaning that it verges on meaninglessness, so replete with interpretations that in the end they all seem to cancel out. It is this tantalizing but ungraspable quality of the great Sperm Whale, we are later told— his facelessness, his imposing "pyramidical silence," but also the immensely amplified sense of the "Deity and the dread powers" that lurk within his brow—it is this unrelenting but also unyielding mystery that stands at the center of the universe. "I but put that brow before you," a central character says. "Read it if you can."[15]

The question for the novel, perhaps its central philosophical question, is not just what the character of this mystery is, but also how we are to understand ourselves in its midst. A preliminary indication is found in the opening passages of the book.

Ishmael is the name of the book's narrator, or at least his pseudonym. "Call me Ishmael," he says, in the novel's famous opening line. Ultimately he will be the sole survivor of the *Pequod*'s ill-fated voyage, and he is probably something like the hero of the tale. He is a strange hero, however, a relatively minor character on the ship itself, and an exceedingly moody one at that, but his perspective is one we learn to trust. The book makes a lot out of different ways of seeing the world; and Ishmael—named as he is after the biblical outcast destined to a life of homeless wandering—our Ishmael, is a character who is friendly not only with all the niceties but also all the horrors the world has to offer. "Not ignoring what is good," he tells us, "I am quick to perceive a horror, and could still be social with it."[16]

Ishmael recalls Melville himself, who in his various voyages on whaling ships and frigates, as well as during his three-week turn among the cannibals of the Typee Valley, seems to have made a virtue—not to mention a profession—of getting along well with all types of people. Like Melville, Ishmael has spent some time at the head of a classroom, "lording it as a country schoolmaster, making the tallest boys stand in awe of you."[17] And there is even a suggestion from Melville's own biography that this wandering, homeless existence—a life in which one leaves the certainties of one's own civilization and becomes sociable with all the goods and horrors of the world—is itself the best way to discover a path out of our troubles. "Brooding under the southern constellations," one commentator reports Melville to have said, "makes me receptive to new ideas."[18]

This is the Ishmael, then, in whose hands we must place ourselves. Can this moody, sociable character, this outcast and wanderer without a home, can this Ishmael tell us something about the mystery of the whale? Can he tell us how to understand ourselves in its midst?

Ishmael has determined to "sail about and see the watery part of the world,"[19] and as usual in this tale, it is his moodiness that sends him on his way. Wandering about the boundless sea, he explains, is "a way I have of driving off the spleen, and regulating the circulation."

> Whenever I find myself growing grim about the mouth; whenever it is a damp, drizzly November in my soul; whenever I find myself involuntarily pausing before coffin warehouses, and bringing up the rear of every funeral I meet; and especially whenever my hypos get such an upper hand of me, that it requires a strong moral principle to prevent me from deliberately stepping into the street and methodically knocking people's hats off—then, I account it high time to get to sea as soon as I can.[20]

And it is in the context of Ishmael's determination to take to sea, of his drive to repel an advancing despair, that he finds himself before a painting in the Spouter Inn. The huge canvas dominates the entry, but it is poorly lit, "thoroughly besmoked and every way defaced," and extremely difficult to get a handle on. It is a "marvelous painting" that demands the attention of the viewer, but it seems to resist every attempt to plumb its depths. "Ever and anon a bright, but, alas, deceptive idea would dart you through," Ishmael tells us.

> It's the Black Sea in a midnight gale.—It's the unnatural combat of the four primal elements.—It's a blasted heath.—It's a Hyperborean winter scene.—It's the breaking-up of the icebound stream of Time.

Or perhaps, it occurs to him at a different point, "some ambitious young artist, in the time of the New England hags, has endeavored to delineate chaos bewitched."

The painting is the bulging mystery that stands at the entry to the Spouter Inn, itself a "wide, low, straggling entry" whose "old-fashioned wainscots" remind one "of the bulwarks of some condemned old craft."[21] This old seacraft of an inn, therefore, this ancient vessel, is the place from which Ishmael's whaling voyage begins; and at its very entry stands a beguiling mystery of a pictorial representation, an ancient, besmoked, and beleaguered mystery that calls out for resolution and resists it in nearly equal measure.

Involuntarily taken in by the sublimity of this mysterious painting, Ishmael finds himself determined to sound its depths.

> Yet was there a sort of indefinite, half-attained, unimaginable sublimity about it that fairly froze you to it, till you involuntarily took an oath with yourself to find out what that marvelous painting meant.[22]

One might think that the seemingly endless range of possible meanings for the painting would lead Ishmael to despair, that its indecipherable mystery would be intolerable. There is precedent for such a response—albeit generations later, to be sure—in the twentieth-century literature of despair that extends from Eliot's Prufrock to Allen Ginsberg's "Howl" and beyond. And Ahab himself, as we shall see, cannot abide the thought that such a mystery infects the world. But Ishmael is not a nervous man like Ahab, and his is a journey to drive away a temporary despair, not to revel in its poetry or demand its eternal relief in life. After long conversations "with many aged persons," therefore, after "much and earnest contemplation, and oft repeated ponderings," at last Ishmael rests content with one final interpretation of the painting in the Spouter Inn. Perhaps it is not the truth of the matter in any deep sense, he admits; it is only "a final theory of my own."

> [A]t last all these fancies yielded to that one portentous something in the picture's midst. *That* once found out, and all the rest were plain. But stop; does it not bear a faint resemblance to a gigantic fish? even the great leviathan himself? In fact, the artist's design seemed this. . . . The picture represents a Cape-Horner in a great hurricane; the half-foundered ship weltering there with its three dismantled masts alone visible; and an exasperated whale, purposing to spring clean over the craft, is in the enormous act of impaling himself upon the three mast-heads.

A whale, then, impaling himself upon a dismantled trinity of masts, as the half-foundering ship from which the masts arise is swallowed up by the hurricane-bestirred waves of the boundless sea.

A moving interpretation that speaks eloquently to the whaler. You can see why Ishmael wants to stop with that.

"THIS IS A LONG LETTER," Melville once wrote to Hawthorne, "but you are not at all bound to answer it."[23]

> Possibly, if you do answer it, and direct it to Herman Melville, you will missend it—for the very fingers that now guide this pen are not precisely the same that just took it up and put it on this paper. Lord, when shall we be done changing?

Never, is the answer to that question. We shall never be done changing. And that is true for Ishmael and Melville alike. For Ishmael, like his ever-changing creator, is moody and constantly redefined by his moods; he is a Catskill mountain eagle, as Melville suggests, a noble bird who can soar to the highest heights and descend into the blackest mountain gorges. And in all of these moody flights some godlike truth and meaning is revealed. In Ishmael, as in Melville himself, "divine magnanimities are spontaneous and instantaneous—catch them while you can."[24]

Perhaps, therefore, if some other mood had driven Ishmael to the Spouter Inn—some mood other than the "damp, drizzly November in [his] soul"—then in that case some other interpretation of the painting would have left him content. But what makes Melville's book so thrilling, what makes it speak so forcefully to the modern age, is that Ishmael's drizzly mood is our own. And his determination to "drive off the spleen"—well, that ought to be ours as well. Even if it sometimes isn't.

If our interpretations—if the meanings we find in the events of our lives or in paintings or artworks or literature or whales; in anything, in fact, that is deep and important and true—if these interpretations are filtered through our moods, then doesn't that show we haven't gotten to the bottom of things after all? Doesn't it cast doubt, in other words, upon how satisfying—or maybe even how true—we can find these moody, filtered accounts? Science, for instance, is supposed to reveal the ultimate truth about the world; and as everyone knows, calm, reflective, neutral inquiry is its central prerequisite.

Melville doesn't think so. When it comes to the most important aspects of our existence—to the most challenging and important mysteries about us, about the universe, about the whale itself—neutral, scientific inquiry is inert. This is clearest in the famous Cetology chapter, in which Melville offers what he claims to be a scientific classification of the whale. But this classification promises "nothing complete," Ishmael says. "[A]ny human thing supposed to be complete, must for that very reason infallibly be faulty."[25] And so it must be with the classification of the whale. It cannot be objective and incontrovertible; it cannot be perfected and final—precisely because it can never be complete. As he says at the conclusion of the Cetology chapter:

> It was stated at the outset, that this system would not be here, and at once, perfected. You cannot but plainly see that I have kept my word. But I now leave my cetological System standing thus unfinished, even as the great Cathedral of Cologne was left, with the crane still standing upon the top of the uncompleted tower. For small erections may be finished by their first architects; grand ones, true ones, ever leave the copestone to posterity. God keep me from ever completing anything. This whole book is but a draught—nay, but the draught of a draught. Oh, Time, Strength, Cash, Patience![26]

Divine truths, therefore, insofar as there are any, must be changeable and never completed. The divine magnanimities that Melville claims to have are divine precisely because they are spontaneous and changeable; they are godlike and true, in other words, because they are incomplete, unfinished; because they are revealed only by the current mood. And it is for this reason that the moody Catskill eagle flies high above all the other birds. For "even if he for ever flies within the gorge," Ishmael tells us,

> that gorge is in the mountains; so that even in his lowest swoop the mountain eagle is still higher than other birds upon the plain, even though they soar.[27]

To take seriously our moods—both our highest soaring joys and our deepest, darkest descents—to live in each of them as moody Ishmael can, to do this is to be open to the manifold truths our moods reveal.

These truths are not final and permanent, they are not completed any more than is the mystery of the whale. But it is precisely because of their incompleteness that they are divine and true.

ISHMAEL TAKES HIS MOODINESS seriously, allowing him to connect with modes of existence radically different from his own. Take Queequeg, for example.

Queequeg could recall only once having suffered from indigestion. It was a memorable occasion. A great battle successfully completed, his father the king had prepared a stupendous feast. "Fifty of the enemy had been killed by about two o'clock in the afternoon, and all cooked and eaten that very evening."[28]

Queequeg is the rainbow-colored Kokovokan cannibal with whom Ishmael is forced to share a room—and therefore a bed—during his first night at the Spouter Inn. He has just returned from a long day peddling shrunken human heads, and is quite a sight. His body is "tattoed all over with an interminable Cretan labyrinth of a figure, no two parts of which were of one precise shade"[29]; his arm is so full of colors and designs that it "looked for all the world like a strip of . . . [particolored] patchwork quilt"[30]; his "bald, purplish head"[31] and facial tattoos were so intensely hued, their variegation so complete, that "barred with various tints" they "seemed like the Andes' western slope, to show forth in one array, contrasting climates, zone by zone."[32]

Despite this inauspicious introduction, and despite too an initial meeting that is marred by a misunderstanding of the sort that involved some unfortunate "flourishings of the tomahawk,"[33] Ishmael and Queequeg are nevertheless quickly bosom friends. "Better sleep with a sober cannibal than a drunken Christian," reasons our hero. When Ishmael wakes up the next morning, he finds Queequeg's colorful arm thrown over him "in the most loving and affectionate manner." "You had almost thought I had been his wife."[34]

A pagan harpooner of the finest sort, Queequeg will become the lead harpooner on Captain Ahab's ship. His lack of Christian charity is prized among the old Quaker proprietors of the *Pequod*. "Pious harpooners never make good voyagers," one of them says, "it takes the shark out of 'em."[35] Queequeg's pagan blood is that in which Ahab perversely baptizes the harpoon intended for Moby Dick.

There is no doubt that, in the minds of Melville's mid-nineteenth-century readers, Queequeg must have seemed like the worst of the world's horrors; and Ishmael's social satisfaction in his presence must have seemed nothing less than wicked. The anticolonialist message that we may have more to learn from the cannibalist pagans than they from us, would have looked perverse, its perversity exemplified in the way Queequeg dresses himself: first, stark naked, donning his enormous beaver hat, then in a bizarre application of modesty retreating under the bedcovers to squeeze into his boots, and only later, after many entreating admonitions from his partner and after swinging about indecorously for a while before the open window, managing to end the indecency by stepping into his pantaloons.[36] The erotic overlay of the entire episode with Queequeg probably escaped most Victorian eyes, but at some unconscious level it must have added to its cast of perversity and wickedness. As you can imagine, it is easy fodder for today's postmodern and psychoanalytic critique.[37]

Perhaps, then, this is the wickedness at the center of Melville's book. Perhaps, in other words, the guiding force behind Melville's evil art lies in the apparently preposterous suggestion that we should prefer the company of the pagan cannibal to the company of our Christian neighbor; or even that we should embrace such pagan cannibalism over Christianity ourselves.

There is certainly something to this line. Queequeg, after all, evinces a deep and serious skepticism about Christian life. He had set about on his whaling journey in order to learn about Christendom, in the hope that through its practices he might help his people to be happier, and better, than they already are. But after performing his due diligence in the matter, he decides that Christianity only makes things worse. "[A]las!" he tells Ishmael,

> the practices of whalemen soon convinced him that even Christians could be both miserable and wicked, infinitely more so, than all his father's heathens. . . . Thought he, it's a wicked world in all meridians; I'll die a pagan.[38]

More than that, Queequeg actually worried that his exposure to Christianity, and especially to Christians, had somehow defiled him, that it had made him unfit to return to the pagan purity of his native Kokovokan land:

> By hints, I asked him whether he did not propose going back, and having a coronation; since he might now consider his father dead and gone, he being very old and feeble at the last accounts. He answered no, not yet; and added that he was fearful Christianity, or rather Christians, had unfitted him for ascending the pure and undefiled throne of thirty pagan Kings before him.[39]

Ishmael suggests in other ways, too, that Queequeg's life is not just better than the Christian life—as if leaping over this evidently low bar were some accomplishment—but that even in some more absolute sense Queequeg is deeply admirable and full of spiritual health. At a certain point, for example, when Queequeg has taken ill and looks on the verge of death, Ishmael admires the "immortal health" that shines in his eyes:

> How he wasted and wasted away in those few long-lingering days, till there seemed but little left of him but his frame and tattooing. But as all else in him thinned, and his cheek-bones grew sharper, his eyes, nevertheless, seemed growing fuller and

fuller; they became of a strange softness of lustre; and mildly but deeply looked out at you there from his sickness, a wondrous testimony to that immortal health in him which could not die, or be weakened.[40]

But although Melville sees something deeply admirable in Queequeg, his message does not seem to be that we should return to Queequeg's pre-Christian, pagan ways. How could we manage this, after all, having lived through two thousand years of Christianity? Indeed, Queequeg and Ishmael seem to stand as bookends to the history of the West, Queequeg transitioning into Christian civilization and Ishmael transitioning out of it.[41] And although Queequeg does not end up dying before the final confrontation with the whale, he does not survive that confrontation. His pre-Christian, pagan existence is not, after all, the way forward.

If there is some kind of wickedness, therefore, in Melville's portrayal of Queequeg's pagan existence—and in Ishmael's admiring friendship with him—nevertheless the deepest kind of wickedness must lie elsewhere in the book.

ISHMAEL'S SATISFACTION WITH his interpretation of the picture at the Spouter Inn reflects Melville's content with his wicked book. "[N]o hopefulness is in it," Melville says, "no despair. Content—that is it." The account is a good one, in both cases, an interpretation that makes much sense of things as they stand. But there is no hope that it is more than this, no longing for some further, final, ultimate truth; and there is no despair, either, at the thought that such a deep and final truth might not be found. The medieval picture of a secure and final and certain foundation—of God as the deep and final source of all that is—has been left behind. As Ishmael says, "I have perceived that in all cases man must eventually lower, or at least shift, his conceit of attainable felicity."[42]

Captain Ahab is not capable of such a shift. Ahab was probably always tormented in some fashion or another, and questions of religious significance seem always to have been involved. There are mysterious and unexplained references to an event off Cape Horn long ago, when he "lay like dead" for the biblically significant period of three days and nights. There is the "deadly skrimmage" he had with a Spaniard—presumably a Catholic—a skirmish that took place "afore the altar in Santa." And there is the silver calabash into which he spat—a mysterious reference itself that remains unexplained.[43] But could this be the bowl—the calabash—that holds the Eucharist in a Catholic church? Could this insult to the Catholic God have been the provocative act that began his skirmish with the Spaniard? The resonances are rich with religious significance, but the details must forever remain untold.

Whatever Captain Ahab's ancient torments, however, they found a new focus on his previous whaling voyage, when the great white Sperm Whale Moby Dick bit off Ahab's leg. From that point forward the whale is his chief tormentor. Ahab's monomaniacal purpose, his "quenchless feud,"[44] is to force a confrontation—face to face—with that "inscrutable thing,"[45] to delve beneath its inscrutability and find out whether its attack upon him was truly malicious or whether in fact the whale is merely a dumb and meaningless brute. In an important passage Ahab lays out the metaphysical picture of the universe that animates his hatred: that every act, every object, and every event in the world has a deep truth standing behind its surface affairs, and that man's purpose is to uncover these final, eternal truths. "All visible objects, man, are but as pasteboard masks," Ahab says.

> But in each event—in the living act, the undoubted deed—
> there, some unknown but still reasoning thing puts forth the
> mouldings of its features from behind the unreasoning mask. If
> man will strike, strike through the mask! How can the prisoner
> reach outside except by thrusting through the wall? To me, the

white whale is that wall, shoved near to me. Sometimes I think there's naught beyond. But 'tis enough. He tasks me; he heaps me; I see in him outrageous strength, with an inscrutable malice sinewing it. That inscrutable thing is chiefly what I hate; and be the white whale agent, or be the white whale principal, I will wreak that hate upon him. Talk not to me of blasphemy, man; I'd strike the sun if it insulted me.[46]

This is a man whose greatest wish is to find the kind of certainty that a final truth provides. Later in the book, talking with the ship's carpenter, he picks up the carpenter's workshop vise and tightens it around his fingers. "Oh, sir, it will break bones—beware, beware!" shouts the astonished carpenter. "No fear," says Ahab, "I like a good grip; I like to feel something in this slippery world that can hold, man."[47] And so he does. No happiness will come for Ahab until that faceless pasteboard mask has revealed every final and ultimate secret he feels certain it must be hiding. Felicity, if Ahab can ever attain it, will not be the result of a lowered conceit.

THERE IS SOMETHING ADMIRABLE about Ahab's pursuit. It recalls those hallowed scenes of dogged determination in American history, of "Don't fire until you see the whites of their eyes!" or "Win one for the Gipper!" It is a strength of purpose and determination of will to keep up a "quenchless feud" against the odds. And it is not just individual determination either, but the ability to lead, to bring others along with you, to rally the troops in support of the cause. Ahab has this effect upon all; even moody Ishmael falls under his spell:

> I, Ishmael, was one of that crew; my shouts had gone up with the rest; my oath had been welded with theirs; and stronger I shouted, and more did I hammer and clinch my oath, because of the dread in my soul. A wild, mystical, sympathetical feeling

was in me; Ahab's quenchless feud seemed mine. With greedy ears I learned the history of the murderous monster against whom I and all the others had taken our oaths of violence and revenge.[48]

But if there is something admirable about Ahab, if he evokes our sympathy and draws us to his side, then perhaps this is the ultimate wickedness of the book. For a long tradition of Melville criticism sees in the eloquent and driven Ahab a reflection of that Satan whom one can find in Milton's *Paradise Lost*. And it sees in Melville a talent worthy of Milton, an ability to evince an "unconscious sympathy for the devil."[49] Fifty years ago, for example, Henry A. Murray claimed that "Melville's Satan is the spitting image of Milton's hero . . . the stricken, passionate, indignant, and often eloquent rebel angel of *Paradise Lost*, whose role is played by Ahab."[50] On such an interpretation Melville's Moby Dick takes the place of Milton's God, and Ahab's prideful, passionate battle against him puts him as the leader of the rebel angels. To the extent that we find some sympathy with Ahab, then we are in league with the devil as well.

Further evidence for such an interpretation might be found if we uncover some of the many biblical references in *Moby Dick*. Captain Ahab's name itself, for example, is a reference to that King of Israel from the Bible's Book of Kings. The husband of the infamous Jezebel, he would go down in history as the most evil of all the kings before him (1 Kings 16:30). The prophet Elijah foresaw King Ahab's demise, finding in his murderous and rebellious actions against God the seeds of Ahab's undoing. So too does Melville give us an Elijah, an old sailor who goes by that name and who prophesizes that Ahab is beyond redemption. "Look ye; when captain Ahab is all right," Elijah says, "then this left arm of mine will be all right; not before."[51] The left arm, of course, is the sinister one—*sinister* in Latin just means left. When left is right, in other words, when evil has taken the place of good, then Ahab's sickness will be over.

There is certainly something suggestive about these connections, and we agree with these traditional readings that there is a sense in which Ahab is wicked. But we believe that his wickedness is not the same as that of Milton's Satan, if only because Moby Dick is not the same as Milton's God. Indeed, Ahab's wickedness is in some sense the opposite of Lucifer's, since it consists not in his rebellion against God, but in his determination to find out whether there is a God against whom to rebel. Ahab's pursuit of Moby Dick is, in effect, a monomaniacal pursuit of the *final, ultimate truth* about the way things are. "If man will strike, strike through the mask!" But there are no such final truths in Melville's world; no reasoning thing stands behind the unreasoning mask. Ahab's determination to find such a foundation—that is the wicked core of his monomaniacal monotheism.

We get closer, therefore, to the true wickedness of Melville's book, when we see this reversal. What Ahab hates most thoroughly is the idea that the universe might be inscrutable to the last; that ultimately there might be "naught beyond." He therefore holds desperately and passionately to the idea that there is an ultimate, final, and universal truth about how things are; that there is, in other words, a traditional kind of monotheistic God. This misguided passion for monotheism, the book reveals, is the most dangerous and deadly kind there is. Melville's genuine wickedness, in other words, consists in his portrayal of Ahab's monomaniacal monotheism as itself the incarnation of what the universe most abhors.

By contrast with this wickedness, the book's spotlessness consists in the polytheistic alternative it offers instead. To get clearer on this alternative we will have to look more carefully at the whale, and eventually at the appalling whiteness of Moby Dick.

WE HAVE SEEN ALREADY that the whale is a mystery, that he supports an indefinite range of meanings and that ultimately, in fact, he is unrepresentable. This quality is first suggested in the extracts that stand as Preface to the book, and then amplified by the discussion of the mysterious whale painting in the Spouter Inn. The cetology chapter clinches the claim, arguing as it does that nothing worthwhile and true can ever be complete. But if the whale is God then he is a polytheistic god, and his is a world of multiple meanings and truths. Look at the extraordinary distinction that Melville draws between the Sperm Whale and the Bible's God.

By tradition the Hebraic God refuses to show his face. When Moses asks God to show His glory, the Lord replies:

> "I shall make all my goodness pass before you, and I shall pro-
> nounce in your hearing the name, 'Lord.' I shall be gracious to
> whom I shall be gracious, and I shall have compassion on whom
> I shall have compassion." But he added, "My face you cannot
> see, for no mortal may see me and live." [Exodus 33:18–20]

Melville has this Hebraic tradition firmly in mind when he proposes the Sperm Whale as a new kind of god, and he intends to go one step beyond the Bible's account. The extraordinary and sacred power of Melville's Sperm Whale consists not in its hiding its face from man. Rather, the Sperm Whale has no face at all:

> But in the great Sperm Whale, this high and mighty god-like
> dignity inherent in the brow is so immensely amplified, that
> gazing on it, in that full front view, you feel the Deity and the
> dread powers more forcibly than in beholding any other object
> in living nature. For you see no one point precisely; not one
> distinct feature is revealed; no nose, eyes, ears, or mouth; no
> face; he has none, proper; nothing but that one broad firma-
> ment of a forehead, pleated with riddles . . . [52]

To say that the Sperm Whale has no face at all is to go beyond any traditional kind of religious mysticism. It is not just that his face is too awesome to look at or too complex to grasp. It is not a matter of his exceeding the bounds of our capacity to understand him. Rather, the god of Melville's universe, and therefore Melville's universe itself, lacks a hidden truth. Its face is not hidden behind some pasteboard mask. The mask—the skin, the riddled brow—is all there is.

At the center of Melville's understanding of the whale is the idea that there is no meaning to the universe hidden behind its surface events, that the surface events themselves—contradictory and mysterious and multiple as they may be—are nevertheless all the meaning there is. As he says in a later chapter, "Dissect him how I may, then, I but go skin deep."[53] Ishmael's amazing strength is that he is able to live in these surface meanings and find a genuine range of joys and comforts there, without wishing they stood for something more. This is what he means by "lowering the conceit of one's attainable felicity":

> I have perceived that in all cases man must eventually lower, or at least shift, his conceit of attainable felicity; not placing it anywhere in the intellect or the fancy; but in the wife, the heart, the bed, the table, the saddle, the fire-side, the country.[54]

This ability to live at the surface, to take the events of daily life with the meanings they present rather than to seek their hidden purpose, to find happiness and joy in what there already is, finds its easiest expression in a pre-Christian age. Indeed, not just a pre-Christian age, but a pre-Buddhist, pre-Platonic, pre-Hinduist, and pre-Confucian one as well.

SINCE KARL JASPERS's 1949 book *The Origin and Goal of History,* historians and sociologists have emphasized a cross-cultural turn in the first millennium BC that Jaspers called the Axial Revolution.[55] This revolution introduced the idea—through Plato's metaphysical philosophy, the Buddha's conception of Nirvana, and various religious notions of Eternal Life—that there is a good beyond what we can find in the everyday conception of human flourishing; that there is a transcendent good that is the nature of the Divine. As Charles Taylor explains it:

> The Axial Revolution tended to place the Divine on the side of the ultimate good; while at the same time redefining this as something which goes beyond what is understood as ordinary human flourishing: Nirvana, Eternal Life.[56]

It is precisely this conception of "going beyond" that Melville's faceless whale encourages us to resist. Rather than searching for some reasoning thing behind the mask as Ahab insists on doing, Ishmael thinks we should nurture the moods of everyday existence—the moods of the wife, the heart, the bed, the table, and any others we can learn about or discover—for the meanings they already offer. As Nietzsche points out, such a life is at its best in the pre-Axial wonder of the Homeric Age:

> Oh, those [Homeric] Greeks! They knew how to live. What is required for that is to stop courageously at the surface, the fold, the skin, to adore appearance, to believe in forms, tones, words, in the whole Olympus of appearance. Those Greeks were superficial—out of profundity.[57]

The profundity of this kind of superficial life consists not only in its ability to find genuine meaning in the rituals of the family table or, like Helen for example, in the wonder of Aphrodite's erotic world. It consists in the ability to live in the contradictions that these meanings present. Shining Helen is perhaps the most extreme example of this, as we have seen already: first she is drawn by Aphrodite's light to run away with the charming and handsome houseguest Paris, and then later she is happy to return to the domestic life of ease exemplified by Hera and enabled by her first husband, Menelaus. Throughout these turns and contradictions, indeed perhaps even because of them, Menelaus, and even Homer himself, sings her praise.

Ishmael is also full of meaningful contradictions. His, however, take on a more explicitly religious tone. Ishmael is perfectly happy to transition, for example, from the joy of Father Mapple's powerful Presbyterian sermon to the wonders of Queequeg's weird idol-worshipping rites. Father Mapple is the former whaleman turned minister who preaches at the Whaleman's Chapel, down the road from the Spouter-Inn. When Ishmael visits his church one Sunday, before starting out on the *Pequod*'s voyage, Mapple's sermon focuses (naturally) on the biblical story of Jonah and the whale. Unlike Queequeg, who slips out of the church sometime before the benediction, Ishmael stays for the entire sermon and seems to think that there is something worth retrieving in Mapple's Presbyterian vision of the universe. At the end of the sermon, for example, he reports that Mapple "showed a deep joy in his eyes."[58] (Presumably this joy is something that Queequeg, in his complete rejection of Christianity, couldn't appreciate or even detect.) If Ishmael's goal is to chase away the "damp, drizzly November in his soul," then perhaps this kind of Christian joy is one of the moods for which to aim. But there is clearly something in Mapple's view that Ishmael wants to reject as well. For Mapple's real goal is not just earthly joy but the highest ecstasy of heavenly delight. "Delight," he says, "top-gallant delight is to him, who acknowledges no law or lord, but the Lord his God, and is only a patriot to heaven."[59] This rejection both of the joys of everyday communal existence and of all religions other than Christianity—this all-enveloping idea that the Christian God brooks no other and that Christian joy is the perfect heavenly delight—is undermined by Ishmael's very next act. For after he leaves Father Mapple's sermon, he returns to the Spouter Inn to join in Queequeg's idol rite.

There is no doubt that this transition is at odds with Mapple's traditional conception of Christianity. But Ishmael, who was "born and bred in the bosom of the infallible Presbyterian Church,"[60] gives a wonderful kind of Christian argument against this closed and total-izing interpretation of Christianity. It is by this argument that he con-vinces himself to stop at the surface and enter into Queequeg's rite. The argument goes something like this:

1. To worship is to do the will of God.
2. The will of God is to do unto others as I would have others do unto me.
3. I wish Queequeg would unite with me in my form of (Presbyterian) worship.

Therefore: I should unite with him in his form of (idol) worship.[61]

This argument, if taken seriously, seems to speak against the closed, inward, and totalizing isolation of Mapple's version of Christianity. It speaks, of course, against Queequeg's utter rejection of Chris-tianity as well. It suggests instead that Christianity in its essence requires openness to and community with others—even openness to other forms of (non-Christian) worship. Christianity itself, in other words, requires that one "cherish the greatest respect towards everybody's religious obligations,"[62] even, perhaps, to the point of joining in them. The implicit criticism is that Christianity goes astray not in its basic religious impulse, but rather in its totalizing turn. When Christianity accounts itself the one true faith, when it claims a total, unique, and transcendent truth, then it leads to isolation and lack of community. For in its search for some tran-scendent Divine it forsakes the multiple, communal goods that are already to be found here on earth.

Ishmael's polytheistic view finds in the communal rituals of daily life, contradictory and polysemic and plural as they are, the meanings that can drive away the drizzly November of the soul. This is perhaps clearest in the famous chapter titled "A Squeeze of the Hand." At this rather late point in the story the *Pequod* has managed to kill a sperm whale. Sperm whales are so named for the milky-white, waxy substance called spermaceti that is found in their heads; it was originally mistaken for sperm or semen. This was one of the very valuable substances that could be harvested from the whale, since it was used to make wax candles as well as oils, sweeteners, softeners, ointments, and so on. In the chapter in question the spermaceti has been collected into a large bath, where it has formed brilliant white crystals that are hard but oily to the touch. Ishmael finds himself, along with several other shipmates, assigned to the task of "squeezing these lumps back into fluid."[63] During this task he sometimes finds himself unwittingly squeezing his co-laborers' hands. His description of this kind of loving, communal experience seems to be the essence of Melville's understanding of the Christian mood of agape, or Christian love for others. In what might have seemed a dreary and monotonous task, Ishmael manages to find Christian joy:

> Squeeze! squeeze! squeeze! all the morning long; I squeezed that sperm till I myself almost melted into it; I squeezed that sperm till a strange sort of insanity came over me; and I found myself unwittingly squeezing my co-laborers' hands in it, mistaking their hands for the gentle globules. Such an abounding, affectionate, friendly, loving feeling did this avocation beget; that at last I was continually squeezing their hands, and looking up into their eyes sentimentally; as much as to say,—Oh! My dear fellow beings, why should we longer cherish any social acerbities, or know the slightest ill-humor or envy! Come; let us squeeze hands all round; nay let us all squeeze ourselves into each other; let us squeeze ourselves universally into the very milk and sperm of kindness.[64]

In this joint, communal task Ishmael has the experience of "an abounding, affectionate, friendly, loving feeling," which seems clearly to be his characterization of agape love. As if to leave no doubt, however, Ishmael goes on to tell us that this earthly feeling, this feeling got by a communal ritual performed with others, is in fact the very feeling the angels have in paradise:

> Would that I could keep squeezing that sperm for ever! . . . In thoughts of the visions of the night, I saw long rows of angels in paradise, each with his hands in a jar of spermaceti.

Ishmael's position, therefore, is not so much a rejection of Christianity as an appropriation of it. In Ishmael's view the Christian kind of joy that one can experience is already all around us, if only we'd pay attention to it. It is in "the wife, the heart, the bed, the table, the saddle, the fire-side, the country." All of these, presumably, are places where we can find the "abounding, affectionate, friendly, loving feeling," that he found in the task of squeezing spermaceti with his co-laborers, and this is the kind of joy that the angels in paradise feel. This kind of Christian joy, however, is hidden from us because we're trying to look past it, to find something deeper. We have joy—real joy of the sort promised by Christianity, in Ishmael's view—all around us; we just need to be attentive. That is ultimately why we must lower, or at least shift, our conceit of attainable felicity. For Ahab's determined monotheism covers up the very real and polytheistic joys that are already to be found right here on earth. If you recognize the kind of joy that is already around you, at least some of the time, then you will see that this is a mood that you have in the here and now. Not forever, and not always. But you can appreciate it when the opportunity presents itself.

It is in this context that we can begin to understand Melville's bizarre prophecy, his call to lure back the gods of old. His current world is Ahab's world—a world in which the universe is a set of deep meanings we can strike through to with the strength of our autonomous will. Ahab is a combination of Kant's theory of human beings as autonomous selves and Dante's religious hope for eternal bliss. But these accounts, each unlivable on its own, are the worst kind of wickedness when brought together. They account for the "now egotistical sky" under which we live, and its inability to admit meaning beyond what our self-sufficient will can achieve. And they explain how we have chased away the gods of the earth, leaving only our "now unhaunted hill." It will take a "highly cultured, poetical nation" to lure back "the merry May-day gods of old": a nation of people who can find meaning in the rituals of their daily lives. The meaning they find will be unrepresentable in the sense both that there is nothing deep behind it and that it nevertheless will give us something beyond what we contribute ourselves. That is why the great Sperm Whale shall take the place of Zeus in the coming pantheon of gods. For the overpowering mystery of his blank, unrepresentable brow is what makes every ritual, if properly lived, a site of contentedness, joy, and meaning to wipe away the drizzly November of the soul.

MOBY DICK IS NOT just any sperm whale. The sailors recognize him immediately by various traits—the way he waves his tail, his curious spout, the number of harpoons still stuck in him. But what is especially notable about Moby Dick is that he is completely and utterly white. This makes him unusual even among sperm whales, and makes him stand out as the paradigm of paradigms, the king of the "kings of the boundless sea." And it is this very whiteness that Ishmael finds both appalling and essential:

> It was the whiteness of the whale that above all things appalled me. But how can I hope to explain myself here; and yet, in some dim, random way, explain myself I must, else all these chapters might be naught.[65]

The forbidding and often unread chapter on the whiteness of the whale is an attempt to explain this essential feature of Moby Dick. The chapter consists almost entirely of citations and examples showing the enormous range of meanings that whiteness can take on in our culture. After a full page of examples showing the various ways in which whiteness "refiningly enhances beauty, as if imparting some special virtue of its own,"[66] Melville concludes that it is nevertheless terrifying in its basic aspect:

> yet for all these accumulated associations, with whatever is sweet and honorable, and sublime, there yet lurks an elusive something in the innermost idea of this hue, which strikes more of panic to the soul than that redness which affrights in blood.[67]

Melville then goes on for several pages exemplifying the terrifying associations we have with whiteness. From the White Steed of the Prairies to the pallor of the dead, from the white bear of the poles to the white shark of the tropics, whiteness has the ability to "enforce a certain nameless terror" and "to heighten that terror to the furthest bounds." The question is why whiteness *itself*—not the whiteness of the polar bear or the shark or the corpse or the terrible steed or even the whale, but whiteness *as a color*—is terrifying. The amazing answer helps us to understand the particular wickedness of Ahab's world.

It is crucial to Ishmael that the terror he feels is a response to whiteness itself. He knows that others will find this strange, but he is convinced that he is onto a deep truth about the nature of the universe. Indeed, he says that this sensibility of his is something built into him like an instinct, the way a colt raised in Vermont, who has never seen a buffalo or any other predator, will be terrified by its smell.

So what is it about whiteness per se that Ishmael finds terrifying? It has to do with the way in which it can stand for anything from the most holy and pure to the most abject and horrifying. That it is

> at once the most meaning symbol of spiritual things, nay the very veil of the Christian's Deity; and yet should be as it is, the intensifying agent in things the most appalling to mankind.[68]

What is terrifying about whiteness is not any particular meaning or connotation that it can have. Rather, it is the fact that it seems so meaningful and yet, precisely in virtue of its ability to take on such a radical range of meanings, is nothing like a meaning at all. It is instead, he says, a "dumb blankness full of meaning."[69]

To understand this idea you have to think of whiteness of the sort that we get in so-called "white light." As a color, the perception of whiteness is evoked by light that stimulates all three types of color-sensitive cone cells in the retina to a nearly equal degree. So in this sense white is the color you get when you add all the colors together. But white light is itself invisible or colorless—you can't see white light, but it is that which allows you to see everything else; it is, as Melville says, the "visible absence of color."[70] In the terminology of this book, white light, or whiteness itself, acts like the background practices for a culture. The background—like white light—is what you can't see, but which allows you to see everything else:

> [T]he great principle of light, for ever remains white or color-less in itself, and if operating without medium upon matter, would touch all objects, even tulips and roses, with its own blank tinge.[71]

If you try to look at whiteness per se, if you try to focus on the white light "operating without medium upon matter," then it is like trying to see the background practices as they are in themselves. But there is nothing one can say about the background as it is in itself; one can only say what it looks like when it touches a tulip or a rose. It only shows itself insofar as it allows you to fix upon something else.

This sense of whiteness as the background, of its being present in our experience but only by means of what it allows us to see, applies to the Sperm Whale in an amazing way. We have seen already that the Sperm Whale has no face. But it turns out that even his back side cannot be clearly seen. Like the background practices of a culture, the tail seems at once to be familiar and meaningful and also incapable of being described. In another astounding reference to the Hebraic God, Melville says this of the Sperm Whale's tail:

> The more I consider this mighty tail, the more do I deplore my inability to express it. . . . But if I know not even the tail of this whale, how understand his head? Much more, how comprehend his face, when face he has none? Thou shalt see my back parts, my tail, he seems to say, but my face shall not be seen. But I cannot completely make out his back parts; and hint what he will about his face, I say again he has no face.[72]

The penultimate line of this passage recalls in detail the Hebraic God. When the Lord promises to reveal Himself to Moses, He sets up the situation carefully:

> The Lord said, "Here is a place beside me. Take your stand on the rock and, when my glory passes by, I shall put you in a crevice of the rock and cover you with my hand until I have passed by. Then I shall take away my hand, and you will see my back, but my face must not be seen." [Exodus 33:21–23]

In the Hebraic tradition, therefore, God's face is ever-hidden but his back may be revealed. In Melville's version of the story, by contrast, the new god has no face at all, and his back side cannot be clearly seen. There are no deep and hidden truths to the universe, and the meanings that there are cannot be seen with any clarity. Instead, the meanings we can find are made available through our engagement with the rituals and practices of our culture and others. But these background practices are not the kinds of things about which one could ever get clear. The terror of whiteness consists in its looking as if it were a color like any other—a color whose meanings one could understand—though it's only a dumb blankness. It's full of meaning, of course, full of every possible meaning there is. The striking similarity between this claim about whiteness and the analogous claim about the whale itself becomes even clearer in a chapter toward the end of the book.

WHITENESS HAS TWO EXTREME FORMS that are especially terrifying. Ishmael speaks of the "terror in those appearances . . . especially when exhibited under any form at all approaching to muteness or universality."[73] It is clear that the universal form of whiteness is the form combining all the colors of the spectrum. But what is the form approaching "muteness"? How can Melville possibly pull off the conceit of the terror of whiteness using an auditory metaphor?

We discover the answer in a later chapter called "A Bower in the Arsacides."[74] This chapter seems to be added on almost as an afterthought. It has literally nothing to do with the narrative of the text, and is couched in the form of a reminiscence from some earlier journey that Ishmael undertook. We hear nothing about the journey itself, or the circumstances surrounding it. What we do know is that on the journey Ishmael landed on a small island, somewhere to the northeast of Australia in a group of islands called the Arsacides, and made friends with the locals. He says he spent the holidays there—indicating that he was invited to and stayed for their local religious festivals:

> I was invited to spend part of the Arsacidean holidays with the lord of Tranque, at his retired palm villa at Pupella; a sea-side glen not very far distant from what our sailors called Bamboo-Town, his capital.[75]

Among the things he notices on the way is a wide range of "wonders" that Tranquo—the king of the island—has collected. At the top of his list is the skeleton of a whale that had beached itself on the shore many years before and died. When the locals had stripped the "fathom-deep enfoldings" from the animal they dragged the skeleton to a glen by the sea and used it for a chapel. By the time Ishmael saw it the grasses and ferns and branches and shrubs had woven themselves through the skeleton to make a kind of carpet. We get here a description of God as a weaver—recalling the various ancient accounts of gods at their loom—and the sound of his weaving as something so deafening that through it he hears no mortal voice. Indeed, if we were to pay attention to his weaving, Ishmael tells us, we would be deafened too. It's only when you get far enough away that you are able to hear the "thousand voices that speak through it."

> The weaver-god, he weaves; and by that weaving is deafened, that he hears no mortal voice; and by that humming, we, too, who look on the loom are deafened; and only when we escape it shall we hear the thousand voices that speak through it.[76]

If you tried to listen to all the sounds of the universe at once it would be deafening. All the various meanings would cancel each other out. You would hear the chaos of white noise instead of the single, hidden truth of a rational universe. This is exactly parallel to what would happen if you tried to see all the colors in the world at once. It would look like something that has a meaning, you would be driven to find out what that ultimate meaning was, but you would be driven mad in the search. Because when it is universal it is deafening, it is a chaos; and although this chaos is itself the ultimate nature of the universe, you can only fathom it from one perspective at a time.

That is why, on Melville's account, Ahab's fanaticism is ultimately mad. The multiple meanings of the universe simply don't add up to a single, universal truth. Our only hope is to engage in each of them fully, live contentedly in the truths they reveal, but feel no urge to reconcile them to one another. The image for this kind of plural polytheism is neither the deafening chaos of white noise nor the dumb blankness of the color white. Rather, it is the rainbow that separates out the colors of the spectrum, and reveals each in its own wonderful hue.

Ishmael makes this clear in his discussion of the fountain—the spray from the great sperm whale's spout. In the chapter on the fountain[77] the whale-spray makes a rainbow above the head of the whale, "as if Heaven itself had put its seal upon his thoughts."[78] Each of these colors is one of many true perspectives on the universe, and the most we can ever have is a series of these true perspectives. They are what Ishmael finds in his many moods. The perspectives, were you to try to reconcile them, would clash and conflict, so the best that one can hope for is to "lower the conceit of attainable felicity." Don't try to see what all the colors look like when they're added up. Instead, try to get into as many (revealing) moods as possible, as many ways of responding to the sacred as you can—and this life of serial resonances with the sacred is ultimately a kind of contentedness, happiness, even joy. But it is not one that gives ultimate and final meaning to one's life; it makes instead a man who takes all the meanings with an equal eye:

> And how nobly it raises our conceit of the mighty, misty monster, to behold him solemnly sailing through a calm tropical sea; his vast, mild head overhung by a canopy of vapor, engendered by his incommunicable contemplations, and that vapor—as you will sometimes see it—glorified by a rainbow, as if Heaven itself had put its seal upon his thoughts. For, d'ye see, rainbows do not visit the clear air; they only irradiate vapor. And so, through all the thick mists of the dim doubts in my mind, divine intuitions now and then shoot, enkindling my fog with a heavenly ray. And for this I thank God; for all have doubts; many deny; but doubts or denials, few along with them, have intuitions. Doubts of all things earthly, and intuitions of some things heavenly; this combination makes

neither believer nor infidel, but makes a man who regards them both with equal eye.[79]

THERE IS ONE FIGURE in the book who sees all of this, and who is described early on as a hero. In the context of the figures on the ship he is the lowliest of them all—the "ship-keeper" who stays back on the ship when the others go out in the boats to hunt the whale. Pip is small and ungainly, weak and nervous, dark as the night, an antihero by Homeric lights:

> As a general thing, these ship-keepers are as hardy fellows as the men comprising the boats' crews. But if there happen to be an unduly slender, clumsy, or timorous wight in the ship, that wight is certain to be made a ship-keeper. It was so in the Pequod with the little negro Pippin, by nick-name, Pip by abbreviation.[80]

Despite these disadvantages—or perhaps because of them—Ishmael introduces Pip early on as a kind of hero:

> Black Little Pip . . . Poor Alabama boy! On the grim Pequod's forecastle, ye shall ere long see him, beating his tambourine; prelusive of the eternal time, when sent for, to the great quarter-deck on high, he was bid strike in with angels, and beat his tambourine in glory; called a coward here, hailed a hero there![81]

What does Pip see that makes him a hero in Melville's eyes?

Pip's trouble starts when he has to take the place of one of the regular boatsmen on a whale hunt. The first time it happens he gets so scared when they are bumped by the whale's tail that he jumps out of the boat and gets caught up in the line. The other sailors have to cut the line in order to save him, and they lose the whale as a result. Pip is execrated by the crew and given a stern rebuke by Stubb, the second mate of the *Pequod* and leader of the mission, who warns Pip never to jump out of the boat again. But he does jump out a second time, and on this occasion he is left behind as Stubb's boat is dragged at a rapid pace by the retreating whale. Pip is left alone at sea and there confronts something that changes him forever.

What happens to Pip at sea? The problem is not that he almost drowns. That would be a particular thing to fear. What Pip confronted was a kind of horror that is worse than simple fear for one's life. In Ishmael's eloquent description of it Pip confronts the possibility of becoming a castaway, of losing all connection with human beings, of becoming completely isolated on the infinite sea. As the boat takes off before him Pip sees

> Stubb's inexorable back . . . turned upon him; and the whale was winged. In three minutes, a whole mile of shoreless ocean was between Pip and Stubb. Out from the centre of the sea, poor Pip turned his crisp, curling, black head to the sun, another lonely castaway, though the loftiest and the brightest.[82]

Pip has lost all his connections with other men and the *Pequod,* which is his center. The ship is the stable, human thing that grounds one on the infinite sea. It is the loss of everything connected with this final human thing that Pip finds horrifying:

> Now, in calm weather, to swim in the open ocean is as easy to the practised swimmer as to ride in a spring-carriage ashore. But the awful lonesomeness is intolerable. The intense concentration of self in the middle of such a heartless immensity, my God! who can tell it?[83]

Pip's sense of being completely lost is beautifully expressed when he looks up and sees the sun as "another lonely castaway." This expresses a sense that even the sun (the symbol of the Good in Plato and of God in Dante) has lost its place at the center of the universe. Pip's loneliness is not just the loneliness of the individual in the vast, indefinite sea; it is the loneliness of our culture as we realize we are cut loose from everything that ultimately gives us ground. It was the horror of this loneliness that Pip experienced and that—in one sense at least—ultimately drove him mad.

Pip's madness, however, is also a kind of truth. Pip has seen the total emptiness of the universe—the absence that is all that is left of God. As Ishmael puts it, he saw the "heartless immensity." He saw that the universe is the random result of random actions like those performed by the coral insects who, through their unintelligent activity, had created the rainbow-colored, "colossal orbs" of coral that stand as the "firmament of waters." He'd seen, in other words, not just the whiteness—the ultimate absence of any deep, single, unified meaning to the universe—but also the rainbow—the presence of a multiplicity of interpretations. It is as if he saw both that what ultimately grounds the universe is meaningless—like the unintelligent coral insects—and also that there are nevertheless wonderful meanings—like the rainbow-colored colossal orbs of coral they produce. Both of these insights are true, according to Melville, but one cannot live in them simultaneously. Together they drove poor, insubstantial Pip across the precipice of sanity:

> By the merest chance the ship itself at last rescued him; but from that hour the little negro went about the deck an idiot; such, at least, they said he was. The sea had jeeringly kept his finite body up, but drowned the infinite of his soul. Not drowned entirely, though. Rather carried down alive to wondrous depths, where strange shapes of the unwarped primal world glided to and fro before his passive eyes; and the miser-merman, Wisdom, revealed his hoarded heaps; and among the joyous, heartless, ever-juvenile eternities, Pip saw the multi-

tudinous, God-omnipresent, coral insects, that out of the firmament of waters heaved the colossal orbs. He saw God's foot upon the treadle of the loom, and spoke it; and therefore his shipmates called him mad. So man's insanity is heaven's sense; and wandering from all mortal reason, man comes at last to that celestial thought, which, to reason, is absurd and frantic; and weal or woe, feels then uncompromised, indifferent as his God.[84]

Pip is a kind of hero because he doesn't deny the lack of any ultimate meaning to the universe, but instead becomes a pure openness to it. To see God's foot upon the treadle of the loom and live, as Pip does, is to be deafened, to be made unfit for hearing any meaning as a human can. Indeed, after this event Pip has no identity at all; he becomes open to all interpretations because he has none himself:

> Pip? whom call ye Pip? Pip jumped from the whale-boat. Pip's missing.[85]

In losing his identity, and having no perspective of his own, Pip can see that all the meanings in the world are meanings taken from one perspective or another. He can see the selfishness involved in thinking of these meanings as ultimate or final precisely because he can see that ultimately each is a perspectival rendering of something that has no deeper truth. This becomes clear in the fascinating chapter on the doubloon.[86]

Early in the book Ahab has nailed up a doubloon on the main mast and told the crew that anyone who can site Moby Dick will win it.[87] Much later in the novel many of the characters inspect the doubloon to see what the markings upon it mean. It becomes clear very quickly that each sailor finds something of himself and his understanding of the universe written in the mysterious markings of the doubloon: Ahab finds nothing but himself: "There's something ever egotistical in mountain-tops and towers, and all other grand and lofty things." Starbuck, the chief mate of Quaker persuasion, finds a representation of the Trinity (plus some lurking threat to it); "easy-going, unfearing"[88] Stubb finds nothing but the natural cycle of life; the sturdy, practical third mate Flask finds sixteen dollars upon the mast and notes that "at two cents the cigar, that's nine-hundred and sixty cigars." (The un-flappable editors of the NCE point out that the "the arithmetic seems shaky" here.) Others take their turn as well.[89] In this way we learn something important about many of the characters in the book.

But what's particularly interesting for our purposes is what Pip sees. Pip sees not only the doubloon, but everyone else looking at the doubloon. And his take on the doubloon itself is to notice that it is something different each time someone new looks upon it.

Thus the doubloon itself is nothing deeper than people's various perceptions of it. That's why when Pip finally walks up to the dou-bloon he doesn't give another substantive interpretation as if to say what its final truth was. Instead, he begins to conjugate the verb:

> I look, you look, he looks; we look, ye look, they look. . . . And I, you, and he; and we, ye, and they, are all bats; and I'm a crow, especially when I stand a'top of this pine tree here. Caw! caw! caw! caw! caw! caw! Ain't I a crow? . . . Here's the ship's navel, this doubloon here, and they are all on fire to unscrew it. But, unscrew your navel, and what's the consequence?[90]

In a sense Pip has had his navel unscrewed: he has seen the ultimate meaning of the universe, he has seen God's foot upon the treadle of the loom. And what he has learned is that there is no deep, underly-ing truth there to see. There are only the practices within which one already lives. But to take these practices as something deeply true, as the mark of an ultimate and final ground, to do, in other words, what all these sailors try to do—is simply bats. The person who does this, in other words, is blind like a bat, crazy like a bat (batty), and he will ultimately be driven bats if he tries to hold on to his particular perspective as if it were a final truth.

Pip, by contrast, is a crow. He is black as a crow, of course, and he caws inarticulately like the bird. But he is also a crow because, from the crow's nest at the top of his pine tree mast, he sees all interpretations as interpretations and is left with no interpretations of his own.

There is an important sense in which Pip and Ahab are counterparts of one another. Pip sees that there are only perceptions of the world and no final answer, and he becomes open to all perspectives while managing to live in none. This makes him crazy in a worldly sense, since he has no identity to live by. Ahab, by contrast, has the strongest identity possible. Indeed:

> There was an infinity of firmest fortitude, a determinate, unsurrenderable wilfulness, in the fixed and fearless, forward dedication of [his] glance.[91]

But Ahab's willfulness is set upon the universe, driven to force it to reveal its final truth. This makes him crazy in a different way. For he is determined to see what Pip already has, and equally determined to make it something other than it is. Melville ties these two types of craziness together when he describes the surprising relationship between the captain and his keeper. After Pip's accident, Ahab takes the boy under his wing. Once, as they go off together to the captain's cabin, an old Manx sailor makes the crucial remark:

> There go two daft ones now. . . . One daft with strength, the other daft with weakness. But here's the end of the rotten line—all dripping, too. Mend it, eh? I think we had best have a new line altogether.[92]

Pip and Ahab contain within them the two basic possibilities left for the West if we hang on to the Axial intuition that there is an ultimate truth behind everything that is. Either we become crazy at the recognition that there is no such truth, or we drive ourselves crazy trying to prove there is. The end of a rotten line indeed, suggests the Manxman. Perhaps we had best have a new line altogether.

IT IS ONE THING to *say* that the line is rotten, but Melville attempts to *show* it as well. For Ahab finally gets what his heart desires—a forehead to forehead confrontation with the dread Moby Dick—and dies in the event. But the details of Ahab's encounters with the whale are important for understanding the subtle nuance of Melville's view.

The book ends with a three-day chase of the whale. The chase is clearly set up as Ahab's opportunity to have an outright conversation with the gods—not to communicate by way of omens or prophecies, but to speak with the authors of the universe direct. At least that is what Ahab imagines it will be. At one point, for example, he derides Starbuck's superstitious idea that a certain event is an ill-boding omen for the chase:

Omen? Omen?—the dictionary! If the gods think to speak outright to man, they will honorably speak outright; not shake their heads, and give an old wives' darkling hint.[93]

And indeed, on the first day Ahab does achieve a face-to-face encounter with Moby Dick. As he scrambles forward to the bow of his boat, and the boat spins around upon its axis, Ahab comes directly before the head of the whale:

But as if perceiving this stratagem, Moby Dick, with that malicious intelligence ascribed to him, sidelingly transplanted himself, as it were, in an instant, shooting his pleated head lengthwise beneath the boat.[94]

As he stove the boat to pieces, "the bluish pearl-white of the inside of the jaw was within six inches of Ahab's head."[95] The confrontation on this day evinces a malicious intelligence in Moby Dick. He is variously described as devilish, crafty, malicious, cruel, intelligent, and vindictive in the encounter.[96] Perhaps, then, this is the ultimate truth about the nature of the universe. It clearly has Ahab in its sights, and wishes to do him the ultimate harm.

The second day of the chase, however, reveals a different Moby Dick. Once again Ahab meets him head to head, this time as part of a strategy to keep from being spied by the whale's side-set eyes. But on this occasion there is nothing devilish or malicious about him; the whale is described instead as merely an instinctive brute, his body responding as if by reflex to the touch of any surrounding thing:

> [W]henever a stray oar, bit of plank, the least chip or crumb of
> the boats touched his skin, his tail swiftly drew back, and came
> sideways smiting the sea.[97]

In this confrontation Moby Dick once again staves Ahab's boat, but this time his intention seems more undirected; instead of Ahab, it is merely the wooden planks of Ahab's boat that Moby Dick seems to have in view:

> [T]he White Whale . . . seemed only intent on annihilating
> each separate plank of which those boats were made.[98]

The whale does manage in this encounter to drag under a mysterious character named Fedallah, albeit by accident, and this seems the partial fulfillment of a dire, Macbeth-like prophecy that Fedallah himself once uttered. Furthermore, Ahab is more willing to take this omen seriously than he was the last, as if the whale's apparent degree of intelligence is inversely proportional to his communicative intent. But what had seemed a devilish and malicious universe on the first day now seems merely brutish and lacking intent.

The third day shows a different universe still. As Ahab's boat ranges along the White Whale's flank, Moby Dick is completely oblivious; he takes no notice of Ahab or his boat at all. It is not just that the whale is now an unintelligent brute. Rather, whether he is intelligent or not, Ahab's existence is completely irrelevant to him: "he seemed strangely oblivious of [the boat's] advance—as the whale sometimes will."[99] This completely meaningless encounter, Ahab's total irrelevance to him, is oddly reminiscent of the episode when Moby Dick bit off Ahab's leg:

> [S]uddenly sweeping his sickle-shaped lower jaw beneath him, Moby Dick had reaped away Ahab's leg, as a mower a blade of grass in the field.[100]

To be insignificant as a blade of grass to a mower, to have no role in the universe at all, is Ahab's greatest fear. His will is set inexorably upon the task of revealing once and for all his true place in the universe. But Ahab's final confrontation with the whale turns out to be so swift and surprising, his death so instant and unexpected, that nobody has time even to notice that he is gone. As Ahab shoots a final harpoon at Moby Dick, Ahab gets caught in the fast receding line, and is pulled under to his death before anyone—even he himself—can notice that the deadly event has occurred:

> The harpoon was darted; the stricken whale flew forward; with igniting velocity the line ran through the groove;—ran foul. Ahab stooped to clear it; he did clear it; but the flying turn caught him round the neck, and voicelessly as Turkish mutes bowstring their victim, he was shot out of the boat, ere the crew knew he was gone.[101]

The ultimate indifference of Moby Dick toward Ahab could be an indication that this is the way the world really is. Perhaps there really are no meanings, no truths about the purpose of our lives; perhaps the nihilistic story is the final truth. But Melville's account is subtler than this. Sometimes the universe is meaningless, it is true—sometimes a death is senseless or dumb. But the universe has its brute and reflex-like moments as well, in addition to malicious and vindictive and devilish ones. And in addition to all these, it is also gently joyous and divine. On the first day of the chase, for instance, Ishmael describes Moby Dick:

> A gentle joyousness—a mighty mildness of repose in swiftness, invested the gliding whale. Not the white bull Jupiter swimming away with ravished Europa clinging to his graceful horns; his lovely, leering eyes sideways intent upon the maid; with smooth bewitching fleetness, rippling straight for the nuptial bower in Crete; not Jove; not that great majesty Supreme! did surpass the glorified White Whale as he so divinely swam.[102]

The ultimate story of the universe is not that it is indifferent to us, though Pip and Ahab have a god that is indifferent to us in precisely this way. Recall Pip's final thought in the sea that he had been left there like a castaway, the world "indifferent as his God." But there are other gods as well—malicious and vindictive and joyous and divine—and the universe is all of these by turns. Which is to say that ultimately it is no one of them. A whole pantheon of gods is really there.

QUEEQUEG IS NOT FROM our rotten line, and we have seen already that he exhibits a kind of hale, eternal health. His pagan culture is too far from our own to be the saving possibility to which the wise old Manxman alludes, but there is nevertheless something we can learn from Queequeg's way of life. For the great warrior's immortal health comes from his native recognition that one must embody the truths of one's culture, even if one can never get clear about what they mean. This is emphasized most clearly in the story of Quequeeg's extraordinary tattoos.

The tattoos that cover Queequeg's body are of mystical origin, and they don't so much represent as embody his understanding of both himself and the world. Like the Maorian chief Te Pehi Kupe on whom he is almost certainly modeled,[103] Queequeg signs his name by copying from memory a central portion of his tattoos.[104] Taken as a whole, the markings seem to incarnate his culture's understanding of everything that is, and the way that it is; they manifest a whole Kokovokan understanding of being. And they are thoroughly indecipherable. It is as if Queequeg were a prospective comment on a famous saying by Yeats. In one of his last letters, written only weeks before he died, Yeats rejects all aspiration to abstract knowledge of the deepest truths. "Man can embody the truth," he writes, "but he cannot know it."[105] Just so Queequeg embodies his culture's truth:

> [His] tattooing had been the work of a departed prophet and seer of his island, who, by those hieroglyphic marks, had written out on his body a complete theory of the heavens and the earth, and a mystical treatise on the art of attaining truth; so that Queequeg in his own proper person was a riddle to unfold; a wondrous work in one volume; but whose mysteries not even he himself could read, though his own live heart beat against them; and these mysteries were therefore destined in the end to moulder away with the living parchment whereon they were inscribed, and so be unsolved to the last.[106]

But even though Queequeg's way of life is healthy, in the end he goes down with the entire ship and crew when Moby Dick rams this "larger and nobler foe."[107] And indeed the *Pequod* is so large and noble, that in one of Melville's final tours de force the sinking of Ahab's ship might stand for the sinking of the entire history of the West. In an image that recalls the painting in the Spouter Inn from the beginning of the book, the ship's trinity of masts sinks slowly beneath the water's edge under the force of the Sperm Whale's powerful head. But unlike in the painting, upon the tallest of the *Pequod*'s masts stands Tashtego, another of the pagan harpooners, valiantly nailing Ahab's devil-red flag to the mainmast until only inches remain above water. Tashtego's red arm hammers faster and faster as the certainty of his impending fate comes clear. With a final blow, he pins a sky-hawk between the hammer and mast, and Tashtego's death-grasp holds it there, dragging the bird with him down from heaven to the watery depths below. Melville writes:

> A sky-hawk that tauntingly had followed the main-truck downwards from its natural home among the stars, pecking at the flag, and incommoding Tashtego there; this bird now chanced to intercept its broad fluttering wing between the hammer and the wood; and simultaneously feeling that ethereal thrill, the submerged savage beneath, in his death-grasp, kept his hammer frozen there; and so the bird of heaven, with archangelic shrieks, and his imperial beak thrust upwards, and his whole captive form folded in the flag of Ahab, went down with his ship, which, like Satan, would not sink to hell till she had dragged a living part of heaven along with her, and helmeted herself with it.[108]

The imagery here is complete. The archangelic shrieks of the bird from heaven indicate that Christianity itself has sunk with the *Pequod;* the imperial beak that the bird thrusts upward might suggest the death of the Roman tradition as well; and finally it is Ahab's folded flag that brings this tradition to the bottom of the sea. Ahab's complete and total commitment to the transcendent truth that defines the history of the West, in other words, ultimately sinks this historic tradition from within.

Where, then, are we to go from here? Although Queequeg himself does not survive the sinking of the *Pequod,* he and the embodied, ritualistic practices of his culture do play an importantly redemptive role. For it is Queequeg's very coffin, scrupulously carved by Queequeg himself "in his rude way"[109] with a replica of the tattoos that were etched upon his body, it is this pagan hieroglyphic coffin life-buoy that saves Ishmael from the final descent of the ship. As the Pequod sinks to the bottom of the ocean, in the Epilogue of the book, it takes down all its passengers but one. Out of the closing vortex that is left behind by the suction of the sinking ship Queequeg's coffin bursts. It "shot lengthwise from the sea, fell over, and floated by my side," Ishmael tells us.

> Buoyed up by that coffin, for almost one whole day and night,
> I floated on a soft and dirge-like main. The unharming sharks,
> they glided by as if with padlocks on their mouths; the savage
> sea-hawks sailed with sheathed beaks.[110]

WHAT, FINALLY, CAN BE SAID about the secret motto of Melville's book? Here there is one more, final trick to reveal. Whether Melville himself understood this trick or not is something we will probably never know. He is happy to claim, as a good writer should, that the metaphorical meanings of the book are beyond his grasp.[111] But still, his intuitions are good. He was certainly right, for example, to find in *Moby Dick* something wicked, and yet something that left him spotless as the lamb. But if the secret motto of the book is none other than Ahab's own baptismal incantation, then doesn't that put Melville in Ahab's place? And isn't this an awkward position for him to take? For after all, Ahab has nothing whatsoever to do with the polytheistic future that Ishmael prophesizes.

The trick is all in what is left unsaid. When Melville writes to Hawthorne of the secret motto of the book, he leaves the motto mysteriously incomplete. "Ego non baptiso te in nomine," he writes, "but make out the rest yourself." Isn't this the crucial difference between Melville and Ahab? Ahab completes the diabolical incantation, aligning himself with the wickedness of that devil that will bring down the Roman Christian world. But Melville seems intent upon not completing the phrase. Indeed, he says Hawthorne must complete it himself; and so too, presumably, must everyone else who reads the book. "I baptize you not in the name of . . ." whatever totalizing and inward kind of religion that closes itself off to the surface truths, he seems to say. Rather, I let you find all those polytheistic truths yourself; live in them, find joy in them, and even sorrow. But in these joys and sorrows rest content with the thought that they give meaning to our world.

7

Conclusion: Lives Worth Living
in a Secular Age

I N YANKEE STADIUM on the Fourth of July, even the loss of the
opening game couldn't spoil the mood of the crowd. Fans craned
their necks for a glimpse of the big, shy man and current Yankee captain, Henry Louis Gehrig. Known as The Iron Horse, Gehrig had recently ended his record-setting streak of 2,130 straight games, played
over the course of fourteen seasons of baseball.

The long run dated back to the beginning of the 1925 season,
and during that period Gehrig had played through broken bones,
crippling attacks of lumbago, and even pitches taken to the head.
Despite his legendary toughness, however, on May 2 the captain
of the Yankees had voluntarily removed himself from the lineup.
A mysterious and debilitating weakness in his muscles had led to
increasingly erratic play; he felt he was becoming a burden to the
team. Gehrig stayed on as captain and watched the games from the
dugout, but speculation about his health filled the papers. Finally in
late June, after an extended trip to the specialists at the Mayo Clinic,
Gehrig was diagnosed with amyotrophic lateral sclerosis—the fatal
wasting disease of the motor neurons in the brain and spinal cord
that now bears his name. Although nobody knew for sure at the
time, in fact the disease was already at a relatively advanced stage.

Less than two years later, at the age of thirty-seven, Gehrig would be dead.

Lou Gehrig was perhaps the most revered player in all of baseball—admired not only for his skill and stamina, but as a shining example of "sportsmanship and clean living."[1] Despite his virtual allergy to the spotlight, Gehrig's friends, fans, and teammates would not be denied the opportunity to celebrate his life. In what was described as "perhaps as colorful and dramatic a pageant as ever was enacted on a baseball field," the capacity crowd had gathered at Yankee Stadium on the Fourth of July to "thunder a hail and farewell" to Henry Lou Gehrig.[2]

The event did not disappoint. During the break between the games a bed of microphones sprouted up around home plate, and Gehrig's teammates gathered behind him there in support. A long line of well-wishers—from the mayor of New York City to the janitorial staff at the stadium—showered him with gifts and praise.

When the time came for Gehrig to give his thanks, he was too moved to speak. Sid Mercer, the MC of the event, noticed Gehrig's fragile state and stepped to the microphone to offer thanks on his behalf, before calling the ceremony to an end. But as Gehrig was walking away, and the crew was taking down the microphones, the crowd broke into loud chants of "We want Lou! We want Lou!" In a moment of resolution Gehrig turned back toward home plate. When his shaky legs made it almost impossible for him to approach the microphone, his friend and manager Joe McCarthy took him by the arm. Then, speaking without notes, and in a voice that was on the verge of breaking, Lou began his short speech to the crowd with two famous sentences:

> Fans, for the past two weeks you have been reading about a bad break I got. Yet today I consider myself the luckiest man on the face of the earth.

He described his heartfelt gratitude for the kindness and encouragement he had gotten from the fans over the course of his career, for the honor he felt in playing with his teammates and for his coaches, and for the blessing of a good family and a wife who is a "tower of strength and courage." He concluded with another now famous sentence. "So I close in saying," he said, "that I might have been given a bad break, but I've got an awful lot to live for."

The thundering applause filled the stadium for two full minutes.

At fewer than three hundred words, Lou Gehrig's farewell speech stands as perhaps the most powerful example of American rhetoric ever produced outside the political sphere.[3] Film clips from the event show a stadium that vacillates between pin-drop silence and thunderous applause. The papers described it as "without doubt one of the most touching scenes ever witnessed on a ball field and one that made even case-hardened ball players and chroniclers of the game swallow hard."[4] It is a fair bet that nobody in the stadium that day felt even a tinge of T. S. Eliot's indecision, or Samuel Beckett's sense of an interminable wait, or David Foster Wallace's anger and frustration at his inability to find meaningful differences in life. For the moments that led up to and were held together by Gehrig's speech, 62,000 people knew exactly what they were about. And paramount among them was a great man on the verge of death—Henry Lou Gehrig himself.[5]

SPORTS MAY BE THE place in contemporary life where Americans find sacred community most easily. We saw already in our opening chapter that a great athlete can shine like a Greek god, and that in the presence of such an athlete the sense of greatness is palpable. It has even become popular to argue that in recent years sport has come to form a kind of folk religion in American society, standing in for more traditional kinds of religious practice and belief. Whether or not it is true as a matter of historical and sociological fact that sport now plays this kind of religious role in America, a related phenomenological claim seems harder to dispute. There is no essential difference, really, in how it feels to rise as one in joy to sing the praises of the Lord, or to rise as one in joy to sing the praises of the Hail Mary pass, the Immaculate Reception, the Angels, the Saints, the Friars, or the Demon Deacons.

In part this association between sport and religion derives from the importance of community in each. The sense that one is joined with one's fellow human beings in the celebration of something great reinforces the sense that what one is celebrating really is great. It is one thing to sit alone on the living room sofa and be astonished by some amazing feat of athleticism seen on the television as David Foster Wallace sometimes did. But moments like this take on greater meaning when they are shared with a community of like-minded folks who are experiencing the same kind of awe. Whether it is in the church or in the baseball stadium, the awesomeness of the moment is reinforced when it is felt as shared by others. When it is also shared *that it is shared*—when you all recognize together that you are sharing in the celebration of this great thing—then the awesomeness of the moment itself bursts forth and shines. When you find yourself spontaneously high-fiving the stranger sitting next to you at the stadium, the mood of "Do I dare to eat a peach?" is far away.

In the best cases events like this do more than draw you into a simple mood of exultation; they bring out everything that is important in the situation, letting each thing shine at its very best. A great baseball game, for example, played in a ballpark that highlights the most beautiful or exciting aspects of the city, can gather people together and focus them on what is best about the season, the community, the game, and themselves. Albert Borgmann, the philosopher of technology, writes movingly about this possibility, tying it explicitly to a notion of the presence of divinities. "A rich reality is needed to sponsor a sense of community," Borgmann writes.

A thoughtful and graceful ballpark tunes people to the same harmonies. It inspires common pride and pleasure, a shared sense of season and place, a joint anticipation of drama. Given such attunement, banter and laughter flow naturally across strangers and unite them into a community. When reality and community conspire this way, divinity descends on the game, divinity of an impersonal and yet potent kind.[7]

As Borgmann says, the divinities that descend upon a game are impersonal ones. They bear no metaphysical issues—no questions, for instance, about how to reconcile three persons in one God, or how many angels can dance on the head of a pin—and the impersonal gods of baseball encourage no questions about the afterlife or the nature of the soul. But this lack of any personal element strips the notion of the sacred to its essential core. Nietzsche said that the sacred is whatever it is in a culture at which one is not allowed to laugh. One can laugh, of course, at the spectacle of grown men trying to hit a hard ball with a wooden stick, or carry a spheroid across a line. It is not that sports are sacred to the culture in any absolute sense. But there are moments in sport—either in the playing of them or in the witnessing of them—during which something so overpowering happens that it wells up before you as a palpable presence and carries you along as on a powerful wave. At that moment there is no question of ironic distance from the event. That is the moment when the sacred shines.

DAVID FOSTER WALLACE, more than most, had a strong sense for sacred moments like this. Perhaps such a claim will sound surprising: after all, the main point of our chapter on Wallace was to highlight the nihilistic strain in his thought. But although a kind of willful Nietzschean nihilism dominates Wallace's work, he was an amazingly receptive writer. Indeed, he seems to have resonated with most of the varied and incompatible phenomena that animate our contemporary world. In particular, one finds a strong counterstrain to Wallace's nihilism in his writings on the sacred moments of sport.

Wallace was a special devotee of tennis, and among his pantheon of players there he rates Roger Federer at the top. Wallace's principle hymn to Federer appeared in the *New York Times Magazine* article he wrote titled "Federer as Religious Experience."[8] "[I]f you've never seen the young man play live," Wallace writes,

> and then do, in person, on the sacred grass of Wimbledon, through the literally withering heat and then wind and rain of the '06 fortnight, then you are apt to have what one of the tournament's press bus drivers describes as a "bloody near-religious experience." It may be tempting, at first, to hear a phrase like this as just one more of the overheated tropes that people resort to. . . . But the driver's phrase turns out to be true—literally, for an instant ecstatically—though it takes some time and serious watching to see this truth emerge.[9]

Wallace's analysis of Federer is masterful. He argues that Federer's combination of power and beauty has revivified a power baseline game that others worried had reached its evolutionary endpoint. In this way, he shows, Federer has "figuratively and literally re-embodied men's tennis." Because of the way he embodies this new style of playing, for the first time in years the game's future is open, unpredictable, alive. If Wallace is right about this then his interpretation makes sense—really, literal sense—of the claim that watching Federer play is like having a religious experience: it focuses a new understanding of human beings and their pursuits.

This new understanding of the sacred highlights a tension, perhaps even an irreconcilable conflict, both in Wallace's writing and in our culture more generally. For the redeeming value that Wallace finds in Federer, literally the salvation he finds in the experience of Federer's kind of athletic grace and beauty, is not just at odds with but turns completely on its head the disembodied kind of bliss he had hoped to find in the levitating tax-return examiner Mitchell Drinion.

The best way to see the conflict between these notions of the sacred is to focus on the body. Most human tasks—even intellectual or spiritual tasks—are related in some way or another to the body. The pain from Don Gately's gunshot wound, for example, instigates his long reverie at the end of *Infinite Jest*. But the revelation that this reverie generates involves a repudiation of the body as enfeebling. Like Augustine, Gately is ultimately aiming for a kind of *disembodied* state—a state in which the body and its limitations melt away and there is nothing left but the alive, exhilarating bliss of the eternal present. Wallace wrote the Gately passages quickly—perhaps in a kind of Gately-esque trance himself—and he seems to have had a very personal relationship to them. At the time he told a friend he was working so well he "couldn't feel my ass in the chair."[10]

The point of Gately's experience, of Wallace's own ass-lessness, and of course the point of the levitating Mitchell Drinion, is that the body is a hindrance. True bliss, true deliverance, on this traditional, Augustinian view, comes from sloughing off the burden of the body. No doubt this is one way of approaching the body that is clearly recognizable today.

But Federer's athletic grace reveals a different, more nuanced understanding of the role of the body in the experience of the sacred. Indeed, far from repudiating it, Federer's tennis mastery becomes an episode in "human beings' reconciliation with the fact of having a body." This does not mean that bodies are always and entirely good:

> There's a great deal that's bad about having a body. If this is not so obviously true that no one needs examples, we can just quickly mention pain, sores, odors, nausea, aging, gravity, sepsis, clumsiness, illness, limits—every last schism between our physical wills and our actual capacities. Can anyone doubt we need help being reconciled? Crave it? It's your body that dies, after all.

But if one focuses only on these bodily miseries, then salvation lies in not having a body: ecstatic bliss in feeling the absence of one's ass. Federer's bodily, athletic grace, by contrast, drives one to extol the sacred wonders of the body instead:

> There are wonderful things about having a body, too, obviously—it's just that these things are much harder to feel and appreciate in real time. Rather like certain kinds of rare, peak-type sensuous epiphanies ("I'm so glad I have eyes to see this sunrise!" etc.), great athletes seem to catalyze our awareness of how glorious it is to touch and perceive, move through space, interact with matter. Granted, what great athletes can do with their bodies are things that the rest of us can only dream of. But these dreams are important—they make up for a lot.

Federer's athletic grace, in other words, focuses the possibility of a fully embodied, this-worldly kind of sacred. This notion of the sacred embraces the limitations of the body precisely because exploring, extending, and reforming bodily constraints can open up new kinds of experiences for us.

And more than that, it allows us to find a kind of mystery and magic right here upon the earth: a metaphysical mystery, as Wallace himself insists, in "those rare, preternatural athletes"—athletes like Federer and Michael Jordan and Muhammad Ali—"who appear to be exempt, at least in part, from certain physical laws." It allows us to find something sacred and divine in Jordan the human being, as Wallace once wrote, "hanging in the air like a Chagall bride."[11] It allows us to rise as one in ecstatic and spontaneous joy at the human greatness of Bill Bradley splitting the defenders or Wesley Autrey diving on the subway tracks. Indeed, it accounts for Wallace's own reaction to seeing—on the television, no less[12]—that impossible shot by Federer, like something out of *The Matrix*:

I don't know what-all sounds were involved, but my spouse says she hurried in and there was popcorn all over the couch and I was down on one knee and my eyeballs looked like novelty-shop eyeballs.

This kind of encounter with fully embodied athletic grace—like our encounters with other kinds of fully embodied joys—can give us a genuine kind of religious experience. But it differs from the Augustinian notion of the sacred we encountered before. It is a religious experience that—unlike Gately's eternal Present—cannot be approached directly, cannot be uncovered through control and will and confrontation:

> You more have to come at the aesthetic stuff obliquely, to talk around it, or to try to define it in terms of what it is not.

This glancing approach is inclined toward reconciliation instead of purification. It involves a fully human notion of the sacred that lives not in the repudiation or transcendence of pain and boredom and anger and angst, but rather in the recognition that these difficult aspects of our existence live together with the sacred moments, that they complete one another, and make sense of one another. It is a notion of the sacred that is reconciled with the idea that you cannot have gods that care about you without having gods that sometimes get angry as well.[13]

And finally—for that reason—it is an experience that requires recognizing the need for practices to "propitiate the divine."[14] These are the practices that Wallace cannot envision, but that this conclusion will focus and describe. For all his sensitivity to embodied, athletic grace, Wallace nevertheless remains deeply entrenched in a nihilistic Nietzschean world. For him these practices look like naive superstitions[15] instead of genuinely sacred rites, because after all he lives still beneath Descartes' "egotistical sky" beside his "now-unhaunted hill."

That's why he has not yet been able to lure back the gods. And yet, even so, he cannot help but to be amazed and awed by the world in which this kind of fully human religious experience lives. "It's hard to describe," he says,

> [I]t's like a thought that's also a feeling. One wouldn't want to make too much of it, or to pretend that it's any sort of equitable balance; that would be grotesque. But the truth is that whatever deity, entity, energy, or random genetic flux produces sick children also produced Roger Federer, and just look at him down there. Look at that.

There are four points to notice about the sacred moments in sport, points that start to fill in what Wallace could not see. First, in the truly extraordinary moments, something overwhelming occurs. It wells up and carries you along as on a powerful wave. The wave metaphor is crucial here. When a wave is at its most powerful it is a solid foundation that can support as many riders as will fit upon it. It can even sweep up more as it runs along. But when the wave passes, nothing but its memory survives. Try to stand upon the still water and you'll find that the supporting foundation is gone. These moments of sport are like that. When you are in the midst of them, riding the wave, they carry you along and give meaning to life. As Borgmann says:

> At the beginning of a real game, there is no way of predicting or controlling what will happen. No one can produce or guarantee the flow of a game. It unfolds and reveals itself in the playing. It inspires grace and despair, it provokes heroics and failure, it infuses enthusiasm and inflicts misery. It is always greater than the individuals it unites.[16]

But the meaning they give is temporary. One can remember having been caught up in the excitement of the play, having been taken over and directed by the situation. But the memory tells you nothing about how to act once the situation is gone. This makes our contemporary notion of the sacred and the real radically different from many others we are familiar with. This situational notion of what grounds our existence, for example, is nothing like the eternal, everlasting kind of certainty and security that philosophers from Plato to Descartes to Kant desired. And it is nothing like the monotheistic, unified kind of certainty that the Judeo-Christian religions offer either. Rather, this pre-Axial kind of certainty is transient and multiple and it requires care. As Homer knows it carries you along for a while but it cannot last forever.

Second, this characteristic of the sacred as we experience it in our culture ties it very closely to the Homeric Greek conception of what is real. In Homer's age the name for nature, or what there is, was *physis*. This is the word from which our word *physics* derives. Physics today is likewise the study of what there is, but we now have a very different conception of what there is than Homer had. For us, the ultimate elements of nature are quarks and leptons and other subatomic particles that have mass and charge. Or perhaps the ultimate constituents are minuscule multidimensional strings that vibrate. Or maybe the final physics will tell us something different still. But whatever physics ends up saying about the universe, the story it gives will be a story about basic constituents and the laws that govern how they casually interact. For Homer this notion of reality isn't wrong on the facts, as if some other physical, causal story could get it right.[17] Instead, for Homer, the causal account starts in the wrong place altogether. For the word *physis* in Homeric times wasn't the name of some ultimate *constituent* of the universe; it was the name for the *way* the most real things in the world present themselves to us.

The most important things, the most real things in Homer's world, well up and take us over, hold us for a while, and then, finally, let us go. If we had to translate Homer's word *physis,* then whooshing is about as close as we can get. What there really is, for Homer, is whooshing up: the whooshing up of shining Achilles in the midst of battle, or of an overwhelming eroticism in the presence of a radiant stranger like Paris; the whooshing up of a rock in the turbulent sea that calls forth Odysseus's hand to grab it. These were the shining moments of reality in Homer's world. And whooshing up is what happens in the context of the great moment in contemporary sport as well. When something whooshes up it focuses and organizes everything around it. The great athlete in the midst of the play rises up and shines—all attention is drawn to him. And everyone around him—the players on the field, the coaches on the sidelines, the fans in the stadium, the announcers in the booth—everyone understands who they are and what they are to do immediately in relation to the sacred event that is occurring. In Homer's world what whooshes up is what really shines and matters most. And we can still sense this in the moment of sport.

It is worth emphasizing that this Homeric notion of reality is orthogonal to our contemporary scientific understanding—they are simply not explaining the same kinds of things. Indeed, one could embrace both notions—and we think one should embrace both notions—without any conflict. The scientific conception of what there is focuses on the causal basis of reality; Homer's account, by contrast, describes the way the most important or meaningful moments of existence present themselves to us. Of course it is true that meaningful events—like great moments in sport—involve entities that have a causal basis. But the causal structure of the leg muscles in Lou Gehrig's left thigh is neither here nor there when it comes to the question what it is like to be caught up in the response to one of his extraordinary plays or his moving farewell.

The third point to make is that the *physis* phenomenon is not unique to sport. It may be that in our culture sport provides the central locus for the phenomenon—that in general it is in the context of sport that contemporary Americans are most likely to feel this sense of community and focused meaning, this sense of understanding exactly what one is about, if only for a while. But that is not to say it can't happen in other contexts too. Many people, for instance, felt their sense of themselves and their world come into focus during the speech by Martin Luther King Jr. on the National Mall. For someone else it might happen occasionally in the context of an important family meal at Thanksgiving. Perhaps some other folks feel this kind of focused, communal meaning taking them over in the context of the classroom. There is nothing in our position that requires the story to focus on sports. It's just that this is the place in contemporary American culture where the phenomenon seems most familiar.

But the sports example is important for another reason too, and this brings us to the fourth point we want to make. Namely, there is something inherently dangerous in the phenomenon we are describing. Inherently dangerous, and perhaps even repellent. We need now to address this final point about *physis*.

AT A DINNER PARTY recently one of us was describing the phenomenon of whooshing up. A colleague at the table—himself a kind and clearheaded philosopher who thinks deeply about related issues—had an immediate response. "I know exactly what it's like to feel that kind of energy pulsing through a crowd," he said. "And every time I'm near it I want to get as far away as possible." The discussion was cut short at this point, as social conversations often are, and the source of this colleague's concern was never explicitly articulated. It is clear, however, what someone might mean by a comment like this, and there is a very serious worry behind it. Without attributing any of the following views to our friend, therefore, we need to lay out the danger of whooshing up.

First we need to notice that to be overtaken by some potent force is to have one's actions no longer completely under one's control. When I find myself rising as one with the crowd in the presence of some great athletic feat, there is an important sense in which I am not the source of my own activity. It is my muscles, of course, that generate the motor actions—straightening the legs, raising the arms, emitting the inarticulate utterance that means "Hooray!" But there is a strong sense in which I perform these movements without ever having decided to do so. The activity is out of my control in the sense that I do not perform it voluntarily. It's not as if I was *forced* to jump up and cheer either, of course. It was always an option for me to adopt a kind of ironic distance from the situation, or even, as our colleague recommends, to walk away. But so long as I find myself taken over by the situation, there is an important sense in which I am no longer the source of my own activity.

From the point of view of the Enlightenment, this condition is appalling. In a famous essay, Kant argued that "enlightenment is man's emergence from his self-imposed immaturity."[18] To be immature, in the Kantian sense, just is to allow oneself to act in ways that one has not chosen freely on one's own. Failing to resist the madness of crowds is a prime example. Maturity, by contrast, is having the resolve and courage to use one's own understanding in choosing how to act, without guidance from anyone or anything external to oneself. The mature thing to do at the baseball game therefore, in this Kantian sense of maturity, is to resist the power of the community response in order to decide as a rational individual what the appropriate response to the situation should be. One might well decide that an athletic feat merits applause, and if so, one might express one's approval appropriately. But rising as one with the crowd is out of the question.

This might sound like a boring way to act at a baseball game, but there is sense behind Kant's caution. There is, after all, a vanishingly small distance between rising as one with the crowd at a baseball game and rising as one with the crowd at a Hitler rally. Indeed, insofar as Lou Gehrig's farewell address is properly considered an act of rhetoric instead of an act of athletic greatness proper, perhaps the distance there is smaller still. So the power of the whooshing up phenomenon is revealed to be Janus-faced. If we cannot articulate a distinction between Lou Gehrig's farewell and Hitler's taking over, then perhaps Kantian maturity, though relatively boring, really is the wisest course.

IS THE CHOICE WE FACE, then, one between a life of boring but mature and moral activities, on the one hand, and a life of risky—potentially even abhorrent—but nevertheless meaningful ones, on the other? No. The stakes are even higher. The Englightenment's metaphysical embrace of the autonomous individual leads not just to a boring life. It leads almost inevitably to a nearly unlivable one. Already in Dante, for example, the assertion of the individual's autonomous will was a rebellion against the source of meaning in the world. And Melville's Ahab was "daft from strength" in something like this sense as well. His need to find a clear, articulate, and completely certain answer to the question of his individual place in the universe, that monomaniacal need to find out whether he is at the center of it all, was in Melville's view, a deeply tragic flaw.

And perhaps our contemporary situation is even worse. David Foster Wallace's need to create meaning ex nihilo out of the individual puts him in the traditional position of God, a position that Nietzsche embraced as well. But Wallace's exploration of this God-like position led him ultimately to feel both that it was necessary for a meaningful existence and that he could neither understand nor live it himself. If these authors have got the phenomena clearly in mind, then individualist autonomy, it seems, leads at least to wickedness or tragedy, and more likely to nihilism or even suicide. The Enlightenment embrace of this kind of metaphysical individualism, in such a view, was indeed a dramatic turn in the history of the West. But rather than standing as the final and most advanced stage in the history of our understanding of who we are, it seems instead to be the final step in the decline from Luther to Descartes to Kant to Nietzsche, a self-conception that destroys the possibility of a meaningful and worthwhile existence.

As an antidote to this condition we have been arguing that the basic phenomenon of Homeric polytheism—the whooshing up that focuses one for a while and then lets one go—is still available in American culture today. This source of meaning, of course, stands in direct contrast with the ideals of Enlightenment individualism, for at least the simple reason that whooshing up takes its start in the response of a community rather than of the individual. It is in this kind of community, for example, that Ishmael felt he could go on squeezing spermaceti forever. And the moment of exultation in a ballgame can be like that as well: one wishes it would last forever while knowing that it can't. That sort of moment offers what autonomy cannot: a sense that you are participating in something that transcends what you can contribute to it.

There is something enormously hopeful in the idea that we might be able to resist the sense that life is meaningless by appropriating and developing our receptivity to this ancient phenomenon. And if things were easy we would be able to stop the story here. But the potential cost of this appropriation is apparently prohibitive. For surely no way of living that leaves us open to fascist rhetoricians is tenable. We are stuck, therefore, between Scylla and Charybdis: a nihilistic and meaningless life on one side, a meaningful but potentially abhorrent one on the other.

Unfortunately, we cannot steer between these dangers simply by embracing Homer's polytheism. There are things in Homer by which we are rightly repulsed, and it would be regressive to call for a return to them. In the *Iliad*, for example, after Achilles kills Hector, he drags the body around the walls of the city of Troy for three days straight in a kind of manic heroic madness. Homer does not applaud this notorious action. But he doesn't condemn it either; he just describes how it affects Hector's father Priam. We must position ourselves so that we can condemn an act like this even if we find ourselves in a crowd drawn to applaud it at the time. Homer is dangerously noncommittal on this crucial point.

EVERYTHING WE HAVE SAID so far is in vain if we can't avoid the danger to which Homer leaves himself open. The correct response to this danger begins with the observation that fortunately, besides ecstatic *physis,* there are other sacred practices left in our culture. Properly understood and appropriated, these other notions of the sacred preserve *physis* at its best while forbidding its repellent manifestations. Before we can understand this response to the dangers of *physis,* however, we need to examine a kind of sacred practice still available at the margins of our culture that will lay the groundwork for putting *physis* in its proper place.

That nurturing practice was called *poiesis.* Until about a hundred years ago, the cultivating and nurturing practices of *poiesis* organized a central way things mattered. The *poietic* style manifested itself, among other places, in the craftsman's skills for bringing things out at their best. This is an ancient practice in the culture that was already recognized in Homer's world where Hephaestus, the craft god, brought forth shining things, and Homer's Greeks stood in wonder before them. But Hephaestus was a marginal figure in the Homeric Greek pantheon. It wasn't until Aeschylus that Athena's *poietic* style of bringing the culture out at its best organized the understanding of everything that is. This cultivating, craftsman-like, *poietic* understanding of how to bring out meanings at their best was alive and well into the late nineteenth century, but it is under attack in our technological age.

Despite the general trend away from the development of *poietic* skills, there are some domains in which they are still essential. The skill of playing baseball, or tennis, or piano, for example, is still something that we teach in a relatively traditional way. We assign exercises that teach the aspiring athlete or musician how to respond automatically and well to certain kinds of situations—a groundball to the left side, a three-octave run—and on the basis of these exercises we expect the beginner to gain technical proficiency in the domain. Still, this method of learning strikes some as drudgery, and the kind of automaticity that it develops can seem too trivial a prize for such hard work

In fact, skills are a much richer phenomenon than this picture suggests. We can begin to understand this by noticing that the achievement of skill involves substantially more than the mere acquisition of a physical ability. Learning a skill is learning to see the world differently. The skilled surgeon, for example, sees something more than a broken and bloody leg; he sees a particular kind of break, one that requires this precise surgical technique to fix it. Likewise, we hear people say that the successful running back has "great vision," the point guard has extraordinary "court sense." In each case this means that the person's skill at surgery or running or passing allows them to see meaningful distinctions that others without their skill cannot.

To get a fuller sense for this phenomenon, we need to think about something more wide-ranging than mere physical skills. We need to return to a time when craftsmen's skills were central to the way people lived their lives.

Take the wheelwright at the end of the nineteenth century, for example. The wheelwright's shop was inhabited by workmen who had learned their skill by apprenticing to masters of the craft. This notion of skill, or more broadly of craftsmanship, that organized the life of the wheelwright was much wider and more pervasive than our own. Whereas we understand skill primarily in terms of technical proficiency, the wheelwright's conception goes beyond this in at least three important ways. George Sturt, the last in a succession of wheelwrights, wrote about this traditional conception of his craft nearly one hundred years ago.[19] We can begin with the wheelwright's skilled understanding of the wood itself. Sturt writes:

> I have known old-fashioned workmen refuse to use likely-looking timber because they held it to be unfit for the job.
> And they knew. The skilled workman was the final judge.
> Under the plane (it is little used now) or under the axe (it is

all but obsolete) timber disclosed qualities hardly to be found otherwise. My own eyes know because my own hands have felt, but I cannot teach an outsider, the difference between ash that is "tough as whipcord," and ash that is "frow as a carrot," or "doaty," or "biscuity." In oak, in beech, these differences are equally plain, yet only to those who have been initiated by practical work.[20]

Sturt is emphasizing here what we have glimpsed in the skilled athlete; like the running back who immediately sees the hole, the skilled workman has learned from years of experience how to discern distinctions of worth that those without his skill cannot see. But Sturt highlights something that we have not noticed yet: the precise connection between the worker's physical abilities and the distinctions he can discern. The timber discloses qualities under the axe or the plane, according to Sturt, that it does not reveal otherwise. It is only because one has felt these distinctions in one's hands that one can identify them by sight. This ability to see what is worthwhile cannot be taught to the outsider, since it is not a matter of distinguishing shades of color or texture or some other merely visible property in the wood. Rather, it is seeing immediately how the wood will respond to an axe or saw or plane, seeing immediately how it will bear up or collapse under the weight of a carriage. To see these distinctions in the environment requires skill in chopping and sawing and planing the wood, in building the wheels and putting them on the carriage in a way that suits the needs of the farmer for whom it is made. This vision of skill is essentially practical and embodied.

It is worth noting that although there is nothing *mysterious* about this vision of the master wheelwright—it is in no way magical or supernatural—nevertheless this phenomenon is already a revelation. For considered properly it is the clue to a whole new understanding of who we are. The wheelwright sees meaningful distinctions *in the wood*—distinctions of worth and of quality—that in no way find their source in him. The skilled craftsman does not *decide* to treat the ash as if it were "frow as a carrot," the way David Foster Wallace decides to treat the lady in the checkout line as if she were on her way to the hospital. Rather, the fact of the matter is out in the world. The task of the craftsman is not to *generate* the meaning, but rather to *cultivate* in himself the skill for *discerning* the meanings that are *already there.*

But there is more to this phenomenon as well. For it is not just that the wheelwright can discern a few distinctions; his understanding of the wood is detailed and rich. Sturt is clear about this in a way that the contemporary examples are not. Indeed, the truly skilled craftsman, according to Sturt, understands that every piece of wood he works with is distinct and has its own personality, its own individuality. Each piece throws up different obstacles than the last, or makes possible approaches to it that the previous pieces did not. To be a true master of the wood, one must be able to recognize precisely how *it* requires to be worked:

> [The woodworker] had no band-saw (as now) to drive, with ruthless unintelligence, through every resistance. The timber was far from being a prey, a helpless victim, to a machine. Rather it would lend its own subtle virtues to the man who knew how to humour it: with him, as with an understanding friend, it would co-operate.[21]

Sturt's description here gives us a second enrichment of the notion of skill. For the master of wood, each piece he works with, and therefore more generally each woodworking situation in which he finds himself, is unique. The master's skill for working with wood, therefore, involves intelligence and flexibility rather than rote and automatic response. This does not mean that the master is constantly planning out his actions; his ingenuity is practical, embodied, and in the moment. The master workman will rarely do the same thing twice.

Finally, and perhaps most important, the uniqueness of each situation gives a sacred dimension to the craftsmanship. Because each piece of wood is distinct, has its own personality, on Sturt's account, the woodworker has an intimate relationship with the wood he is working. Its subtle virtues call out to be cultivated and cared for. This sense of intimacy with the wood initiates in the woodworker a feeling of care and respect for it. But it is not just the wood alone, as if it sprang fully cut and dried into his workshop. The wood has a place of origin, too, so the master becomes familiar with the local soil, the terrain, and the sources of water that nourish the trees. He comes to know intimately the weather and the seasons, since they change the way the trees will respond to his saw; and he knows that timber cut in the wintertime dries differently from that cut in the late spring or summer or fall. Ultimately this diverse practical knowledge instills in the woodworker a connection to his countryside and his land that goes beyond a mere sense of responsibility to it. Indeed, Sturt speaks of the *craftsman's reverence for the land and countryside* in which he lives. This sense of reverence for a place goes far beyond our notion of skill as automatic technical proficiency and begins to tie it to a sense of the sacred—and ultimately to bringing ourselves out at our best.

Sturt is perhaps most eloquent about the wheelwright's reverence for his countryside when he contrasts it with the development of the modern world. As the craftsman's skill and intelligence for working with the land is replaced by the "ruthless unintelligence" of machines, the sense of reverence for the countryside is quickly lost.

[T]here had been a close relationship between the tree-clad country-side and the English who dwelt there. But now, the affection and the reverence bred of this—for it had been with something near to reverence that a true provincial beheld his native trees—was all but gone. A sort of greedy prostitution desecrated the ancient woods. All round me I saw and heard of things being done with a light heart that had always seemed to me wicked—things as painful to my sympathies as harnessing a carriage-horse to a heavy dray, or as pulling down a cathedral to get building-stone.[22]

The trees that furnish the material for the wheelwright's craft, therefore, are much more than the collection of physical properties that describe them. Like the stones of the cathedral, they are sacred and must be treated with care and reverence. To do otherwise is desecration.

Sturt's account establishes a rich and appealing notion of skill. In place of the technical proficiency of an isolated and autonomous individual, Sturt's craftsman exists entirely in relation with his domain. Like any good relationship, each side brings out the other at its best. It is because the craftsman is an intelligent observer of wood and not a ruthless and unintelligent machine, that the wood can reveal to him its subtle virtues. But it is because the wood has these virtues already that the craftsman can cultivate in himself the skill for discerning them and ultimately can come to feel reverence and responsibility for the wood and where it lives. There is, therefore, a kind of feedback loop between craftsman and craft: each jointly cultivates the other into a state of mutual understanding and respect.[23] We have seen the name Aristotle gave to this dual cultivation of craftsman and craft. He called it *poiesis*.

Unfortunately, the cultivation of *craftsman-like* skill will not by itself annul the dangers of *physis*. Even master wheelwrights with reverence for the land were swept up by the power of Hitler's rhetoric. But the notion that skills reveal meaningful differences is crucial nevertheless. There is another kind of *poietic* skill that no one has noticed yet, although it is already at work in people's lives: the higher-order skill for responding to meaningful distinctions between dangerous and benign ways of being swept away. The person who has acquired this skill knows that it's not *always* appropriate to walk away from the crowd—getting caught up in the mood of "I have a dream," and rising with 200,000 people to cheer Dr. King, is not an event one should be proud to have walked away from. Indeed, if everyone on the National Mall that day had walked away or merely responded with coolly considered rational approval, the event would have failed to have the effect it did, and the world we live in would be poorer for it.

To recognize when it's appropriate to let oneself be swept up and when it's appropriate to walk away is a higher-order skill that is crucial for us in the contemporary world. To acquire this skill, like any skill, requires taking risks as we shall see later. For the moment, however, it is sufficient to note that such a skill allows us to cultivate one prominent form of the sacred available in the culture today. *Meta-poiesis,* as one might call it, steers between the twin dangers of the secular age: it resists nihilism by reappropriating the sacred phenomenon of *physis,* but cultivates the skill to resist *physis* in its abhorrent, fanatical form. Living well in our secular, nihilistic age, therefore, requires the higher-order skill of recognizing when to rise up as one with the ecstatic crowd and when to turn heel and walk rapidly away.

We shall return to *meta-poiesis* in a moment. But first we need to see how the understanding of ourselves on which it depends—the understanding of human beings as beings who reveal meaningful differences through the cultivation of skills—is itself under attack in the technological age.

IF WILD, ECSTATIC *PHYSIS* is the sacred realm of meaning still evident today, gentle, nurturing *poiesis* is a dying art. In part this is the result of our own success: advances in technology have diminished the importance of specialized skills in contemporary life. Indeed, perhaps the central goal of modern technology is to make every domain accessible to everyone, no matter what his or her level of skill. "Even a child can do it!" is the mantra of the technological age. To cook a meal is to press a button, to travel across the country is to step on a plane.

To navigate an unfamiliar terrain is to turn left or right whenever the Global Positioning System (GPS) says. Technology improves our lives by making hard things easier. That is a basic axiom of the contemporary world.

But the improvements of technology are impoverishments as well. The GPS covers over the meaningful distinctions that the art of skilled navigation revealed. To the extent that technology strips away the need for skill, it strips away the possibility of meaning as well. To have a skill is to know what counts or is worthwhile in a certain domain. Skills reveal meaningful differences to us and cultivate in us a sense of responsibility to bring these out at their best. To the extent that it takes away the need for skill, technology flattens out human life.

There are two aspects to this flattening. First, the world itself begins to look increasingly nondescript. That is what Sturt means when he says that the local knowledge of timber has died: for most people nowadays the distinction between ash that is "frow as a carrot" and ash that is "tough as whipcord"—a genuine distinction of meaning and worth—is no longer recognizable. Myriad other endangered distinctions, previously revealed by the skillful craft of woodwork, have slipped into obscurity with its death. Because the band saw never met a knot it couldn't tackle, for example, there is no need anymore for one to see the distinction between the knot that is an obstacle to be deftly avoided and the knot that can be turned to advantage, to strengthen the piece. The inability to recognize this distinction lowers the quality of the product: as Sturt says, the felloes produced by machine may look better to some "theorist from the office," but the skilled craftsman can see that they were made completely without intelligence. Even worse than losing quality, however, is losing the skill for telling the difference. As we lose our knowledge of craft, the world looks increasingly devoid of distinctions of worth.

Flattened out along with this worldly loss of meaning is our understanding of ourselves. Moods of affection and reverence—born of close and skillful attention to distinctions of worth in a domain—are nearly lost to us. Perhaps Lou Gehrig's speech was moving not just because Gehrig was a dying hero, but because the crowd's response to him proved that these moods are available to us still. But the loss of reverence is important for another reason. Reverence reveals us as cultivators of meaningful distinctions. To revere the timber, after all, is not just to hold it up as worthy of our amazement, but to care for it and bring it out at its best—to let it shine. As technology strips away the need for skill, it strips away too this noble understanding of ourselves as cultivators of meaning.

Understood in this context, the march of technology presents a grave danger. The danger lies not in particular technological advances or technological gadgets, but in the understanding of ourselves and of what we can aspire to that a technological *way of life* encourages. To aspire to a life that requires no skill to live it well is to embrace the flattened world of contemporary nihilism. The appropriate response to this danger is not to reject technology per se, but to accept individual technological advances while preserving the *poietic* practices that resist a technological way of life.

Take the GPS, for example. There is something convenient about this device with which you are never lost. Occasionally, of course, it tells you to take a sharp right turn when you are in the middle of a long bridge. But this kind of inadequacy will soon be ironed out. For those of us who are directionally challenged (and both authors count ourselves among this group) the GPS seems to offer a great technological advance.

But notice the hidden cost to this advance. When the GPS is navigating for you, your understanding of the environment is about as minimal as it can possibly be. It consists of knowing things like "I should turn right now." In the best case—and we want to take the best case here—this method of navigating gets you to your destination quickly and easily. But it completely trivializes the noble art of navigation, which was the province of great cultures from the seafaring Phoenicians to the navigators of the Age of Discovery. To navigate by GPS requires no sense of where you are, no sense of where you're going, and no sense whatsoever for how to get there. Indeed, the whole point of the GPS is to spare you the trouble of navigating.

But to lose the sense of struggle is to lose the sensitivities—to landmarks, street signs, wind direction, the height of the sun, the stars—all the meaningful distinctions that navigational skill reveals. To navigate by GPS is to endure a series of meaningless pauses at the end of which you do precisely what you are told. There is something deeply dehumanizing about this: it's like being the central figure in a Beckett play without the jokes. Indeed, in an important sense this experience turns you into an automated device the GPS can use to arrive at its destination. This is one of the ways the world can be, and at times it is the best the world can be. But to aim for this as an entire way of life is to lose touch with the skill and care, the reverence and awe, that are some of the moods that bring out human beings at their best.

Caring for the goods of a worthwhile domain and cultivating the skill for revealing meaningful distinctions within it are necessary for resisting the technological way of life. But you can't just decide to care about a domain, any more than you can make a decision about whom to love. How is anyone to discover what is worth caring about?

The fact is, whether you know it or not, you already care about a whole range of goods. Just as the world is pregnant with meanings waiting to be revealed, human beings are filled with modes of caring that they have hidden from themselves. This may seem surprising. The idea that our cares exceed our understanding of them seems an affront to fundamental principles of self-knowledge. Surely, if I care about something then I am in a position to know that I do. The Enlightenment tradition of autonomy suggests such a principle, and contemporary philosophy takes it virtually as an article of faith. But to be an embodied being as we are, open to moods that can direct us and reveal the world as meaningful, just is to be a being who extends beyond what we can know about ourselves. The project, then, is not to *decide* what to care about, but to *discover* what it is about which one already cares.

Let's take a simple example. You get up in the morning, stumble down to the kitchen, and make coffee. Does it matter which cup you choose as the vessel for your morning drink? Or is the cup completely irrelevant to the morning coffee drinking routine? If it could have been any old cup, if the Styrofoam cup would have done as well as the fine china, then we can say that you are using the cup as a mere resource. That's because you are treating it as something that is completely exchangeable. The particular cup, the cup in all its uniqueness, has become completely generic and banal.

Notice the strong contrast between the banality of the generic cup and the uniqueness of the wood in the wheelwright's shop. The intimacy that characterized the wheelwright's relation to his wood—the sense that it was an understanding friend, that it would reveal its subtle virtues to the skilled individual who knew how to bring them out at their best—that sense of the routine of woodworking as a sacred ritual shot through with intimacy, meaning, and worth, is completely lacking from the generic coffee drinking routine. To treat the cup as totally irrelevant to the task is to approach the coffee with ruthless unintelligence; to turn what might have been a revered domain into something completely devoid of worth.

But what is there to a cup, you might well ask, beyond the generic function of holding liquid? Surely any appropriately shaped object can perform such a function equally well. It is worth noting in passing how strange this observation would sound if made about certain kinds of cups: the simple cups of the Japanese tea ceremony, for instance, or the Holy Grail used by Jesus at the Last Supper. But perhaps these are exceptional cases. How can it be any insult to the cup, or indeed to the coffee-drinking routine as a whole, for me to care so little about it?

This generic way of treating the cup, and the coffee it holds, obscures its meaningful distinctions, diminishing the quality of the coffee we drink, as the unskilled coffee drinker necessarily fails to choose better ways of serving it over worse. The situation is eerily reminiscent of Sturt's complaint. Indeed, the ruthless unintelligence of Sturt's hated band saw mirrors the generic unintelligence of the Styrofoam cup. The generic cup, in its stupidity, treats every coffee and every coffee-drinking situation as if it were indistinguishable from the last.

To approach the domain of coffee drinking this way is to dehumanize yourself as well. Like navigating by GPS, the coffee-drinking routine that recognizes no distinctions of worth is a routine in which the coffee drinker becomes exchangeable: assimilable to all of the millions of others who are sleepwalking through the same generic routine. If the cup is exchangeable in the activity, then so are you. To treat the cup as a mere resource is to treat yourself as a mere resource too, to dehumanize yourself by failing to recognize the care you might have shown for that domain.

Now, perhaps there is nothing wrong with this some of the time. One cannot expect every moment of one's existence to be a sacred celebration of meaning and worth. Indeed, there is probably something about us that resists this or even makes it impossible. But to endure the absence of meaning is one thing, to embrace it another. If we are to be human beings at all, we must distinguish ourselves from others; there must be moments when we rise up out of the generic and banal and into the particular and skillfully engaged. But how is one to know whether the coffee-drinking ritual is one of these moments?

The answer is that one must learn to see. That you already care about coffee drinking is something you may have hidden from yourself. To find out whether this is so, ask whether you take the routine to be functionally exchangeable. The morning ritual is delightful in part because it wakes you up. But would anything that woke you up be equally good? Would a quick snort of cocaine substitute in a pinch? Or if that's too extreme, then perhaps a small caffeine pill that one could swallow on the way to the car? To the extent that these exchanges seem appealing, then the coffee really is just performing the function of waking you up. In that case any form of stimulant would do. But to the extent that these do not seem appealing substitutes, there are aspects of the coffee-drinking ritual that go beyond its function, aspects about which you already care.

If you do care about drinking coffee in the morning, then there are meaningful distinctions to the ritual that are worth uncovering. The clue to revealing these distinctions lies in further simple questions you must ask yourself. Why exactly do you prefer a cup of coffee to a caffeine pill or to a cup of tea? Is there something in the coffee itself, not just in its stimulating effect but in its aroma, its warmth, the ritual of drinking it, or something else—that drives you to this activity rather than some other? And to the extent that there is, then what kind of coffee, what kind of coffee-making process, what kind of coffee-drinking companions or coffee-drinking places, what kind of coffee cup would bring these things out best?

These are not questions you can answer in the abstract. You need to try it out and see. If it is the warmth of the coffee on a winter's day that you like, then drinking it in a cozy corner of the house, perhaps by a fire with a blanket, in a cup that transmits the warmth to your hands might well help to bring out the best in this ritual. If it is the striking black color of the coffee that attracts your eye and enhances the aroma, then perhaps a cup with a shiny white ceramic interior will bring this out. But there is no single answer to the question of what makes the ritual appealing, and it takes experimentation and observation, with its risks and rewards, to discover the meaningful distinctions yourself. This experimentation with and observation of the coffee ultimately develops in you the skill for seeing the relevant features of the ritual and ultimately develops the skills for bringing them out at their best. These skills are manifold: the skill for knowing how to pick exactly the right coffee, exactly the right cup, exactly the right place to drink it, and to cultivate exactly the right companions to drink it with. When one has learned these skills and cultivated one's environment so that it is precisely suited to them, then one has a ritual rather than a routine, a meaningful celebration of oneself and one's environment rather than a generic and meaningless performance of a function.

There are a wide variety of domains worth caring about and there are no objective, context-independent principles for determining which domains these are. You just have to try it out and see. Some people care about mathematics, others about music, some prefer baseball and others bullfighting. Some prefer drinking a local wine with their friends. Whether a domain is worth caring about is determined by whether it appropriately elicits further and further meaningful involvement with it.

Because there are no objective rules about this, one must constantly be open to the possibility that the domain to which one is drawn will reveal itself as too brutal or too trivial or too isolating or too dull or in some other way inappropriate for bringing out everything at its best. One must be prepared, as Helen was, to regret having been drawn into such a world and to allow oneself to be drawn to a more rich and meaningful one. This risk of regret is the risk associated with everything meaningful, a risk without which our lives would descend to meaninglessness and boredom, expressionlessness and angst.

THIS BRINGS US BACK to *meta-poiesis*. For recall that in addition to the first-order skills for operating within a domain, we moderns must also develop the higher-order, *meta-poietic* skills for bringing out *physis* at its best. In addition to the gentle, nurturing skills of the craftsman's sacred domains, our culture also harbors a wild, ecstatic form of the sacred. But we saw that this has a dangerous side. How can we develop the skills to distinguish when it's appropriate to rise up as one with the ecstatic crowd and when it's appropriate to walk away?

The stakes are high here. We've seen already that without the ecstatic form of the sacred our world would be a poorer place. After all, crowds can rise up as one to change the mood of a culture in positive and transformative ways; without the phenomenon of *physis* such radical, paradigm-shifting changes would never occur. We need to find a way, therefore, to skillfully appropriate the phenomenon of *physis,* to bring out this form of the sacred at its best. We cannot rest content with the safe but lazy, rational approach of rejecting *physis* altogether.

A new kind of courage is required for this path. In place of the Kantian courage to resist the madness of crowds, we need the courage to leap in and experience it. Sometimes, as with Martin Luther King on the Mall, things will turn out extraordinarily well: paradigms will shift and the culture will come to understand itself in new and more shining and meaningful ways. Sometimes, by contrast, one dances with the devil. Like Ishmael being drawn into the contagious mood of Ahab's monomaniacal quest, one can only survive its fiery darkness if one learns by experience the dangerous world it reveals. Only by having been taken over by the fanatical leader's totalizing rhetoric, and experienced the dangerous and devastating consequences it has, does one learn to discriminate between leaders worth following and those upon whom one must turn one's back.

Developing any skill necessarily involves risk. Whether it is the skill of fielding ground balls or making coffee, or the meta-skill of bringing out *physis* at its best, one does not become a master without taking chances and learning from the consequences of one's mistakes. But our culture calls for a special kind of skill. The hidden history of the West—the history of the ways the practices have gathered to reveal the possibility of sacred, shining things—has bequeathed to us not one form of the sacred, but a variety of different and incompatible types. *Physis, poiesis,* and technology show us, respectively, a wild, ecstatic sacred that lifts us up like a wave; a gentle, nurturing style that brings things out at their sacred best; and an autonomous and self-sufficient way of life that laughs at everything of sacred worth.

Having taken the risk required in learning, the special, *meta-poietic* skill called for at this stage of our history, then, is the skill to give each of these sacred modes of gathering its due. The master of living in our poly-sacred world will understand immediately and without reflection that one moment calls for the microwave, while another moment calls for a grateful feast. He will have acquired the skill to let himself be overwhelmed by the ecstatic and wild gods of sport, but the discrimination to keep himself from being drawn in by the rhetoric of the fanatical and dangerous demagogue. He will live a life attuned to the shining things and so will have opened a place to which all the gods may return.

Are we saying that everyone *ought* to live a polytheistic life? No. Ours is not a moralistic claim, but a claim about what the gods are calling us to do. It is a natural temptation to ask why one *should* hear the call, or why one *should* heed it if it makes itself heard. But these moralizing temptations must be avoided. There is no *reason* why one ought to hear or respond to the call of the gods: callings just demand to be heard and obeyed. We in our culture are being called to cultivate ourselves as beings who are sensitive to what we are called to do. The calling is there, and those who are sensitive enough to the culture and to its rich heritage will hear it. But our focus on ourselves as isolated, autonomous agents has had the effect of banishing the gods—that is to say, covering up or blocking our sensitivity to what is sacred in the world. The gods are calling us but we have ceased to listen. They are calling us to cultivate our sensitivity, but like Dante's sinners, we have closed ourselves off by telling ourselves that we ought to be self-sufficient.

As autonomous subjects we have closed ourselves off to the calling of the gods, and it is in this sense that we have banished them. Nobody seems to have noticed this. Martin Buber talks about the eclipse of God, Beckett about how we are waiting for God to return. Others talk about God's absence, withdrawal, or death. But the picture we are offering turns on its head the traditional twentieth-century narrative.

The gods have not withdrawn or abandoned us: we have kicked them out. They are waiting plaintively for us to hear their call. Ask not why the gods have abandoned you, but why you have abandoned the gods.

THE INTENSE AND MEANINGFUL world of Homer's Greeks evidently shone with sacred force. Our technological world, by contrast, seems impoverished and dull. We cannot return to Homer's world, and we should not hope to do so. But we can become receptive to a modern pantheon of gods—to the ways in which Gehrig and Federer shine, the ways in which Marilyn Monroe or Albert Einstein changed how we see the world in which we live. And we can also lure back the gods of old—the great works that were venerated once before and now can be re-experienced in their sacred worth. To do this requires more than simply canonizing these works on reading lists and classroom syllabi. It requires developing the skills for responding to the manifold senses of the sacred that still linger unappreciated at the margins of our disenchanted world.

These notions of the sacred are richer and more varied than anything Homer ever knew. For his gods shared a common style; they literally had a family resemblance with one another. Whether it was Aphrodite's sacred erotic world or Ares's sacred world of war, Athena's world of practical wisdom or Hephaestus's world of beautifully wrought, shining things, the sacred worlds of all the Homeric gods had something in common: they whooshed up like a wave and carried one for a while, before finally losing power and letting one go. This sense of the sacred as *physis* is still available at the margins of our culture today, but it is not the only kind of sacred open to us.

In addition to *physis*, we also have a *poietic* conception of the sacred that was completely absent in Homer's age, a sense of being able to cultivate the world, to develop the skills needed to bring it out at its shining best. This *poietic* understanding of the sacred comes in many forms. Whether it is Jesus' sense that the world is best revealed through the light of His mood of agape love, or Dante's sense that we can teach ourselves the skill to be receptive to the love that moves the sun and the other stars; whether it is Aeschylus's sense that we can bring out the culture at its best by finding an appropriate place for all its nascent forces or Sturt's sense that we can dwell in a natural world of sacred worth, these *poietic* accounts of the sacred are gentle and nurturing in a way that was alien to Homer's world.

And in addition to all these accounts of the sacred, we also have a technological conception of the world, an efficient and resourceful understanding of things that allows us to produce and control what is. The world is this way too at times—not sacred but devoid of intrinsic worth, ready to be molded to our desires and will.

The practices have gathered throughout the history of the West to reveal these manifold ways the world is. Perhaps there are other ways the practices have gathered too. But only now, released from the ancient temptation to monotheism, can we find a place for each of these ways of being in our contemporary world. The polytheism that gets all these ways in balance will be more varied and more vibrant than anything Homer ever knew.[24]

This contemporary Polytheistic world will be a wonderful world of sacred shining things.

EPILOGUE

TWO STUDENTS HAD STUDIED for many years with a wise old master. One day the master said to them, "Students, the time has come for you to go out into the world. Your life there will be felicitous if you find in it all things shining."

The students left the master with a mixture of sadness and excitement, and each of them went a separate way. Many years later they met up by chance. They were happy to see one another again, and each was excited to learn how the other's life had gone.

Said the first to the second, glumly, "I have learned to see many shining things in the world, but alas I remain unhappy. For I also find many sad and disappointing things, and I feel I have failed to heed the master's advice. Perhaps I will never be filled with happiness and joy, because I am simply unable to find all things shining."

Said the second to the first, radiant with happiness, "All things are not shining, but all the shining things are."

ACKNOWLEDGMENTS

Isaac Newton said famously, "If I have seen further than other men, it is because I have stood upon the shoulders of giants." Unable to climb to such lofty heights, we have articulated in this book intuitions that have come primarily from standing upon each other's shoulders. Each of us is, therefore, grateful in the first place to his coauthor for the contortions, extensions, offerings, suppressions, and support that have made such a wonderful working relationship come to be.

Moreover, we are grateful to the many people around us who have made this acrobatic act possible: Liv Duesund, who invited us to the University of Oslo in 2006 to work out our nascent ideas on embodiment in Homer; Michael Sandel and Charles Taylor, who encouraged us to introduce the issue of polytheism to a seminar on Taylor's book *A Secular Age* at Harvard University in 2009; Joseph Schear and Wayne Martin, who offered us the opportunity to discuss a portion of the final manuscript with philosophers at Christ Church College, Oxford, in 2010; Taylor Carman, Eugene Chislenko, Stephen Mulhall, George Pattison, and Mark Wrathall, who discussed the issues with us there at a deep and satisfying level; Tao Ruspoli, whose fantastic film *Being in the World* was being produced at the same time as our book and whose probing questions were a great opportunity to explore the issues in the book from another perspective; Charles Spinosa, whose feedback was always fascinating and instantaneous and often led us in new directions; Jill Kneerim, our literary agent, who helped us navigate the foreign but marvelous world of trade publishing;

Hilary Redmon, our editor at Free Press, whose initiative began this project and whose patient and steady hand kept it on track throughout many deviations and much craziness; and Geneviève Boissier-Dreyfus and Cheryl Kelly Chen, whose support—both technical, philosophical, and otherwise—made this book possible and to whom in part it is dedicated.

We would also like to thank various students and former students who gave us feedback, technical advice, and in some cases extraordinary research assistance. Julie Rhee put in an enormous amount of work on the copyediting, and it is no exaggeration to say that this book would not exist without her help; Adam Spinosa, Billy Eck, and Céline Leboeuf all helped in one way or another as research assistants or discussants and would gladly have helped more if we'd asked them to; and, of course, all the students of Philosophy 6: From Gods to God and Back at U.C. Berkeley and of Culture and Belief 14: The Experience of the Sacred in the History of the West at Harvard, who have suffered through poorer versions of this story and have helped it to become richer and more relevant.

And thanks, finally, to the gods, who show themselves little by little or sometimes all at once and for whom we hope this book provides an appropriate landing place to welcome you back home.

Chapter 1. Our Contemporary Nihilism

1. "Early Blooms in Brooklyn," *New York Sun,* January 3, 2007.
2. The following account is taken from Cara Buckley, "Man Is Rescued by Stranger on Subway Tracks," *New York Times,* January 3, 2007, as well as from several other *Times* articles that appeared in the days following the incident.
3. "State of the Union," *New York Times,* January 24, 2007. See also, "Subway Rescuer Receives the City's Highest Award," *New York Times,* January 5, 2007.
4. "Why Our Hero Leapt onto the Tracks and We Might Not," *New York Times,* January 7, 2007.
5. "A Big Hero in the Big City," *New York Times,* January 4, 2007.
6. "Heroes Rush In, but What Would Average Joe Do?" *New York Times,* January 7, 2007.
7. Op. cit., "Man Is Rescued by Stranger."
8. Quoted in op. cit., "Heroes Rush In."
9. John McPhee, *A Sense of Where You Are: A Profile of Bill Bradley at Princeton* (New York: Farrar, Straus and Giroux, 1999). Originally published in 1965.
10. Ibid., p. 156.
11. Ibid., p. 61.
12. Ibid., pp. 86–88.
13. We shall see in the Dante chapter that this characterization is a bit of an exaggeration. For it was not strictly speaking inconceivable to Dante that a person should willfully choose his own identity. But far from its being the natural or necessary condition of man, as we assume in the contemporary world, Dante took this kind of willful choice to be the worst kind of rebellion against God. Indeed, he reserves the lowest levels of Hell for people engaged in such activity.
14. See his new magnum opus, *A Secular Age* (Cambridge, MA: Harvard University Press, 2007). See also, Charles M. Blow, "Heaven for the Godless?" *New York Times,* December 27, 2008, an op-ed piece that reports on a recent survey from the Pew Forum on Religion and Public Life. The survey shows that 70 percent of Americans believe that people from religions other than their own can achieve eternal life.

Chapter 2. David Foster Wallace's Nihilism

1. See, for example, David Lipsky, "The Lost Years and Last Days of David Foster Wallace," *Rolling Stone,* October 30, 2008, for an example of the former claim. See A. O. Scott, "The Best Mind of His Generation," *New York Times,* September 21, 2008, for an example of the latter.

2. Quoted in D. T. Max, "The Unfinished," *The New Yorker,* March 9, 2009. Original from Larry McCaffery's 1991 interview available at: www.dalkeyarchive .com/interviews/show/21

3. Lipsky, op. cit.

4. See Bruce Weber's obituary "David Foster Wallace, Influential Writer, Dies at 46," *New York Times,* September 15, 2008.

5. See Mary Karr, *Lit: A Memoir* (New York: Harper, 2009).

6. Available at: www.salon.com/09/features/wallace1.html

7. Quoted in D. T. Max, op. cit., p. 54.

8. Interview with Bookreporter at: www.bookreporter.com/authors/au-gilbert-elizabeth.asp#view060324.

9. Elizabeth Gilbert, *Eat, Pray, Love* (New York: Penguin Books, 2006), p. 10 (hereafter, EPL, followed by page number.)

10. McCaffery interview available at: www.dalkeyarchive.com/interviews/show/21.

11. Quoted in Max, op. cit., p. 58.

12. Quoted in Max, op. cit., p. 60.

13. Quoted in Max, op. cit., p. 57.

14. Interview available at: www.charlierose.com/view/interview/5639. The quoted passage begins at 3:16. No reference to the famous biblical passage is implied or intended.

15. *Infinite Jest,* p. 230. David Foster Wallace, *Infinite Jest* (Boston: Little, Brown, 1996), p. 230 (hereafter, *Infinite Jest,* followed by page number).

16. Ibid., p. 940.

17. Ibid., p. 54.

18. *Hamlet,* Act V, Scene 1, line 185.

19. As the world of Hank Hoyne was collapsed, after an accidental viewing of the film. See *Infinite Jest,* pp. 507–508.

20. Wallace complained constantly that critics—even those who thought highly of his book—had missed the deep sadness in it. See, for example, the Salon interview from 1996 and the Charlie Rose interview from the following year.

21. Quoted in Max, op. cit., p. 57.

22. These include "Good People," *The New Yorker,* February 5, 2007; "The Compliance Branch," *Harper's Magazine,* February 2008; "Wiggle Room," *The New Yorker,* March 9, 2009. In addition, further passages from the manuscript are quoted in D. T. Max's article.

23. "Wiggle Room," p. 63.

24. Ibid.

25. As reported in D. T. Max.

26. *Infinite Jest,* pp. 859–60.

27. Ibid., p. 860.
28. Ibid.
29. Ibid., pp. 860–61.
30. *Salon* interview.
31. Ibid.
32. D. T. Max.
33. Quoted in D. T. Max.
34. Romans 7:7–10, in the New International Version translation.
35. *Infinite Jest*, p. 205.
36. Friederich Nietzsche, *The Gay Science*, trans. Walter Kaufmann (New York: Vintage Books, 1974), p. 242.
37. Indeed, there is amazingly little discussion of God at all in the book. To the extent there is, it is mostly dismissive. Early on, for example, it is intimated that Hal is asked on a regular basis by his brother Mario—whom he sometimes calls "Boo"—whether he believes in God. Hal hates the question, avoids it at all cost. At one point, however, when forced to take a stand, he suggests that if there is a God then he is not to be admired:

> So tonight to shush you how about if I say I have administrative bones to pick with God, Boo. I'll say God seems to have a kind of laid-back management style I'm not crazy about. I'm pretty much anti-death. God looks by all accounts to be pro-death. I'm not seeing how we can get together on this issue, he and I, Boo. (*Infinite Jest*, p. 40)

38. This Nietzschean interpretation of Wallace is contradicted by certain passages in *Infinite Jest*. Not surprisingly. Wallace's position is nothing like a single, well-developed philosophical view; it is more like a pastiche of observations, many of which conflict with one another but seem somehow not, in virtue of this, to weaken one another. Nietzsche's own perspectivism about truth comes to mind. In any case, one important passage in this context appears on p. 291. The narrator reports there that:

> What metro Boston AAs are trite but correct about is that both destiny's kisses and its dope-slaps illustrate an individual person's basic personal powerlessness over the really meaningful events in his life: i.e., almost nothing important that ever happens to you happens because you engineer it. Destiny has no beeper; destiny always leans trenchcoated out of an alley with some sort of *Psst* that you usually can't even hear because you're in such a rush to or from something important you've tried to engineer.

The contrast between this view and the view that someone like Gately can engineer his own, personal, blissful experience of pain by willfully attending to it in the right way—this apparently obvious conflict might be explainable by emphasizing the difference between destiny and the eternal present. But it might not, also.

39. Dante Alighierig *Paradiso,* trans. John Ciardi (New York: Signet, 1970), Canto XXXIII, lines 142–50 (hereafter *Paradiso*).
40. Nietzsche, op. cit., §124.
41. Norton Critical Edition, 2nd ed., Hershel Parker and Harrison Hayford, eds. (New York: W. W. Norton, 2002), p. 547 (hereafter cited as NCE), ch. 23, p. 96.
42. Ibid., ch. 3, p. 29.
43. Ibid., ch. 23, p. 97.
44. Ibid.
45. Ibid.
46. Quoted in David Lipsky's *Rolling Stone* article.
47. "Elizabeth Gilbert on Nurturing Creativity," available at: www.ted.com/talks/elizabeth_gilbert_on_genius.html.
48. Nietzsche, op. cit., §125.
49. The idea that we play a completely inert and insubstantial role in our own salvation is probably clearer in Calvin, Luther's successor, than it is in Luther himself. In Calvinism our path to salvation is predestined by God. Calvin's doctrine of predestination makes it completely clear that we can have no impact on the outcome.

Chapter 3. Homer's Polytheism

1. Hom. Od. 4.266. All citations from the *Odyssey* henceforth will be taken from Robert Fitzgerald's fine translation, unless otherwise noted. See: Homer, *The Odyssey,* trans. Robert Fitzgerald (New York: Farrar, Straus, and Giroux, 1998). We will cite this text either as Hom. Od. or simply as Od. as the context dictates, followed by the book and line number in either the original Greek or the translation. Other translations we have consulted and sometimes quote include those by Richmond Lattimore, Robert Fagles, and Allen Mandelbaum. See: Homer, *The Odyssey,* trans. Richmond Lattimore (New York: Harper, 1991); Homer, *The Odyssey,* trans. Robert Fagles, introduction and notes by Bernard Knox (New York: Penguin, 1996); Homer, *The Odyssey,* trans. Allen Mandelbaum (New York: Bantam, 1991). Sometimes, citations will be offered in short form in the body of the text, and if the translation is not by Fitzgerald, the translator's initials will be given there.
2. Hom. Od. 4.305, Lattimore translation.
3. For examples, see Robert E. Bell, *Women of Classical Mythology: A Biographical Dictionary* (New York: Oxford University Press, 1991). Even in the currently accepted version of the text there is a passage suggesting such a treatment: "Helen of Argos, daughter of Zeus and Leda, would she have joined the stranger, lain with him, if she had known her destiny? known the Akhaians in arms would bring her back to her own country? Surely a goddess moved her to adultery . . ." (Hom. Od. 23.218–224, found at lines 247–250 in Fitzgerald). This passage seems to call our interpretation into question, since on our reading Homer

deeply admires Helen instead of thinking she was guilty of some indiscretion for which she should be punished. We were, therefore, delighted to discover that since the earliest times commentators have agreed, for reasons having nothing to do with the issue of Helen's praiseworthiness, that this passage is a later addition to the text.

4. See Snell's classic, *The Discovery of the Mind in Greek Philosophy and Literature* (New York: Dover, 1982). Dodd's rejoinder in *The Greeks and the Irrational* (Berkeley: University of California Press, 1951) and Williams's more recent *Shame and Necessity* (Berkeley: University of California Press, 1993).

5. Martin Heidegger, *Parmenides,* trans. A. Schuwer and R. Rojcewicz (Bloomington and Indianapolis: Indiana University Press, 1992), p. 111.

6. The central Homeric texts, the *Iliad* and *Odyssey,* stand at the foundation of Western culture. As with the Bible, however, little is known about their composition, and littler still about the author or authors who composed them. By tradition Homer was a blind poet, thought to have come from the ancient Ionian city of Smyrna, or the nearby island of Chios. Whether such an individual ever existed, however, and if he did, whether he was the sole author of the epic poems that bear his name, has been the subject of controversy since ancient times. (For an overview of the modern history of this debate and for an account of the current state of the field, see Robert Fowler, "The Homeric Question," *The Cambridge Companion to Homer,* Robert Fowler ed., UK: Cambridge University Press, 2004, pp. 220–32.)

If Homer did exist, he is usually thought to have lived sometime in the eighth century BC; certainly the written texts that have come down to us from antiquity were first transcribed around that time. (We write BC rather than BCE in order to highlight, rather than sideline, the role of belief in Jesus in separating the Christian world from the Hebrew and Pagan worlds.) The events described in the poems, however, assuming they have some basis in fact, probably occurred nearly half a millennium earlier. The *Iliad,* narratively the first of the two books, recounts an important series of events in the ten-year siege of Troy. One traditional date for the Trojan War is 1194 to 1184 BC, and this dating seems to be roughly consistent with the archaeological evidence now available at the most probable site of the war. The *Odyssey* describes Odysseus's adventures during the ten years it took him to return to his home island of Ithaca after the conclusion of the war.

Besides being paradigmatic stories of war and adventure, the songs of the harper played an essential role in the culture of eighth century Greece, focusing for those people their sense of what they were up to as a culture. Even three hundred years later the Athenians living at the time of Aeschylus and Plato knew large parts of the Homeric oeuvre by heart, and appealed to Homer's work to settle moral, legal, and diplomatic disputes. Judging from Classical Greek authors of the day, it was not uncommon for people to quote appropriate bits of Homer on all occasions, the way one might now—or at least until recently—comment on a situation by quoting familiar bits of the Bible.

7. Nineteenth-century pedagogical theories tended dramatically to fall prey to this anachronistic temptation. During that period the unifying purpose of a liberal arts education was simply taken for granted: it was to train the Christian citizen. Greek and Latin classics were read, on this view, in order properly to form one's taste and sense of beauty. (See, for example, the history of the general theory of education discussed in the classic 1945 report of the Harvard faculty entitled *General Education in a Free Society* [Cambridge, MA: Harvard University Press, 1945].) It can hardly be expected in that Victorian age, therefore, that the particular excellence of the most beautiful woman in the world should have been her responsiveness to the Greek way of holding sacred the erotic aspect of existence. Yet that, we will claim, is what Homer himself admired in Helen.

8. See Friedrich Nietzsche, *On the Genealogy of Morals,* trans. Walter Kaufmann (New York: Random House, 1967).

9. See Bernard Knox's notes in *The Odyssey* by Homer, trans. Robert Fagles (London: Penguin Classics, 1996). Knox draws the connection between *arete* and *araomai* in his note to Book 7, line 62, which discusses a character named Arête. But the connection is clear when considering the word *arete* too, on which this character's name is based.

10. Hom. Od. 3.48; Lattimore translation.

11. Hom. Od. 4.499–511; Mandelbaum translation, p. 71.

12. Indeed, before that time *tyche* is sometimes considered in Greek culture to be a force which, if it exists at all, excludes belief in the gods. See, for example, Euripides' play *Cyclops* at line 606.

13. Hom. Od. 22.255ff.; Mandelbaum translation.

14. Hom. Od. 22.272; Mandelbaum translation, p. 446.

15. Quentin Tarantino and Roger Avary, "Pulp Fiction," Internet Movie Script Database, IMSDb, n.d., May 24, 2009 (www.imsdb.com/scripts/Pulp-Fiction.html).

16. See also Hesiod's *Theogony,* especially at 750ff. There Sleep and his brother Death are described as "awful gods"—presumably in the sense that they inspire awe.

17. This phenomenon was so important to the Homeric Greeks that it seems to have been built into the very grammar of their language. In Homeric Greek one finds a rather unusual form of the verb called the middle voice. This verb form is so foreign to us that there is little agreement among scholars about how it was used. The facts, however, are straightforward. Most modern languages have only two verbal voices: active and passive. When the verb is used in the active voice then the subject is the agent of the activity, as in "John *threw* the ball." By contrast, when the verb is in the passive voice then the person becomes more like a passive recipient of the action, as in "John *was thrown.*" But Homeric Greek has a third option: the middle voice. Whatever else is true about the middle voice, it must be intended for situations in which the person in question is neither purely active nor purely passive. But this is just exactly the phenomenon we are describing when we talk of being inhabited or instructed by the gods.

To see how this works, it helps to know that in the example of Odysseus holding on to the rock the verb we have translated in the passive voice as "were put in motion" is actually in the middle voice in the original Greek. And this makes perfect sense. Homer seems to want to indicate that Odysseus was not forced to put his hands out by Athena—as if she made him do it against his will. After all, the phenomenon indicates clearly that there is some sense in which Odysseus was involved in the action. But his involvement was not purely active, either: the whole point of invoking the goddess is that Odysseus on his own could not have done it nearly as well. The middle voice is the perfect grammatical marker to indicate this phenomenon, and it is probably not an accident that Homer is its greatest master; indeed, the form had all but disappeared by the time of the Classical Greek authors of the fifth century BCE.

18. See, inter alia, Hom. Od. 7.22ff. and 13.221ff.; line numbers from the original Greek.

19. See, e.g., Athena's description of Odysseus's winning discuss throw at Hom. Od. 8.193 in the Greek. Fitzgerald translation, line 203.

20. See, e.g., Hom. Od. 8.7ff. in the Greek; Fitzgerald translation, line 7ff.

21. "Film View; Adrift, Fleetingly, in Warhol's World," *New York Times*, April 28, 1996.

22. Jean-Paul Sartre, "Existentialism Is a Humanism," *Existentialism from Dostoyevsky to Nietzsche*, ed. and trans. Walter Kaufmann (New York: Meridian Books, 1995), p. 291.

23. John Donovan, "Head Games: Ankiel, Knoblauch Struggle to Rediscover Their Arms," *CNN Sports Illustrated*, March 23, 2001. Retrieved from http://sportsillustrated.cnn.com/baseball/mlb/2001/spring_training/news/2001/03/23/ankiel_knob/ on June 16, 2009.

24. Naturally, Homer recognizes that a requirement of excellence in any domain is that one must have gone through the process of learning the skills and practices and customs of that domain. It would be silly to think that Chuck Knoblauch could have become the great fielder he was—at least for a while—without the proper kind of coaching and expertise. The point is, however, that the coaching and expertise are not sufficient. Once one has reached the pinnacle of a particular domain, then one is ready to be open to the gods. A case in point here is Telemachus. Athena plays a crucial role in helping Telemachus move from the world of a child, helplessly playing among the suitors, to the world of an adult, who can see that he needs to stand up to them. This move from childhood to adulthood is itself the province of a god, in Homer's view, since no person can make the transition on his own. But of course what it really requires is proper upbringing, and it is no coincidence that Athena helps Telemachus in this regard by inhabiting an important household figure whose name is Mentor. Still, the ability to see the world's demands differently is not sufficient for Telemachus. He also needs experience to be able to make persuasive speeches and command authority. Homer recognizes that Telemachus is lacking the expertise to do this well, and a crucial episode occurs when it becomes clear that

Telemachus's impassioned speech has failed to have its desired effect. (See Hom. Od. 2.270 in the Greek.) (Telemachus himself, like a characteristic young adult, doesn't seem to recognize the importance of experience. At one important point in an important speech he lapses into childhood, throwing his staff to the ground and bursting into tears. [Hom. Od. 2.80 in the Greek.]) The point therefore is not that the gods magically replace our need to develop skills in a domain of excellence. It is that once we have the best skills possible, we need the gods to help us manifest them well.

25. Hom. Od. 19.210ff.

26. See the *Odyssey:*

> The bright doors were shut,
> but like a sudden stir of wind, Athena
> moved to the bedside of the girl, and grew
> visible as the shipman Dymas' daughter . . .
> (Book 6, lines 24–30)

And also:

> So, passing by the strap-slit through the door,
> The image came a-gliding down the room
> to stand at her bedside and murmur to her . . .
> (Book 4, lines 854–856, Fitzgerald translation)

27. An involved episode in this soap opera is presented in Book 8 of the *Odyssey.* It chronicles the adulterous affair between Aphrodite and Ares, with the jealous husband Hephaestus in the role of cuckold.

28. Which is not to say that they are measured with respect to her alone. There are several kinds of great women in Homer. Helen is the standard when it comes to eros, but Penelope's wisdom, for example, makes her stand out in a way that is irreconcilable with Helen's erotic excellence. Indeed, the fidelity and loyalty that Penelope displays—remaining faithful to Odysseus for twenty years—stands in stark contrast with Helen's susceptibility to the present erotic situation. Homer's polytheism allows him to rest content with both these kinds of excellence, feeling no need to rank or compare them.

29. Indeed, one of Odysseus's epithets is "the man of many sorrows."

Chapter 4. From Aeschylus to Augustine: Monotheism on the Rise

1. Aeschylus, *Oresteia,* trans. Richmond Lattimore (Chicago: University of Chicago Press, 1953), *The Eumenides,* lines 614–618.

2. Aeschylus, *The Eumenides,* line 421.

3. Aeschylus, *The Eumenides,* lines 381–384.

4. Aeschylus, *Agamemnon,* lines 206–211.

5. Aeschylus, *Agamemnon,* lines 1522–1527.

6. Aeschylus, *Agamemnon,* lines 1560–1563.

7. Aeschylus, *Agamemnon,* lines 1489–1495.

8. Aeschylus, *Agamemnon,* lines 1563–1566.

9. Aeschylus, *The Eumenides,* lines 385–387.

10. Telémakhos: "[M]y mother's parting curse would call the dread furies to punish me . . ." Hom. Od. 2.144–145 [trans. slightly modified]; "I saw the mother of Oedipus, Epikastê . . . In her noose she swung" and "left him endless agony from a mother's Furies" Hom. Od. 11.310ff.; "[I]f there are Furies pent in the dark to avenge a poor man's wrong, then may Antínöos meet his death before his wedding day!" Hom. Od. 17.622–624; "[A]s hurricane winds took Pandareos' daughters when they were left at home alone. . . . the cyclone wind had ravished them away to serve the loathsome Furies." Hom Od. 20.75ff.

11. Aeschylus, *The Eumenides,* lines 864–866.

12. Aeschylus, *The Eumenides,* lines 914–915.

13. Aeschylus, *The Eumenides,* line 1047.

14. Aeschylus, *Agamemnon,* line 160.

15. Aeschylus, *Agamemnon,* line 1487.

16. Aeschylus, *The Eumenides,* lines 899.

17. Martin Heidegger, "The Origin of the Work of Art," in *Poetry, Language, Thought,* trans. A. Hofstadter (New York: Harper & Row, 1971), p. 42.

18. For a description of the dimensions and directions of moral space, see Charles Taylor's *Sources of the Self* (Cambridge, MA: Harvard University Press, 1989).

19. Heidegger, "The Origin of the Work of Art," p. 41.

20. Ibid., p. 43.

21. Homer is a unique case. Before his work there was only a dim confusion of conflicting myths. He made order by emphasizing what he felt was important, such as gratitude and wonder, and he left out what repelled him, such as the primitive dark force of revenge. He thereby originated a new way of life. We can therefore call him an *originator.*

22. Jesus' new mood of *overflowing* love for all human beings can be contrasted with eros or desire, which Plato defines as a *lack.*

23. Matthew 5:27–28 (The Sermon on the Mount).

24. Romans 7:7 (Paul, Letter to the Romans).

25. Saint Augustine, *Confessions,* trans. R.S. Pine-Coffin (Penguin Classics, 1961), Book VII, ch. 17, pp. 151–52.

26. *Confessions,* Book VII, ch. 18, p. 152.

27. *Confessions,* Book X, ch. 27, p. 232.

28. *Confessions,* Book VII, ch. 18, p. 152.

29. *Confessions,* Book X, ch. 43, p. 250.

30. See David M. Friedman, *A Mind of Its Own: A Cultural History of the Penis* (New York: Penguin, 2003).

31. An early version of Descartes' *cogito* was already explored by Augustine. See inter alia his *Confessions,* Book X, ch. 11, p. 219.

Chapter 5. From Dante to Kant: The Attractions and Dangers of Autonomy

1. A. T. MacAllister, "Historical Introduction," *The Inferno* by Dante Alighieri, trans. John Ciardi (New York: Penguin, 1982), xiii. Hereafter, *Inferno*, followed by Canto and line numbers.
2. *Inferno*, Canto III, line 9.
3. *Inferno*, Canto IV, line 42.
4. *Inferno*, Canto V, line 38.
5. *Inferno*, Canto VIII, lines 101–102.
6. *Inferno*, Canto VIII, lines 109–112.
7. *Inferno*, Canto VIII, line 117.
8. *Inferno*, Canto XI, line 21.
9. *Inferno*, Canto IX, lines 10–105.
10. Monogamous homosexual lovers suffer the least of all sinners. They are purified by fire at the top of Purgatory. There Dante meets several of his friends.
11. Dante never says so in so many words, but his description in *Inferno*, Canto XXXIV, lines 76–77, makes clear what part of Satan's anatomy is at the exact bottom of the material universe.
12. Dante Alighieri, *The Purgatorio*, trans. John Ciardi (New York: Penguin, 1961), Canto XVI, lines 67–87 (hereafter, *Purgatorio*).
13. *Paradiso*, Canto I, lines 91–93.
14. *Purgatorio*, Canto XVIII, line 63.
15. *Paradiso*, Canto XXXI, lines 73–93, 112–117.
16. *Paradiso*, Canto XXXIII, line 102.
17. *Paradiso*, Canto XXII, line 134–135.
18. *Paradiso*, Canto XXII, lines 152–153.
19. *Paradiso*, Canto XXXIII, lines 143–146.
20. *Paradiso*, Canto XXX, line 42.
21. *Paradiso*, Canto XXXIII, line 131.
22. Martin Luther, *Selections from His Writings*, ed. John Dillenberger (New York: Anchor Books, 1962), p. 470.
23. From Luther's list of reforms sent to the German nobility. Preserved Smith, *The Life and Letters of Martin Luther* (Cambridge, UK: The Riverside Press, 1914).
24. Martin Luther, *Martin Luther's Basic Theological Writings*, Timothy Lull, ed. (Minneapolis: Augsburg Fortress, 1989), pp. 43–44.
25. Luther, *Selections*, p. 78.
26. Ibid., p. 76.
27. Ibid., p. 105.
28. Ibid., p. 160. Kierkegaard saw that Jesus' introduction of the agape mood implied that after the Incarnation there is no need and no way to relate directly to God the father. However, he notes in his journals that "Luther acted rightly, but his preaching is not always clear or in agreement with his life—a rare occurrence—his life is better than his preaching." Søren Kierkegaard, *Journals & Papers*, Volume 3: L-R, ed. and trans. Howard V. Hong and Edna H. Hong, assisted by Gregor Malantschuk (Bloomington: Indiana University Press, 1975), p. 78.

29. Luther, *Selections*, pp. 112–13.
30. Luther's love of music was later fully expressed in Bach's church cantatas. They express neither the activity of individual meaning giving, nor passive mystical bliss, but, rather, a community of joyful worshipers who share a sense of the sacred they are swept up by—a mood which they then joyfully cultivate.

   In the *Fourth Preface* to his hymnal's many editions, Luther writes: "Cheerful and merry must we be in heart and mind, when we would sing. . . . For God hath made our heart and mind joyful through his dear Son whom he hath given for us to redeem from sin, death and the devil. Who earnestly believes this cannot but sing thereof with joy and delight, that others also may hear and come."
31. Luther, *Selections*, pp. 24–25.
32. René Descartes, *Meditations on First Philosophy*, Fourth Meditation in *The Philosophical Writings of Descartes*, Vol. II, trans. John Cottingham, Robert Stoothoff, and Dugald Murdoch (New York: Cambridge University Press, 1984), p. 40. Originally published in 1641.
33. René Descartes, *Discourse on Method*, Part III, in *Descartes: Philosophical Writings*, ed. and trans. Norman Kemp Smith (New York: The Modern Library, 1958), p. 111.
34. The words *autonomy* and *heteronomy* will make more sense if we point out their Greek roots. *Nomos* in Greek means law, while the prefixes *auto* and *hetero* refer to the self and to others. Thus, *autonomy* literally means self-law and *heteronomy* literally means other-law.
35. The great lesson of the Enlightenment, according to Kant, is that the mature, fully developed human being uses his own understanding to determine how to act. "Enlightenment is man's emergence from his self-imposed immaturity," he famously writes. See Immanuel Kant, "An Answer to the Question: What Is Enlightenment?" in *Perpetual Peace and Other Essays*, trans. and introduction by Ted Humphrey (Indianapolis: Hackett, 1983), p. 41.
36. Sartre, op. cit., p. 291.

Chapter 6. Fanaticism, Polytheism, and Melville's "Evil Art"

1. Letter to Hawthorne of November 17, 1851. Reprinted in Herman Melville, *Moby Dick*, NCE. The letter appears on pp. 545–47.
2. See discussion in Hershel Parker's "International Controversy over Melville," esp. NCE, p. 468.
3. Review of April 6, 1846, reprinted in part in NCE, pp. 476–77.
4. Parker, op. cit.
5. A report of the *Ann Alexander* event can be found in Alexander Starbuck's *History of the American Whale Fishery from Its Earliest Inception to the Year 1876*, *The Ploughboy Anthology*, April 17, 2003, http://mysite.du.edu/~ttyler/ploughboy/starbuck.htm. See especially Section F, titled "The Dangers of the Whale Fishery."

6. Letter to Evert A. Duyckinck of November 7, 1851. Reprinted in NCE, pp. 544–45. This letter was in response to a letter Melville had received from his friend Duyckinck the night before, which included a news clipping with a report about the sinking of the *Ann Alexander*. The letter, Melville reported, "had a sort of stunning effect on me."

7. Letter to Hawthorne of June 29, 1851. Reprinted in NCE, pp. 541–42.

8. This full version of the incantation was first discovered by the scholarly community during the winter of 1933–34. The American poet Charles Olson—then still a twenty-three-year-old graduate student of American history and literature at Wesleyan—found it on the blank flyleaf of the seventh and final volume of Melville's collected edition of Shakespeare's works. Olson took these and other marginalia from the volumes to indicate the importance of Melville's reading of Shakespeare to the composition of *Moby Dick*. (See Olson's important first book, *Call Me Ishmael*.) Recent scholarship has turned against Olson's interpretation, however, principally in light of the discovery in 1992 that this and other extracts from the flyleaf were in fact copied from an essay about witchcraft published anonymously by Sir Francis Palgrave in the July 1823 issue of *Quarterly Review*. (See Geoffrey Sanborn's article "The Name of the Devil: Melville's Other 'Extracts' for Moby-Dick," published in the September 1992 issue of *Nineteenth-Century Literature*.) The latest speculation from the scholarly world has revolved around several questions: On what day precisely did Melville read this issue? Was he also reading the works of the early-nineteenth-century English essayist Leigh Hunt at the time? And perhaps most important, did he or did he not complete his perusal of these volumes while lounging on his father-in-law's living room sofa? (See Geoffrey Sanborn, "Lounging on the Sofa with Leigh Hunt: A New Source of the Notes in Melville's Shakespeare Volume," in *Nineteenth-Century Literature*, June 2008.) We shall leave the finer details of this discussion to the experts.

9. Melville says Jove here, which is the Roman name for Zeus.

10. NCE, p. 274.

11. NCE, p. 8.

12. Ibid.

13. This use of the name Leviathan to indicate Satan, following Isaiah 27:1, has entered into common usage and then passed out of it again already, now remaining obscure. The last citation that the *Old English Dictionary* can find is from Barnes in 1595, who beseeches the Lord "Breake thou the jawes of olde Levyathan, Victorious Conqueror!"

14. Quoted among the exctracts at NCE, p. 9.

15. Quotes in this paragraph from NCE, ch. 79, pp. 274–75.

16. NCE, p. 22.

17. NCE, p. 20.

18. See Parker, op. cit., NCE, p. 466. Notice the connection to Heidegger's interpretation of Hölderlin. On Heidegger's account, Hölderlin needed to go away to ancient Greece—or at any rate the south of France—to discover how to think about contemporary Germany.

19. NCE, p. 18.
20. Ibid.
21. NCE, ch. 3, p. 26.
22. Ibid.
23. Letter to Hawthorne of November 17, 1851.
24. From earlier in the same letter to Hawthorne.
25. NCE, ch. 32, p. 116.
26. NCE, ch. 32, pp. 124–25.
27. NCE, ch. 96, p. 328.
28. NCE, ch. 17, p. 82.
29. NCE, ch. 4, p. 37.
30. Ibid.
31. NCE, ch. 3, p. 34.
32. NCE, ch. 5, p. 40.
33. NCE, ch. 3, p. 36.
34. NCE, ch. 4, p. 36.
35. NCE, ch. 18, p. 85.
36. See NCE, ch. 4, p. 38.
37. See, for example, Andrew Delbanco's discussion in his biography *Melville: His World and Work* (New York: Vintage, 2005), esp. pp. 130–134.
38. NCE, ch. 13, p. 60.
39. NCE, ch. 12, p. 60.
40. NCE, ch. 110, p. 364.
41. The parallel is even clearer in Melville's prose. Queequeg is in the process of getting a thorough education in the ways of civilized Christian culture. But as his dressing habits show, he is still in a transition state, "neither caterpillar nor butterfly. . . . His education was not yet completed. He was an undergraduate" (NCE, ch. 4, p. 38). By contrast with Queequeg's adaptation to civilization, Ishmael's education takes place at sea. It is a matter of transitioning out of civilized Christian culture, not into it. As he says, "a whaleship was my Yale College and my Harvard" (NCE, ch. 24, p. 101).
42. NCE, ch. 94, p. 323.
43. These episodes are recounted briefly by the prophet Elijah in NCE, ch. 19, p. 87.
44. NCE, ch. 41, p. 152.
45. NCE, ch. 36, p. 140.
46. Ibid.
47. NCE, ch. 108, p. 359.
48. NCE, ch. 41, p. 152.
49. Milton was read this way by the "Romantic" and "Satanic School" interpreters, especially Blake and Shelley. Henry F. Pommer argues that Melville was influenced more by this school of Milton interpretation than by the pious Milton found and praised by his contemporaries. A characteristic passage from Pommer's *Milton and Melville* (New York: Cooper Square Press, 1970) is quoted in

Leslie Sheldon, "Messianic Power and Satanic Decay: Milton in *Moby Dick*," *Leviathan: A Journal of Melville Studies* 4, no. 1 (March 2002): 29–50.

50. Quoted in Sheldon, op. cit.
51. NCE, ch. 19, p. 87.
52. NCE, ch. 79, p. 274.
53. NCE, ch. 87, p. 296.
54. NCE, ch. 94, p. 323.
55. See Karl Jaspers, *The Origin and Goal of History*, trans. Michael Bullock (London: Routledge and Keegan Paul, 1953). Originally published as Karl Jaspers, *Vom Ursprung und Ziel der Geschichte* (Munich: Piper Verlag, 1949).
56. Charles Taylor, *A Secular Age*, p. 687.
57. *Gay Science*, Preface 4.
58. NCE, ch. 9, p. 54.
59. Ibid.
60. NCE, ch. 10, p. 57.
61. Ibid.
62. NCE, ch. 16, p. 79.
63. NCE, ch. 94, p. 322.
64. NCE, ch. 94, pp. 322–23.
65. NCE, ch. 42, p. 159.
66. Ibid.
67. NCE, ch. 42, p. 160.
68. NCE, ch. 42, p. 165.
69. Ibid.
70. Ibid.
71. Ibid.
72. NCE, ch. 87, p. 296.
73. NCE, ch. 42, p. 163.
74. NCE, ch. 102, p. 344.
75. Ibid.
76. NCE, ch. 102, p. 345.
77. NCE, ch. 85, p. 290.
78. NCE, ch. 85, p. 293.
79. Ibid.
80. NCE, ch. 93, p. 319.
81. NCE, ch. 27, p. 107.
82. NCE, ch. 93, p. 321.
83. Ibid.
84. Ibid., pp. 321–22.
85. NCE, ch. 125, p. 391.
86. NCE, ch. 99, p. 332.
87. NCE, ch. 36, p. 138.
88. NCE, ch. 27, p. 105.
89. These various observations are reported in NCE, ch. 99, pp. 332–35.

90. NCE, ch. 99, p. 335.
91. NCE, ch. 28, p. 109.
92. NCE, 125, p. 392.
93. NCE, ch. 133, p. 413.
94. NCE, ch. 133, p. 410.
95. Ibid.
96. All on NCE, ch. 133, p. 410.
97. NCE, ch. 134, p. 417.
98. NCE, ch. 134, p. 416.
99. NCE, ch. 135, p. 424.
100. NCE, ch. 41, p. 156.
101. NCE, ch. 135, p. 426.
102. NCE, ch. 133, p. 409. Jupiter and Jove are both Roman names for the god the Greeks called Zeus.
103. See Geoffrey Sanborn, "Whence Come You Queequeg?" *American Literature* 77, no. 2 (June 2005): 227–57.
104. NCE, ch. 18, p. 85.
105. Letter of January 4, 1939. Yeats died on January 28th of that year.
106. NCE, ch. 110, pp. 366–67.
107. NCE, ch. 135, p. 424.
108. NCE, ch. 135, pp. 426–27.
109. NCE ch. 110, p. 366.
110. NCE Epilogue, p. 427.
111. See, for example, his letter to Sophia Peabody Hawthorne of January 8, 1852, reprinted at NCE, p. 547.

Chapter 7. Conclusion: Lives Worth Living in a Secular Age

1. "End of a Career," *New York Times,* June 22, 1939, p. 18.
2. "61,808 Fans Roar Tribute to Gehrig: Captain of Yankees Honored at Stadium—Calls Himself 'Luckiest Man Alive,'" *New York Times,* July 5, 1939, p. 1.
3. The website American Rhetoric (www.americanrhetoric.com), for example, lists Gehrig's Farewell Speech as number 73 in its list of the top 100 speeches of American history. Most of the speeches listed above it are explicitly political in nature.
4. Ibid.
5. Video footage of the event, including an excerpt from the speech itself, can be found at: www.youtube.com/watch?v=a4msaZTJrTA. The details of this recounting were gathered from various *New York Times* articles, published in May, June, and July of 1939. The complete text of the speech is available at: http://en.wikipedia.org/wiki/Lou_Gehrig#.27The_Luckiest_Man_on_the_Face_of_the_Earth.27.
6. See, for example, *From Season to Season: Sports as American Religion,* Joseph L. Price, ed. (Macon, GA: Mercer University Press, 2001).

7. Albert Borgmann, *Crossing the Postmodern Divide* (Chicago: University of Chicago Press, 1992), p. 135.

8. Published on August 20, 2006, and available at: www.nytimes.com/2006/08 /20/sports/playmagazine/20federer.html?pagewanted=all.

9. Ibid.

10. Quoted in D. T. Max, "The Unfinished," *The New Yorker,* March, 9, 2009.

11. David Foster Wallace, "How Tracy Austin Broke My Heart," reprinted in *Consider the Lobster: And Other Essays* (New York: Little, Brown and Company, 2005).

12. "[A]nd the truth is that TV tennis is to live tennis pretty much as video porn is to the felt reality of human love."

13. Homer's polytheistic Greeks understood this intuitively. They knew that the intense and sacred meaningfulness of the gods is risky and dangerous. They knew that the gods can temporarily abandon you (as Athena does Odysseus) or be angry with you (as Hera often is). But they also knew that this danger is part of what gave the gods meaning such force. The overwhelming power and majesty of Poseidon's wine-dark sea wouldn't have the power it does if it were always beautiful and calm. It's the danger and tempestuousness of it, the way it rises up *physis*-like, that makes it the great, divine force it is.

14. *Infinite Jest,* p. 243.

15. "You don't know from true bug-eyed athletic superstition till you hit the pro ranks, Hallie. When you hit the Show is when you'll understand *primitive.* Winning streaks bring the native bubbling up to the surface. Jock straps unwashed game after game until they stand up by themselves in the overhead luggage compartments of planes. Bizarrely ritualized dressing, eating, peeing." *Infinite Jest,* p. 243.

16. A. Borgmann. Op. Cit., p. 243.

17. The search for the material basis of things, according to the standard historical account, does not begin until the sixth century BC in ancient Greece. Textbooks will typically claim that this is when Greek culture made the transition from a mythological to a scientific explanation of the universe. Although this is a dramatic oversimplification, and it distorts important aspects of the Greek understanding of being, there is nevertheless some surface plausibility to the story. Certainly it is true that Homer was not interested in the material basis of reality; and there is some sense in which the pre-Socratic philosophers were. When Thales claimed that all is water, for example, or perhaps when Heraclitus said that from fire all things begin, there is some sense in which these pre-Socratics were engaged in a protoscientific explanation of what there is.

18. This is the first sentence of Kant's "An Answer to the Question: What Is Enlightenment?"

19. See George Sturt, *The Wheelwright's Shop* (Cambridge, UK: Cambridge University Press, 1976), first published in 1923. Albert Borgmann discusses Sturt's book in his *Technology and the Character of Contemporary Life* (Chicago: University of Chicago Press, 1984). Before Borgmann, F. R. Leavis engaged profit-

ably with Sturt's book in his *Culture and Environment: The Training of Critical Awareness* (London: Chatto and Windus, 1933). Although our presentation owes something to these writers—especially to Borgmann—our take on Sturt's notion of craft was developed independently. Matthew Crawford's recent book *Shop Class as Soulcraft* takes up this notion of the importance of craft in an intriguing way, and draws briefly on Sturt as well. And although he does not explicitly draw on Sturt, Robert Pirsig's classic *Zen and the Art of Motorcycle Maintenance* has an important place for skill at the foundation of meaning too. We are sympathetic with all of these writers, but they remain firmly entrenched in the monotheistic philosophical tradition. Pirsig, like Plato, finds an abstract source of meaning in what he calls "Quality." Crawford, like Aristotle, reacts by emphasizing the hands-on, concrete, socially embedded sources of meaning. We go beyond them both in the details of our treatment of *poietic* skill and also in identifying *poiesis* as one among several ways the world can be. Finally, the idea that there is a skill for getting in balance our receptivity to *physis, poiesis,* technology—and whatever other understandings of reality are left over in the margins of our culture waiting to be revivified and reappropriated—the idea that there is this kind of skill is not found in any of our predecessors, and we take this to be one of the central positive contributions of our book.

20. George Sturt, Op. Cit., p. 24.

21. Ibid., pp. 45–46.

22. Ibid., p. 23.

23. Borgmann makes this point well, if briefly, when he says, "As people adjust to the land, the land discloses itself to the people." (*Technology and the Character of Contemporary Life,* p. 44.)

24. Melville's divine intuitions revealed something like this possibility, and that is what makes him the true prophet for our age. But his Sperm Whale, exalted to Zeus's high seat, is not the same as Homer's Zeus. Having no face, the great Sperm Whale cannot give birth to a family resemblance among his pantheon of gods. For beyond being ways the world can be, *physis, poiesis,* and *technology* don't resemble one another at all. That Melville could have intuited this lack of a grounding unity without being able to recognize these ways the world is and without even having had any sense that we inherit them from our history, is wonderful indeed. And if the masters of our Polytheistic world can learn to embody these sacred practices, they will find a special kinship with wandering Ishmael—the only one saved—who founds a new culture by tattooing on his body the panoply of sacred meanings he comes across and tries on and finds revealing. A polytheistic master like this will have left the security of the land and gone to the sea of hidden history to cultivate a site to which to lure back the gods.

INDEX

The letter *n* after a page number means it is in the note section.

blogs, 7
Borgmann, Albert, 193–94, 199, 243*n*
Bovary, Emma (char.), 15–16
Bradley, Bill, 9–12, 197
Brothers Karamazov, The (Dostoyevsky), 44
Buber, Martin, 221
Buddha, 163
Bulkington (char.), 50–52

Calvin, John, 230*n*
caring, modes of, 215–19
Catskill eagle, 48, 152, 153
charisma, 77–78, 86
chicklit, 26–28
choice, burden of, 3–8, 12–16, 71
Christianity, 105–17, 118–37, 167–68, 187, 200
    critique of, in *Moby Dick,* 155–57, 165–69
    Greek concepts as incompatible with, 112–17, 119, 120, 130, 132–33, 134
    medieval, 14–15, 20–21, 47, 48, 55, 119, 120–21, 157; *see also Divine Comedy, The*
    mood of joy in, 132–33, 134, 135–36, 138, 140, 165, 167–68, 237*n*
    Queequeg's rejection of, 155–56, 165–66
    rebirth in, 135
    Reformed, 136
    saints and sinners of, 105, 116, 121, 137
    virtues of, 61–62
    see also Jesus
Citizen Kane, 5–6
Clytemnestra, 93–95
coffee drinking, ritual of, 216–19
Confessions (Augustine), 114–17, 236*n*
courtly love, 129
craftsmen's skills, 206–11, 213, 219, 243*n*
Crawford, Matthew, 243*n*
cultural paradigms, 100–117, 118–19
    articulators of, 102–3, 104, 105, 107, 108–9, 116, 117, 140

artworks as, 100–105, 120–21
background practices in, 45–46, 99, 104, 105–6, 108, 109–12, 171–73
Queequeg's embodiment of, 185–86, 188
reconfiguring of, 103–12, 137, 140
shifting of, 220

Dante Alighieri, 14–15, 16, 17, 18, 47–49, 89, 101, 103, 117, 119, 120–33, 134, 139, 142, 168, 178, 204, 221, 223
    Beatrice and, 121, 124, 129–32
    Medieval Synthesis and, 133
    passive nihilism of, 133, 135, 136
    political motivations of, 131–32
    see also Divine Comedy, The
Dean, Lane, Jr. (char.), 32–33, 35–36, 38–39, 42
demagogues, rhetoric of, 221
Descartes, René, 19–20, 89, 105, 112, 117, 136, 137–40, 198, 200, 204
Diet of Worms (1521), 136
Divine Comedy, The (Dante), 47, 101, 102, 120–33, 138–39
    Beatrice in, 122, 129–31
    City of Dis in, 124–26, 137, 140
    as cultural paradigm, 119
    ecstatic bliss of contemplating God in, 47–49, 131–33, 134, 135, 136, 138
    free will in, 119, 126, 127–28, 204
    Hell in, 121, 122–26
    Limbo in, 122–23
    opening lines of, 121–22
    Paolo and Francesca in, 15, 16, 123–24
    Paradise in, 121, 122, 124, 130–32
    Purgatory in, 122, 124, 127–28, 129, 236*n*
    romantic love and, 129–31
    Satan in, 17, 125–26, 139, 236*n*
    sinners in, 14–15, 16, 121, 123–26, 221
    suicides in, 18, 126
    Virgil in, 122–23, 124–25, 128

social skills of, 148–49
as sole survivor, 148, 188, 244*n*
Spouter Inn painting interpreted by,
149–52, 157
surface meanings accepted by, 163,
164, 165–68, 175–76
whiteness as viewed by, 169–73

Jackson, Samuel L., 68–70
Jaspers, Karl, 163–64
Jesus, 105–17, 122, 135, 136, 137, 141,
145, 146, 216, 231*n*
agape exemplified by, 108, 112,
113–14, 115, 123, 129, 130,
132–33, 138, 223, 236*n*, 237*n*
The Divine Comedy and, 128–30
griffin as traditional symbol for, 129
Incarnation in, 106, 115–16, 120,
128–29, 133, 237*n*
miracles of, 111, 138
Jezebel, 160
John, Saint, Gospel According to, 89,
106–8, 111, 131, 132, 134, 138
Jordan, Michael, 197
joy, 7, 35, 36, 50, 132–33, 134,
135–36, 138, 140, 165, 167–68,
237*n*
Judeo-Christian monotheism, 21,
61–62, 67, 70, 99, 112, 119,
121, 134, 200
virtues of, 44, 45–46, 61
justice, 91–92

Kane, Charles Foster (char.), 5–6
Kant, Immanuel, 60, 89, 103, 112,
117, 136, 140–42, 168, 200,
220, 243*n*
enlightenment defined as maturity
by, 203–4, 237*n*–38*n*
Karr, Mary, 23
Kenyon College commencement
speech, 36–39, 46–47
Kierkegaard Søren, 106, 130, 237*n*
King, Martin Luther, Jr., 102–3, 220
"I have a dream" speech of, 202,
211–12
Kings, First Book of, 160
Knoblauch, Chuck, 79–80, 234*n*

Knox, Bernard, 62, 232*n*
Kubrick, Stanley, 58, 59
Kuhn, Thomas, 90

Lattimore, Richmond, 230*n*
Leviathan, 147, 239*n*
Libation Bearers, The (Aeschylus), 95–96
Lincoln, Abraham, 102–3
Little, Brown publishers, 32
love, 128, 136
addiction to, 123–24
agape, 108, 112, 113–14, 115, 123,
129, 130, 132–33, 137, 138,
167–68, 223, 236*n*, 237*n*
courtly, 129
heterosexual vs. homosexual, 126,
236*n*
romantic, 129–31
"Love Song of J. Alfred Prufrock, The"
(Eliot), 3–4, 150, 227*n*
luck, 65–66, 68
Luther, Martin, 42–44, 56, 89, 108,
112, 117, 133–37, 138, 204,
230*n*, 237*n*
Aristotle rejected by, 133–34
certainty of, 135–36, 140–41
revelation of, 54–55

MacAllister, Archibald, 120–21
Macbeth (Shakespeare), 17–18
McCaffery, Larry, 28
McCarthy, Joe, 191
McPhee, John, 9–12
Madame Bovary (Flaubert), 15–16
Mandelbaum, Allen, 230*n*
Maoris, 186
Match Point, 65–66
Matrix, The, 19, 197–98
Matthew, Saint, Gospel According to,
110, 111
Max, D. T., 23, 41
meaning, 12, 45, 89, 101, 102, 118,
119, 131, 142, 178–79, 184–85,
189, 193–223
Cartesian, 139
discernment vs. generation of, 209,
211
generic function vs., 216–17, 219

ABOUT THE AUTHORS

HUBERT DREYFUS (BA and PhD, Harvard) is considered a leading interpreter of the work of Michel Foucault, Maurice Merleau-Ponty, and especially Martin Heidegger. From 1960 to 1968 he taught philosophy at the Massachusetts Institute of Technology. Since 1968 Professor Dreyfus has been teaching philosophy and literature at the University of California, Berkeley. He is well known for his decades-long critique of artificial intelligence that culminated in his classic, *What Computers* Still *Can't Do,* translated into twelve languages. The podcasts of his courses on philosophical issues in Western literature have drawn a worldwide audience.

Dreyfus has been a Guggenheim Fellow, and has received research grants from both the National Science Foundation and the National Endowment for the Humanities. He holds a Doctorate Honoris Causa from Erasmus University, Rotterdam, and is a Fellow of the American Academy of Arts and Sciences.

He is also the inspiration behind Tao Ruspoli's 2010 prizewinning documentary *Being in the World: A Celebration of Being Human in a Technological Age.*

SEAN DORRANCE KELLY is Professor of Philosophy and Chair of the Department of Philosophy at Harvard University. He is also a co-chair of Harvard's interdisciplinary committee for the study of mind, brain, and behavior. Before arriving at Harvard, Kelly taught at Stanford and Princeton universities, and he was a visiting professor at the École Normale Supérieure in Paris. He is considered a leading interpreter of the

French and German tradition in phenomenology, as well as a prominent philosopher of mind. Kelly has published articles in numerous journals and anthologies and has received fellowships or awards from the Guggenheim Foundation, the National Endowment for the Humanities, the National Science Foundation, and the James S. McDonnell Foundation, among others.